Woman as Fire, Woman as Sage

SUNY series in Religious Studies
Harold Coward, editor

Woman as Fire, Woman as Sage

Sexual Ideology in the *Mahābhārata*

Arti Dhand

State University of New York Press

Published by
State University of New York Press, Albany

Printed in the United States of America

For information, contact State University of New York Press, Albany, New York
www.sunypress.edu

Production by Judith Block
Marketing by Anne M. Valentine

Library of Congress Cataloging in Publication Data

Dhand, Arti 1966–
Woman as fire, woman as sage : sexual ideology in the Mahabharata / Arti Dhand.
p. cm. — (SUNY series in religious studies)
Includes bibliographical references and index.
ISBN 978-0-7914-7139-5 (hardcover : alk. paper)
ISBN 978-0-7914-7140-1 (pbk. : alk. paper) 1. Mahabharata—Criticism, interpretation, etc. 2. Women in Hinduism. 3. Sex—Religious aspects—Hinduism. I. Title.

BL1138.27.D425 2007
294.5'923048—dc22

2006101104

10 9 8 7 6 5 4 3 2 1

For my two little princes
Rahul and Kai

Contents

Acknowledgments

This work has benefited from the assistance of numerous people. In particular, I owe my thanks to Katherine Young at McGill University, and to my excellent research assistants, John McGee, Patrick McGee, and Maithili Thayanithy.

Introduction

The last decades of the twentieth century have seen a blossoming of interest in the Hindu epics among Hindus, explored through the novel media of television, video, and the Internet. The year 1992, for example, saw the epic *Rāmāyaṇa* developed by B. R. Chopra for a television audience. Shortly thereafter appeared the massive text of the *Mahābhārata* (MBh.) enacted as television drama. For the most part, these modern renditions of ancient but vital Hindu texts have been labors of love and piety, in which the personalities of Rāma and Kṛṣṇa are explored with loving devotion, and every detail of their lives cherished and embellished with worshipful intensity. From this perspective, the novel media are simply new avenues for the manifestation of *bhakti*, not essentially different from the *rāmlīlā*s of folklore and the *kathās* and performances of the *Mahābhārata* elsewhere. There's no denying, however, that the television epics have also had an immense impact on Hindu society and politics. Indeed, it would be no exaggeration to say that the dramatizations have played a critical role in the revival and political self-assertion that has characterized Hinduism in recent years.

One of the many interesting exercises prompted by these celluloid epics is to observe the way that gender is constructed in these works. The producers of these epics, working in the postcolonial context of independent India following its industrial revolution, its multiparty democratic institutions, its bourgeoning middle class, and its increasingly cosmopolitan urban centres, faced the challenge of proving to an ambivalent younger audience that the gender models of epic lore are still of relevance to the modern world. They were called to somehow demonstrate, conscious of feminist critiques, that the traditional gendered structure of Hindu society as represented in the epics continues to be of value, and indeed, that it has the ability to provide the anchoring truths for an age in which women wear skirts, shorts, and trousers, and work alongside men in offices. A gender scheme devised for an ancient audience needed to be updated and rationalized, subjected to the scrutiny of a feminist-transformed consciousness, but at the end of the day still affirmed.

While the invocation of the epics to support gender roles is hardly new—for centuries if not millennia, male siblings have modeled their relationships on Rāma and Lakṣmaṇa; girls have been socialized to "Be like Sītā"—what the new tellings do is prompt a fresh look at what the classical Hindu epics say about gender. For those growing up in Hindu societies, the social and ethical forms found in the Sanskrit epics have always been billed as transcendent models, rooted in an ineffable eternal reality that by virtue of its truth claims demands conformity. A historian of religion, however, can argue otherwise, that all social forms can be historically contextualized. Bruce Lincoln expresses this sardonically, observing that religion often comes across as a "discourse whose defining characteristic is its desire to speak of things eternal and transcendent with an authority equally eternal and transcendent" (225). While this may be the case, the task of the scholar is to be critical; indeed, "to practice history of religions in a fashion consistent with the discipline's claim of title is to insist on discussing the temporal, contextual, situated, interested, human and material dimensions of those discourses, practices and institutions that characteristically represent themselves as eternal, transcendent, spiritual and divine" (225).

This work therefore is an attempt to clear the cobwebs for a new age on the sexual ideology of the classical Sanskrit *Mahābhārata*.[1] It is not an expressly feminist work, albeit feminist analysis is part of the idiom of our time and not only unavoidable but illuminating and desirable. The aim is to produce a critical study of sexuality, to note its embeddedness in conflicting religious worldviews, to observe its organic roots in various types of religious discourse, and to reveal its location in a particular historical, social, and religious moment of Hindu history. My contention in this work is that the *Mahābhārata* evolves a perspective on sexuality that is distinctly ideological, based as it is on political, social, and most of all, religious platforms. These considerations, not obvious to the creators of the television dramas or to their audiences, are nevertheless critical to understanding the direction in which beliefs about sexuality, particularly female sexuality, have evolved in the Hindu tradition.

Defining Sexuality

There have been many volumes published in recent years on the subject of sexuality;[2] surprisingly few of them, however, actually devote time to defining the term. What is sexuality, and what is its relationship to biology? Does anatomy dictate sexuality, and if so, to what extent? The answers to these questions vary depending on the methodology adopted by the scholar.

While psychoanalytic schools have tended to lean toward a biologically-predisposed view of sexuality,[3] in which the psychological development of the individual is premised on the interplay between the biological sex of parent and child, other approaches give less credence to anatomy and psychology, proposing instead that sexuality is a *social* construct localized in cultures, and is therefore of necessity polymorphous and particular to cultures.[4] Jeffrey Weeks puts this contention in the most provocative way, asserting that sexuality "is a fictional unity that once did not exist, and at some time in the future may not exist again. It is an invention of the human mind" (15). It is a subject, he says, that purports to bring together various biological and mental phenomena—gender identity, bodily differences, reproductive capacities, needs, desires, and fantasies. Western cultural history has tended to treat these subjects as if they naturally belonged together, within the realm of the sexual. Weeks, however, like many contemporary theorists, suggests that in fact all of the above are discrete biological or psychical phenomena, which "need not be linked together, and in other cultures have not been" (15). The fact that some cultures do bring these together as being "sexual" and others do not suggests that sexuality is a social construction, telling us more about the assumptions and history of a culture than about sex per se. In truth, argues Weeks, endorsing Kenneth Plummer's 1975 statement on this issue, "nothing is sexual . . . but naming makes it so" (25). While the body and the mind are the necessary terrain of sexuality, they "are given meaning only in social relations" (15).

Weeks' remarks highlight the major pitfalls of talking about sex, a term greatly overutilized in modern times, hence its signification murky and imprecise. I use the term as it is theorized in the disciplines of women's, gender, and cultural Studies: as referring to a set of anatomical features, which are then encoded by cultures with meaning, to yield the concept of gender.[5] A study of sexuality thus embraces the concepts of both sex and gender. What are the sexes? Where did they originate? What are their respective aptitudes, their predilections, their talents and capabilities? What should be their functions? What are appropriate sex-roles? On what basis are these rationalized? A study of sexual ideology in the *Mahābhārata* will theorize the logic of sex and gender in the text, identifying the linkages drawn between one's biological sex and one's social location. It will examine the mythic frames and cosmogonic narratives that support the gendering of sexes, and will study the values with which each gender is inscribed. It will look at the material, social, and political factors that are historically exigent to the development of assumptions about sex, and discuss their impact on the peculiar construction of gender we find in the epic. Most importantly, given that "religions have been the traditional guardians of sexual norms and practices,"[6] it will examine the religious worldview of the text, and seek to contextualize the sexual ideologies of the *Mahābhārata* therein. In sum, the work construes sexuality as a *tool* with which to excavate classical Hindu understandings about the Self, about individuals, their specificities, and their relationships with each other.

Hindu Sexuality

There are a few full-length scholarly works explicitly treating the subject of sexuality in Hinduism: J. J. Meyer's classic 1930 work, *Sexual Life in Ancient India*, Ranjana Kumari's 1988 *Female Sexuality in Hinduism*, and Sudhir Kakar's 1990 psychoanalytic study, *Intimate Relations*. Aside from this, much of Wendy Doniger's work touches on sexuality in its different aspects, particularly in the realm of myth.[7] In addition, numerous smaller-scale works exist, either directly or tangentially analyzing sexuality. Some attempt a broad and general overview of sexual acts and artifacts in Hinduism.[8] Others trace the same through Vedic and classical texts, using particular modes of inquiry.[9] Yet others target particular aspects of sexuality, such as homosexuality, or focus on the lives of key religious figures.[10] Several explore the issue using anthropological modes of inquiry[11] and some using psychoanalytic tropes.[12] Most often, works on sexuality are specific to particular traditions and sects. Thus, one can find literature on sexual motifs in the mythology of Kṛṣṇa in Vṛndāvan,[13] on the use of sexual metaphor and practice in Tantric lineages,[14] on sexuality in Śaivite and other Hindu mythology,[15] on the *devadāsī* tradition,[16] and on the sexuality of the Goddess.[17] Several works have also emerged recently on other Indic traditions.[18]

This work appends itself to this line of scholarship by looking at women in one strain of the tradition, the classical literary religio-mytho-epic "historical" work, the *Mahābhārata*.

Early scholarly writing on women in Hinduism was prone to broad generalizations—about the duties of married Hindu women (*strīdharma*), about the "status" of girls and women in society, about the prevalence of *sati* and the prohibitions against widow remarriage, about the practice of female infanticide and dowry deaths. While such work may have had its merits in pointing out problem issues impacting on Hindu women's lives, too much of it was transhistorical in scope, glossed spatial and chronological boundaries, paid scant attention to diversities of class, caste, region and language, and relied rather heavily on citations from a predictable selection of ancient and classical texts, the most ubiquitous being the *Manu Dharmaśāstra*. The unfortunate result of such scholarship was the creation of a monumental stereotype of the Hindu woman from which a critical reader could derive little substantive knowledge of the particular values undergirding Hindu women's lives in different eras and locales, or the historical, social, political, and legal strictures under which they labored at different periods of history.[19] While the worst excesses of these works have been recognized[20] and remedied in the scholarship of the last generation, these works however still condition the *questions* that scholars raise of Hinduism, and the categories by which women's experience is analyzed and assessed.

Perhaps the biggest problem with many works on women in Hinduism is that they presuppose a general category of womanhood, thus creating an essence where none exists.[21] My first conviction in embarking on a discussion of women's sexuality therefore was that it wouldn't be possible to speak of any generalized Hindu womanhood, given that there's no single archetype from which one may extrapolate the truth of millions of other women's lives. One would have to take careful account of at least the spatial, historical, and communitarian specificity of a woman in order to make an academically intelligible statement. The Hindu tradition has a typology of sex extending back to its ancient beginnings. One would need to take due and proper account of this typology and unpack and articulate it, to identify its fundamental ideological moorings and to track its evolution through history. Only then would it be possible to discuss its manifestation in the moment of the *Mahābhārata*, and to painstakingly locate it within the religious, social, political, and literary interests of the text. One would also need to be attentive to the historiography of the standard texts used to discuss women in Hinduism (Manu et al.) and to relativize in this way their claim to authority in the construction of Hindu women's history. It was with these aims that I set out on this discussion of female sexuality in the *Mahābhārata*.

The *Mahābhārata*

The history of *Mahābhārata* scholarship has been very well summarized in numerous works, most extensively by Brockington (1998), so it would be redundant to reproduce more than its highlights here. Suffice it to observe that each generation of scholarship has made different types of contributions to the understanding of the text. The contribution of nineteenth-century scholarship was in creating and refining methods for the text critical study of the *Mahābhārata*. Key players of this era were German scholars such as Franz Bopp, the "father of comparative Indo-European philology," who in 1829 was the first to edit the text from manuscripts and to propose that the text was of uneven antiquity, with some parts reflecting the linguistic conventions of later times than others. Others such as Adolf Holtzmann, Sr., speculated on the historicity of the events recounted in the text, and on the motives of the tradition that had transmitted it. His "inversion" theory proposed lines of development that radically overturned traditional Indian understandings of the text by proposing that the Pāṇḍavas were the belligerent usurpers of a bardic tradition probably initially intended to laud the Kauravas.[22] Holtzmann, Sr.'s nephew Adolf Holtzmann, Jr., argued in an 1895 work that the Pāṇḍavas represented the ideological takeover of an ancient Buddhism-inspired *Śaivism* professed by the Kauravas, by an emerging Brahmanism-inspired *Vaiṣṇavism*, whose votaries were the Pāṇḍavas. His researches were supported by Lassen, Witnernitz, Meyer, and also by MacDonnell and Keith in their *Index to Vedic Names*.

These interpretations, derived from diachronic methods of inquiry, were countered in the nineteenth century itself by Joseph Dahlmann, who in 1895 offered a synchronic interpretation of the text, arguing that the present text is the unified, organic work of a single author, and that the didactic and mythic elements are purposefully and artistically employed to articulate a definite moral design. Dahlmann's theory, later dubbed the 'synthetic' theory, was ridiculed by many of his contemporaries, but has been judged more fairly by twentieth-century scholars.

A third line of scholarship was developed by the "Analytical" school which, while differing from the "Inversion" school, also employed diachronic methods of analysis, with a view to identifying the epic nucleus around which extraneous traditional, religious, and mythic matter agglutinated. Its major proponent was E. W. Hopkins, an American scholar who formulated a five-stage theory of textual development, the earlier stages represented by the "narrative" portions of the epic, while the later "didactic" portions, "it goes without saying" were developed by "the priests," "for their own interests" (1969, 385). Hopkins adduced evidence for this theory by looking at the disparity between the ideology and praxis of ethics in the epic.

> This [original] story is in its details so abhorrent to the writers of the epic that they make every effort to whitewash the heroes, at one time explaining that what they did would have been wicked if it had not been done by divinely inspired heroes, at another frankly stating that the heroes did wrong. It is not then probable that had the writers intended to write a moral tale, they would have built on such material. Hence the tale existed as such before it became the nucleus of a sermon. (1969, 363)

In particular, Hopkins argued that Kṛṣṇa was a late addition to the epic. Originally introduced as a teacher of diplomatic strategy and statecraft, at the third stage of development, Kṛṣṇa was recast as an incarnation of the God Viṣṇu, and at the final stage, he was cast as the "All God."

The euhemerizing interpretations of Kṛṣṇa proposed by nineteenth century scholarship were influential in shaping twentieth-century scholarship, embraced, for example, by J. A. B. van Buitenen. Van Buitenen postulated a similar theory of textual development, along three 'perimeters' of layering. The first, the central epic story, represents a complex genealogical puzzle. The second involves a wholly unnecessary and "inept" "mythification" of the central narrative. This layer represents the theologizing and systematizing efforts of the epic's *brāhmaṇa* custodians (1973, xiii–xxiii). The theme of the "*brāhmaṇization*" of the epic was in turn taken up by other scholars, and refined to the theme of the 'Bhārgavization' of the epic, arguing the takeover of the epic by one particular family of *brāhmaṇa*s, the Bhārgavas. Similarly, although the Inversion school has few adherents today, scholars still postulate theories that challenge the claims of the tradition. In 1991, for example, Ruth Cecily Katz, following an analysis that isolates the *Sauptikaparva* as the original epic core of the text, argued that the original work intended to celebrate the achievements of neither the Pāṇḍavas nor the Kauravas, but rather of the Pāñcāla family (1991), with the war as an enactment of ancient hostilitites between the Pāñcāla king Drupada and the Kaurava guru Droṇācārya.

The conclusions reached by nineteenth-century scholars and their descendants were criticized in successive generations for their speculative liberties, their dependence on methods developed for biblical studies, and their reductive approaches to Indian tradition. Their primary contribution may be in the refinement of philological and linguistic methods of studying the epic. Clearly the most impressive legacy of the approaches developed by nineteenth-century scholars is the massive editing project undertaken by the

Bhandarkar Oriental Research Institute. Through text critical studies of all available *Mahābhārata* manuscripts, the Critical Edition of the text was published between 1933 and 1972. The Critical Edition has not escaped criticism, but with its concordances and appendices, it has become the standard text for *Mahābhārata* Studies in the West.

Twentieth-century *Mahābhārata* scholarship reveals significant divergences in method from its predecessors, and has been dominated by transhistorical, structuralist approaches to the text. One line of study is represented by the French scholar Georges Dumézil, who departs from the methods of his predecessors by viewing the epic as an historicization of mythical events enacted on a larger Indo-European stage. In Dumézil's view, the MBh. is a well-thought literary project consciously undertaken by a school of talented and skilled technical specialists, to interpret common Indo-European myths transposed into a historical narrative of specific ethnicity. This method precludes any discussion of the historicity of the Pāṇḍavas, who are seen primarily as serving the three functions characteristic of Indo-European mythmaking: the sacerdotal-legislative (Yudhiṣṭhira), the martial-kingly (Bhīma and Arjuna), and the popular-fertile (Nakula and Sahadeva).[23] Dumézil's views, building on those of Swedish scholar Stig Wikander, claim one line of adherents; quite another is claimed by the work of French structuralist Madeleine Biardeau, whose method, indebted to Dumézil in many respects, departs from his in its foundational myths. Thus while she, like Dumézil, treats epic events themselves as pure myth rendered in historical idiom, her work finds its mythic antecedents not in Indo-European myths, but in Purāṇic ones, developed from Vedic origins. Biardeau's central argument is that "Hinduism" is not a haphazard cacophony of beliefs and practices, but rather represents multifarious and multivalent movements around a deeply intuited single core of values. These values are derived from the Vedic origins of Hinduism, but achieve their fullest theological expression in the mythology of the Purāṇas.

> It is around this Vedic core that a Hindu structure will emerge, drawing from it a variety of readings which, within certain limits, shift and change over the course of the centuries. The term 'Hinduism' . . . is appropriate to describe this aggregate of readings, together with their structural organization. Closer to the Vedic revelation, orthodox Brahmanism is not the precursor of modern Hinduism; it is the permanent heart, the implicit model for and against which are constituted the *Bhakti* and Tantric traditions with all their sects. (1995, 21)

Biardeau reads in the epic several levels of meaning, in which the symbolism of the Vedic sacrifice is retained, but recast in the devotional idiom of *bhakti*. The epics are thus quintessentially works of *bhakti* (1976), and the deep structure of the epic is modeled on the cyclic eschatology articulated in the *bhakti* worldview of the Purāṇas. In Biardeau's view, historical chronologies should be resisted in favor of discovering the symbolic patterns underlying the text.[24]

The perspectives of Dumézil and Biardeau, not so dissimilar in method as in content, are sought to be conciliated in the works of Alf Hiltebeitel, who views the works of Dumézil and Biardeau as two lenses through which to interpret the material, one Indo-European, and one "Hindu." He translated the first two volumes of Dumézil's *Mythe et Épopee*, and carries Dumézil's Indo-Europeanist analysis further in several of his early writings, particularly *The Ritual of Battle: Kṛṣṇa in the Mahābhārata*. At the same time, he describes Biardeau's work as "one of the most stimulating and beautifully-crafted formulations to come out of the engagement of scholarship with Hinduism" (1983, 206). In Hiltebeitel's work, Dumézil's and Biardeau's insights are more complementary than opposed.

Although Hiltebeitel's recent work looks more closely at questions of history, his early work was dismissive of many text historical exertions as "atomistic historiography, making capital of a situation that now no longer exists, i.e. the seeming scholarly vacuum of the 'epic period'" (1983, 208). With Biardeau, he views extensions, or later additions to the text not so much as tendentious interpolations, but as being amplifications and enlargements rooted in the more ancient material, and illuminating its latent or hidden motifs. In these methods, Hiltebeitel's work is closer to the perspective of various Indian scholars, who insist that the embellishments evident in the text should be read not as the sly and deceitful appropriations of sectarian meddlers, but as the work of individuals themselves steeped in the tradition. Vidya Niwas Misra, for example, views the diverse material of the epic as organically related, on the analogy of a tree that grows branches and roots in all directions. "The changes, additions, and grafts were made by those who themselves were drenched in the *Mahābhārata*. Their individual identities got absorbed within the fathomless epic" (20). Later additions to the text, therefore, do not always represent separate visions or independently willed accounts, but rather, inspired augmentations of the same central concept: "These were the fallout of constant exposure to the oral recital . . . the masses did not listen to the MBh. for new surprises, because the story was absorbed by them even through lullabies. They heard it again and again only to renew and resharpen the old response—to merge themselves into the greater MBh." (20).

The late twentieth century has also seen great advances in the interpretation of the epic. The unfinished translation project of van Buitenen has been resumed by several well-recognized Sanskritists, among them Wendy Doniger and David Gitomer, under the general editorship of James Fitzgerald. Fitzgerald's work has been particularly illuminating in its insights into the political, historical, and social inspirations of themes recurring in the epic. Also significant is John Brockington's text historical work on *The Sanskrit Epics*, that makes careful comparisons between phenomena common to both epics and epitomizes diachronic interpretations of textual development. Bruce Sullivan has worked on interpretations of Vyāsa, and on literary and performative traditions deriving from the Sanskrit text. Nick Sutton has written on the complexity of religious doctrines found in the *Mahābhārata*, Julian Woods on the dialectic of free will and destiny, and Tamar Reich on sacrifice. Gregory Bailey, David Gitomer, David Shulman, James Laine, and a host of other scholars have commented on aspects of the *Mahābhārata* in the light of other genres of Sanskrit literature, often using regional variations to highlight themes in the Sanskrit text.

Trends in Indian Scholarship

Traditional Indian scholarship on the *Mahābhārata* was by way of commentaries on the text. In these commentaries, the purpose of the *Mahābhārata* is "more than exemplary or didactic; it is therapeutic insofar as seekers are challenged to change themselves through confrontation with the kaleidoscopic play of name and form—the panorama of life itself—viewed through the allegories and images of the poet" (Woods 1993, 12). That the purpose of a literary work is to foster self-understanding and emotional tranquillity (*śānti*), leading to *mokṣa*, is taken for granted by the traditional commentators on the *Mahābhārata*. We know of various mediaeval writers who offered whole or part commentaries on the text: Arjunamiśra (c. 1450–1500 C.E.), Caturbhujamiśra (c.1350/1550 C.E.), Devabodha (n.d.), Nīlakaṇṭha Dīkṣita (c. 1700 C.E.), Ratnagarbha (n.d.), Sadānanda Yati (n.d.), Sarvajña Nārāyaṇa (c. 1100/1300 C.E.), Vidyāsāgara (c. 1350 C.E.), Ānandavardhana (9th century C.E.), and Madhvācārya (13th century C.E.). Perhaps the most influential among these was Ānandavardhana, who in his classic work on aesthetic theory *Dhvanyaloka*, articulates the thesis that the purpose of an artistic work is to morally and spiritually elevate the sensitive viewer. He sees the *Mahābhārata* as the quintessential artistic work—offering a broad and varied experience of life in miniscule, generating in its hearers every conceivable human emotion, and through adroit manipulation of the audience's emotions, subtly bringing them to *śānti*, the peace that bespeaks complete wisdom. In Ānandavardhana's reading, the text is geared toward the artistic and didactic purpose of evoking *śāntarasa*, "an intense experience of detachment that comes from reading or witnessing a work of art depicting ruin, impermanence, the transitory character of worldly existence, and the futility of ambition" (Tubb, 200). Ānandavardhana's perspectives deeply influenced the work of other commentators, in particular Nīlkaṇṭha Dīkṣita, the seventeenth-century commentator whose commentary on the Bombay recension of the text is the most complete of those extant today.

In colonial and postcolonial times, Indian scholarship has been as involved in the text critical study of the *Mahābhārata* as its Western counterpart. This is demonstrated by the fact that the Critical Edition of the *Mahābhārata* was produced primarily through the labors of Indian scholars. Some Indian scholars accepted the inversion theories proposed by European scholars; thus R. N. Dandekar accepts the "Jaya," the alleged original core of the epic, as a "Kaurava ballad," adapted in favor of the Pāṇḍavas. In his view, the reversal is a result of "its tendentious redaction so as to make it serve as an efficacious popular vehicle for the propagation of the new *dharma* of Kṛṣṇa, with the *Bhagavad Gītā* as its focal point" (1990, 17–18). The current text then became devoted to "Kṛṣṇaism."

Notwithstanding these text historical engagements, however, Indian scholars have overall been more engrossed in articulating the "inner meaning" of the epic. A key example of this is V. S. Sukthankar himself. Sukthankar was a student of Winternitz, and eventually became the primary editor of the Critical Edition, a project that involved him in the most acute text critical work. Sukthankar also originated the thesis of the "Bhārgavization" of the epic. At the same time, however, Sukthankar is severely critical of what he views as the excesses of Higher Criticism in its search for the "epic nucleus."

> These propositions . . . strike us by their complete vacuity and absolute inanity. They do not help us in any way to understand this remarkable

> legacy of ancient India to the modern man, but serve merely to reveal the utter bankruptcy of modern literary criticism and to convince us of the futile spirit of vandalism which animates modern critics. (1957, 49)

He proposes instead a three-level theory of analysis, which recognizes at the first the narrative level of a fierce fratricidal war. At the second level, it is an ethical battle, in which the mythic personalities of Vedic tradition assume the forms of the epic heroes to represent the binary principles of *dharma* and *adharma*. At the third, or 'transcendental' level, Sukthankar reads the war of Kurukṣetra allegorically, as the perpetual battle between the higher and the lower self of humanity. Arjuna represents the Super-man in his struggle for mastery over ego, desire, and passion (symbolized by the Kaurava enemy); he is guided by his Inner Self, the Supreme Soul (Kṛṣṇa). Sukthankar concludes:

> When we realize these facts [the inner meaning of the MBh.] questions as to the historicity of the polyandrous marriage of Draupadī or the precise ethnic affinities of the Pāṇḍavas, or the exact date of the *Mahābhārata* war, of the origin and development of the epic—these and other favourite topics of academic wrangling—lose some of their glamour and cease to engross us. They are legitimate questions no doubt, and not totally devoid of interest. But we must realize that while disputing about them, we are still on the periphery of this mighty work, which is primarily concerned with finding a solution to the problem of evil in life, nay to the problem of existence itself. (124)

Other Indian scholars have resisted the application of criteria derived from foreign models in analyzing the epic, and argued the necessity for studying the epic within its native literary contexts. Vaidya and Pusalker, coeditors of the Critical Edition, asserted: "Ancient Indian standards of literary criticism, holding moral edification as the chief aim of any work, are to be applied to the *Mahābhārata*, and these need not conform to the definition of an epic in some foreign literature" (1937, 58). Similarly, Matilal searches for the inner meaning of Kṛṣṇa's enigmatic acts (1991), and tries to sensitize his readers to the fine distinctions between Hindu ethics and Western ethics (1989). In all his writings on the subject, his attempt is to read from within the tradition, juxtaposing it against the Western, but analyzing events and actions with reference to Indian formulations and understandings.

Curiously, although text historical studies have engaged Indian scholars, the Structuralist approaches that have dominated twentieth-century study of the epic in the West have found few adherents. Some scholars have argued that the importance given to myth in structural analysis is undue and exaggerated. Such a view is espoused by R. N. Dandekar, who is outright critical of such approaches. He asserts the obsolescence of Vedic culture, and argues its relative irrelevance to later Hinduism.[25] Other scholars, both Indian and Western, point out that the Structural approach contains a weakness in its lack of historical perspective. "Many structuralists tend to ignore the simple fact that social structures exist and function within historical contexts. They are as much subject to change as any historical reality" (Olivelle 1990, 126). Another scholar contends that "they are almost invariably guilty of a selective use of material in constructing a case that appears thoroughly convincing only when alternative passages are overlooked" (Sutton 2000, xx).

An intriguing and integrative contemporary analysis of the epic's apparently inchoate vastness is offered by A. K. Ramanujan in a brief essay entitled "Repetition in the *Mahābhārata*" (1991). Observing that the vast movement of the epic is based on a relatively solid basic structure, Ramanujan reads the text using the categories of Indian aesthetics. Taking the analogy of classical Indian music, Ramanujan suggests that just as music develops, elaborates, and explores in various ways the complex texture of a *rāga*, so the *Mahābhārata* may be seen as a long series of elaborations, expansions, and variations on a finite number of basic themes. Ramanujan argues that these variations are apprehended by the native intuition of the hearer, in the same manner as a native speaker of a language apprehends the correct grammatical form of a sentence. This is a 'structuralist' approach with a difference. It allows for the organic development of the text within certain artistic boundaries, recognizing limits to the improvisational license of storytellers; at the same time, it avoids the heavy emphasis on the decoding of myth that seems to have alienated some Indian scholars.[26] Given Ramanujan's considerable work on folklore and oral narratives, his approach would reward investigation.

Women in the *Mahābhārata*

Studies on women in the *Mahābhārata* are few. There has been some reflection on individual women—Draupadī,[27] Satyavatī, Sāvitrī;[28] and on epic heroines. There is the classic 1966 work of Shakambari Jayal, *The Status of*

Women in the Epics, which is still impressive in its command of the primary literature, and catalogs quite extensively beliefs and practices related to women in both epics. Its method, however, is dated, and some of its assumptions are questionable.[29] More recent is Shalini Shah's 1992 study on *Gender Relations in the Mahābhārata*, which is an anthropological study of social customs and practices evident in the culture of the *Mahābhārata*. Other than these, few full-length works on the topic exist; it is hoped that this work will help to fill some part of that lacuna.

Methodological Problems

As apparent from the above overview, scholars have grappled with the text for generations, using diverse hermeneutical tools, employing various perspectives. Many challenges confront the student of the *Mahābhārata*, which "like an Indian jungle . . . spreads out before us in an endless wilderness of trees entwined and tangled with rank creepers, coloured and scented with manifold flowers and blossoms, and the home of every kind of living creature" (Meyer, 1). Apart from its sheer size, it presents difficulties of several kinds. This is even more the case when one is querying the topic of women.

Textual Materials

The first limitation one must confess is that the entire discussion is based on one text, a text that represents what is in fact a closed dialogue among men—and further, an elite class of men. What we are likely to find in such a text therefore is almost entirely orthodox male opinion. As Stephanie Jamison points out, "folkloric and non-orthodox elements that are found in our preserved texts have no doubt undergone some processes of adaptation to conform better to orthodox norms and aims" (Jamison, 8). Even where one finds apparently newfangled and liberal opinion, therefore, it still represents *male* representations of womanhood and *male* ideals of femininity. Female voices, even bold and powerful ones, nevertheless represent *male* opinion. As Nabaneeta Dev Sen caustically notes, "Epic poets the world over are men singing the glory of other men, armed men, to be precise . . . Out of the thirty-eight basic things upon which most epic narratives of the world are based, only nine are associated with women . . . There is little they can do there—other then get abducted or rescued, or pawned, or molested, or humiliated in some way or other" (108). At no time, therefore, should we harbor any illusions that we are hearing *women's* perspectives and seeing *women's* lives.

To what extent, then, should we hope to glean knowledge of women in texts that are roundly patriarchal, preoccupied with male concerns, composed *by* men, but *for* society? While arguably it is possible to hear women's voices in the pauses punctuating the text, in the things left unsaid, in the things overstated, that is not in fact the aim of this work. Rather, through the hermeneutic of sex I hope to discover the ideals about gender. My interest is in understanding how these were rationalized, with what material and ideological supports, with a longer view to unpacking the gender ideologies that have, per Lincoln, always presented themselves to Hindu women as transcendent and eternal.

Another concern about textual work is in comprehending its relationship to reality. As Ricoeur has noted, a text is by its very nature "in the air," without a world (1976, 149). This is particularly the case in texts that are historically and spatially distant from us. The text represents a complete universe in its own right, an imaginary "quasi-world," in which the world that produced it is eclipsed to the point that all we have left of that world is its "aura," represented in writing. The conclusions that we draw from the text, therefore, are not necessarily conclusions that would hold for history. As Leslie Orr states in another context: these matters raise questions "about the extent to which the normative texts are capable of providing us with a complete or accurate view of how religious life was actually organized in a particular time and place, in terms of the definition of central religious values and practices" (2000, 124). Texts have limits for what light they can shed on history, and we need to be cautious in extrapolating evidence of lived reality from interpretations of texts.

The Nature of the Text: Genres Within a Genre

Another challenge in interpreting the *Mahābhārata* is in understanding its "nature." Our idea of what a text is doing, what is its purpose and its aim, is a key hermeneutical consideration; it inevitably bears on what we find in it. As we have seen above, Western scholarship has for generations characterized the *Mahābhārata* as an *epic*, comparable to the epics of Greece and Rome, and this characterization has colored its interpretation of the text. Similarly, native Indian commentators had their own view of the intent of the text, and this no doubt influenced what they gleaned from the text. While it may be that the interpretation of the text tells us more about the interpreter than the text, the very fact that it lends itself to so many interpretations tells us something more fundamental: that the Bhārata is a highly multiform text, representing several types of literature simultaneously—legal/theoretical, moral/didactic, mythic/narrative, philosophical/reflective. These different types of materials have generally been interpreted as representing varying layers of historical accretion,[30] each successive layer containing the sedimentation of a chronologically older period in history, thus representing a *temporal* ordering of the material in the text. It may, however, be equally instructive to view these materials not as strands of literature temporally removed from each other, but as different *genres* of literature coexisting simultaneously in the text. A challenging scholarly exercise would be to identify common strands of discourse in all these genres. What ideological commitments hold these varied genres together? Indeed, given the many inconsistencies and apparent contradictions that one finds in different genres of the text, is it possible to argue for any congruency of thought between one and another? One might very legitimately wonder: what is the relationship between the lofty reflections of the *mokṣadharma* section that insist all social distinctions are spurious, and the detailed elaboration of social hierarchies to be found in the *Anuśānaparva*? What is the relationship between the quasi-legal injunctions of the *rājadharma* section to the evidence of the narrative? Indeed, what is the relationship between the search for the divine that defies the norms of society, and the insistence that society must be preserved harmoniously? While answers are not easy to come by, an interpreter needs to be sensitive to these complexities. What appear to be inconsistencies in one place may well represent differences of literary genre. While different genres may indeed betray different historical, social, or religious perspectives, it is equally possible that different kinds of allowances were made to meet the needs of individual genres. Is there one uniform ideology to excavate from the *Mahābhārata*? What is one to make of the fact that while genres seem to reinforce each other on the one hand, they appear hopelessly in conflict on the other? These considerations, as we shall see, are of critical importance in interpreting the gender ideologies of the text.

Method

In the main, the *Mahābhārata* is a richly complex yarn, and much of the understanding of sexuality must be sifted from the careless remains, the unintended debris of narratives. With what tools does one interpret narrative? In answering this question, it has been common among theorists of myth and narrative to employ the work of Lévi-Strauss to speak of levels or "slates" of analysis. Thus, following Lévi-Strauss, Wendy Doniger proposes a four-level analysis of myth: the narrative level of the story, the divine level of the metaphorical struggle of divine and demonic powers, the cosmic level of metaphysical principles and symbolic truths, and the human level of the search for meaning in human life (1973, 2). I have, however, chosen to employ an approach that takes greater account of the political and social ramifications of the ways in which narrative is constructed. Narrative, as Eagleton suggests, is inherently ideological; in its apparently naive meanderings is encoded a worldview, a perspective, a way of thinking and being. The concern in this work, therefore, will be not simply to identify the latent and incipient ideologies that define the boundaries of sexuality. In addition, the hope is to identify the systemic structures that support gender ideologies. Ultimately, I hope to demonstrate that sexuality in the *Mahābhārata* is not something that may be summarized in facile statements about male and female roles. It is also far from haphazard or incidental. Rather, sexuality in the *Mahābhārata* is a consciously polymorphous, highly complex matter, where practice is tailored to be consistent with the larger religious ideology of the culture, and is finely differentiated to reflect the distinctions contained within the ideology itself.

To take but one example, one must explain the glaring and considerable disjunction between the way women characters *act*, and the way women are *expected* to do. There are many ways to think about this. One is to propose a diachronic line of development, in which Kuntī, Satyavatī, Draupadī—all women with colorful sexual histories—would represent a hoary past in which women's sexual lives were less rigorously regulated than later. In this line of analysis, their narratives collide with a much more conservative ideology that is evolving in post-Vedic and classical Hinduism, hence they find themselves to be mouthpieces for an ideal of womanly behavior that they themselves cannot reflect. In this interpretation, Draupadī's polyandrous marriage is the curious and anomalous residue of another time, another way of living. Kuntī and Satyavatī represent real Vedic women who operated boldly in the public sphere before that sphere came to be increasingly usurped by upper-class men. There is no shortage of works on Hindu women that have approached the question through such a diachronic lens.

Another way to think about this is about the needs of the narrative conflicting with the needs of a theologically interested group, a group that is concerned about crafting rigorous moral standards for future generations. In this line of interpretation, while it is anathema to the ideology of *pativratya* for a woman to even mentally entertain the idea of sexual involvement with more than man, the *narrative* is much better served by the intrigues arising out of Kuntī's and Satyavatī's premarital alliances. The plot would be much the paler without Draupadī's scandalous polyandrous marriage.

My method here is both diachronic and synchronic. That is to say, while it is clear that the text is a document rooted in identifiable periods of history, and reflects the various concerns of its time, it is also a bounded literary work, unified by considerable thematic coherence. The historical moment was a particularly charged one, in which the religious elite was weighing separate currents of thought and divergent worldviews. In my view, the schizoprenic characterization of women in the epics is a reflection of the fact that the composers were attracted to multiple currents of thought and unwilling to dismiss any out of hand. The ways in which women fit into these currents, and the different ethics they espouse, is one reason for the inherent contrariness in the presentation of women and sexuality.

To me, it is very clear that the epic as we have it was composed with an eye to several things: (1) to preserving archaic material threatened with extinction by an increasingly pluralist, indifferent, and "secular" culture; (2) to counter the attractions of that culture by a loving and extended immersion in the lost glories of Brahmanical culture, rehearsed through nostalgic stories of *ṛṣis* and *munis*, and a time when the gods walked among mortals; (3) to tell a fabulous tale, yes, but most importantly, *to use that tale* to *educate* and *socialize* successive generations into Brahmanical values, Brahmanical perspectives. It must never be forgotten that the *Mahābhārata* is represented then, as now, as *itihāsa*, *history*; the Bhāratas are represented then, as now, as the remote *ancestors* of the Hindu people.[31] It is of crucial significance that in hearing these tales, Hindus are being taught not about disconnected fictional heroes, but *about themselves*; both the epics, but particularly the *Mahābhārata*, are *rehearsals of Hindu identity*. The epics then are fundamentally tools for the creative reflection, crafting, refinement, and ultimate *public political assertion* of Hindu identity. This is the *central narrative agenda* of the epic, and in my view, no analysis of the text should lose sight of this larger backdrop.

Any study of the *Mahābhārata* must take these factors into account, but they are particularly pertinent to a study of gender ideology, which reflects most obviously the composers' didactic and pedagogical aims. In the following, I hope to take due account of all these perspectives.

Outline

The book is composed of six substantive chapters. The first chapter clears the ground for a discussion of sexuality by articulating the religious underpinnings upon which sexual ideologies are premised. Using the *Mahābhārata*'s own lexicon, it treats the two types of religious activity recognized by the text: *nivṛtti dharma*, and *pravṛtti dharma*. It investigates contrasts and continuities between the two, and locates the space of sexuality within these discussions. The second chapter focuses on *nivṛtti dharma*, and analyzes the place and function of sexuality in *nivṛtti* practices. Key among these practices is the tradition of ascetic renunciation. The third chapter targets *pravṛtti dharma* for extended discussion. It itemizes the numerous categories into which sexual practice is classified, and explores relationships situated at the margins of each category. The fourth chapter focuses on myths and stereotypes relating to female sexuality, identifying the cultural logic and function behind social platitudes. It proposes that women's sexuality is a chronic source of anxiety for both streams of religion, leading to the perpetuation of misogynist attitudes. The fifth chapter extends the discussion of the fourth to look at strategies evolved by both *nivṛtti* and *pravṛtti* streams for the management of women's sexuality. The sixth chapter researches the liminal category of *āpaddharma*, 'the law of distress,' to look at ways in which marginal figures and practices are drawn into the text through the logic of exceptions. The concluding chapter brings these congeries of thought together to propose that the logic of sexuality is designed to facilitate the religious aspirations of both types of religious practice, a domestic tradition that valorizes householder ethics, and a renunciant tradition that affirms the personal individual search for the highest ideals.

All references to the *Mahābhārata* text are to the Critical Edition compiled by the Bhandarkar Oriental Research Institute. Translations are my own, unless otherwise specified.

Chapter One

Religion in the *Mahābhārata*

A brief overview of the historical context of the *Mahābhārata* might be appropriate to launch ourselves into the discussion of religion in the Great Epic.

Historical Context of the *Mahābhārata*

In his work *Brāhmaṇas in Ancient India* (1979), Govind Prasad Upadhyay offers a sketch of the historical and social clime that is encompassed in the *Mahābhārata*. I employ it here because it very economically provides the context for the literary preoccupations of the text. While scholars will differ on individual points of Upadhyay's interpretation, most will agree on the broad details. In Upadhyay's assessment, the *Mahābhārata* is a chronicle of the challenges faced by the Brahmanical community[1] between the period of 600 B.C.E. and 400 C.E. He paints a graphic picture of a group besieged by overwhelming varieties of economic, political, and social change.

Upadhyay begins by noting the geographical core of the Brahmanical community—an area known as *madhyadeśa*, "the middle country," "heartland"; or *āryavarta*, "the land of the *ārya*s." This central space is devoted to the ritualistic sacrificial religion developed by the Indo-Aryans. Upadhyay asserts that the most basic factor contributing to the fluctuations in Brahmanical fortunes is the economic changes "which took a vigorous course from Mauryan times onwards" (30). Urbanism, mobility, trade, commerce, agriculture, the formation of guilds and artisans' communities all led to a greater degree of movement in society. More wealth and power was placed in the hands of the lower castes of society, promoting hierarchies based on class over those of *varṇa*. These new "economic ethics" provided common folk in urban society with a greater scope of options[2] (30).

In addition to the economic changes eroding the foundations of Vedic society, Brahmanical tradition was stressed under a variety of social and political developments. The first of these momentous events was the political ascension of Mahāpadmānanda in the Vedic *madhyadeśa* itself (c. 364 B.C.E.; 30). Mahāpadmānanda was the first *śūdra* ruler of *āryavarta*. His accession to rulership represented a mighty blow to the *varṇa*-based triumphalism of the Brahmanical tradition, which reserved this privilege only for its protégés, the *kṣatriyas*. That *śūdras* should exercise hegemony over *dvijas* was seen as a sign of the moral decline of society. Upadhyay notes that as a result of this, the Nandas are uniformly vilified in Purāṇic accounts as usurpers and uncultured barbarians.

The Nandas were overthrown by Candragupta Maurya who, with the collusion of the Greeks, established the Mauryan dynasty (324–187 B.C.E.).[3] The Mauryan rulers, however, became patrons of the heterodox Buddhist tradition, which posed a serious challenge to the Brahmanical tradition. The incursions of the Greeks, moreover, inspired terror and distress. The *Yuga Purāṇa*, for example, describes the state of panic created by *Yāvana* (Greek) inroads into *āryavarta*, saying that they brought the havoc of war with them (28). True political chaos, however, came with the collapse of the Mauryan empire after the death of Aśoka.[4] The northwest frontier of *madhyadeśa* saw a series of foreign incursions. The migration of new tribes such as the Madrakas, the Sindhus, and the Sauviras, generated increasing social upheaval. In addition, the repeated invasions of the Greeks, the Scythians, the Parthians, and the Abhiras, led to immense instability and an impending sense of chaos. In Upadhyay's assessment, Brahmanical orthodoxy was deeply strained by these invasions, which brought with them not only terrible violence, but also large foreign populations who could have no loyalties to Vedic religion, with its highly specialized ritualism and exclusivist bent. Many of the foreigners, moreover, embraced heterodox traditions, adding further to the insecurity of the orthodox. The Kuśānas, for example, became patrons of Buddhism.

Beginning about the sixth century B.C.E., serious social changes were also afoot. On the eastern fringes of this heartland evolved the *śramaṇa* movements, both Brahmanical and heterodox, with their *yogic* and ascetic ideals. Their moral idealism and reformulated soteriological goals represented a severe critique of Vedic religion, a critique that became increasingly influential within the *madhyadeśa* itself. The dissonance arising from this is reflected in the cultural tensions between the orthodox tradition of the *madhyadeśa* and the heterodox Magadha kingdom, which allied itself with the *śramaṇa*-based Buddhist movement (24). The Brahmanical tradition thus saw itself-menaced on both sides, besieged by ideological challenges on the one hand, and increasing economic, political, and social change on the other.

According to Upadhyay, the southwestern fringe of the *madhyadeśa* saw developments of a less strident, but equally significant kind. These were the rise of various devotional movements (31). There was the rise of Bhāgavatism among the Sātvata, Vṛṣṇi, and Andhaka chapters of the Yādava clan. Like Jainism and Buddhism, Bhāgavatism also originated in the tribal republics of *kṣatriya*s (the Vṛṣṇi-Andhaka tribes), and spread beyond these areas after the demise of Aśoka. Bhāgavata religion practised a non-Vedic style of religion, focused around the devotional worship of Vāsudeva-Kṛṣṇa. Upadhyay traces worship of "Sātvata heroes" such as Kṛṣṇa back to the *Upaniṣad*s, and asserts that by the time of Pāṇini, Vāsudeva was a definite recipient of worship (32). In Bhāgavata religion, Vedic acts were held to be of little use and were disparaged in comparison to *bhakti*.

In addition to the Bhāgavatas, there were the *āgamic* cults of the Pancarātras and the various Śaivite cults. Śiva is a full-fledged "monotheistic" god in the *Śvetaśvatara Upaniṣad*. Several schools of Śaivism were influential around the turn of the millennium: the Pāśupata school, the Lākulīśa Pāśupata school, and the Kāpālika school. The Pāśupata school is held to be the earliest of these (33).

Upadhyay argues that the *Mahābhārata* and the Purāṇas are a record of the intense anxiety experienced by orthodox Brahmanism, as a result of the foreign incursions, the changing socioeconomic environment, and the ideological challenges mounted by the various *śramaṇa*s.[5] These apprehensions, he says, were exorcised through the very gloomy thesis of *kaliyuga*, 'the age of distress' (25). Upadhyay states that the four-*yuga* conception is a nostalgic hearkening to a peaceable glorious past, describing the advancement of human history as one of increasing lawlessness and degeneration: "Nowhere is the *Brāhmaṇa* psychology so much deranged as in the delineation of the horror of this age" (25). Purāṇic and epic writings of the *kaliyuga* betray despondency at the apparent disintegration of orthodox culture, as well as disquiet over Brahmanical responsibility as custodians of the Vedic tradition. The many and vivid descriptions of *kaliyuga* in the *Mahābhārata* and *Purāṇa* rehearse the sense of foreboding generated by the age. It is feared that the *varṇa* system will collapse, and all humanity will be of one order. The earth will be full of *mleccha*s (foreigners), without rites and sacrifices. *Brāhmaṇa*s will be killed and persecuted by *śūdra*s, and, afflicted with fear, will rove the earth without protectors. There will be great wars. The *brāhmaṇa*s, without power or fortune, will need to depend on *śūdra*s for their livelihood, and will have to honor *śūdra*s. The male population will shrink as a result of war. Vedic study and sacrifice will decline, non-Aryans will follow the religion of the Aryans. The earth will belong to *mleccha*s, and there will be no more *śrāddha*s (obsequial rites). *Śūdra*s will explain the *dharma*, and *brāhmaṇa*s will follow. There will be the veneration of bones (a clear reference to Buddhist *stūpās*), the construction of tombs over sacred sacrificial grounds and sacred tanks. People will mix with heretics, non-Vedic texts will be the authority of heretics, and *brāhmaṇa*s will mix with anti-Vedic sects. There will be many sects whose followers will be renouncers (25–29; the notion of *kaliyuga* is discussed further in Chapter Six).

In Upadhyay's view, the fervid unease of the age fermented into a period of concentrated literary and theological creativity. The Brahmanical tradition evolved various devices to overcome the setbacks suffered by Vedic religion. "The *Mahābhārata* betrays a conscious attempt on the part of *brāhmaṇa*s to synthesize diverse religious systems" (37). One of the techniques developed, he proposes, is the incorporation and "vedicization" of non-Vedic deities. The Sātvata deity Vāsudeva-Kṛṣṇa becomes identified with the Vedic Viṣṇu (39). The *Mahābhārata* is thought to have been composed during a time when the Brahmanical tradition was reasserting itself through this kind of imaginative theological reconstruction. Upadhyay does not specify this, but implies in other ways that these artful endeavors assume the successful political defense of Brahmanical values made by the Śuṅga dynasty (second–third centuries C.E.).[6] The *Mahābhārata* is thought to reflect the renewed sense of confidence experienced by the tradition, when various philosophical methods had been formulated for dealing with the intellectual challenges posed by the erstwhile *śramaṇa* traditions. It retains in its narrative strain the collective memory of its hoary Vedic past. At the same time, it reflects the psychological turmoil of the immediately preceding centuries, while anticipating the sophisticated theological syntheses to be chiseled and polished in classical Hinduism. The *Mahābhārata* is therefore viewed as a transitional text, synthesizing the most attractive features of all of its adversarial movements. The devotional trends of the Kṛṣṇaite and Śaiva cults are incorporated as the *bhakti* elements of the text. The *śramaṇa* worldview, with its doctrines of *saṃsāra*, rebirth, *karmic* retribution, and *mokṣa* (final liberation), as well as its stern ethical core, is appropriated as the ultimate interpretation of existence, and paid ideological deference. Meanwhile, the Vedic tradition is retained but increasingly reevaluated. Its sacrificial ethos is interpreted metaphorically, and its most offensive edges (animal sacrifice, for example) are intellectually scrutinized.

Elements of Upadhyay's somewhat breathless summary will be controversial—for example, the trend of viewing Kṛṣṇa as a euhemerized local chieftain has been criticized by Alf Hiltebeitel (1995), while the alleged promotion of Kṛṣṇa from local Sātvata deity to universal God also meets resistance (though it is supported by van Buitenen 1973, Brockington 1999, Hopkins 1969, and others). Similarly, scholars will differ on the dates they assign to the composition of the text.[7] The broad details of Upadhyay's overview, are, however, affirmed by other scholars.[8] Hence for the purpose of this study, I have used his outline provisionally, as a platform on which to situate and ground the more focused discussion to follow—with the proviso that scholars differ on individual points of this trajectory of development.[9] There can be no doubt that the *Mahābhārata* is a product of these contested political, economic, social, and religious upheavals.[10]

This brings us to a more focused examination of the religious context of the epic.

Religion in the *Mahābhārata*

Nineteenth-century European stereotypes characterized India as a land steeped in religion, where the whole spectrum of experience—worldly or "otherworldly"; natural or supernatural; human, subhuman, or superhuman—is subsumed and rationalized in the religious. While this was not considered a virtue in the heyday of logical positivism and rationalist Modern thought, there is good reason for treating the subject of sexuality in the *Mahābhārata* as a religious phenomenon. All discussions of sex and gender are framed within the theological and metaethical discourses of *dharma* and *adharma*, righteousness and unrighteousness, and the study of sexuality in the *Mahābhārata* is therefore inalienable from the study of religion. It is necessary at the outset then, to take some account of the religious platform on which discussions of sex are premised.

The question of the religion of the *Mahābhārata* is complex enough to deserve a separate monograph, and there is no dearth of writing on this subject, particularly that focused on the *Gītā*.[11] In these texts, however, there is little consensus on the larger religious orientation of the *Mahābhārata*. As we have seen, scholars dispute whether the *Mahābhārata* was originally a Śaivite or a Vaiṣṇavite work; they dispute whether Kṛṣṇa is original to the epic; some contend that the *Mahābhārata* was not a religious text at all, but originally a heroic ballad; others view it as quintessentially religious. Nor is there any particular consensus among traditional commentators. Śaṃkara interpreted the *Gītā* along Advaitin lines, Rāmānuja and Madhva along theist ones, the eleventh-century Abhinavagupta took an Advaitin perspective, as did the major seventeenth-century commentator Nīlakaṇṭha Dīkṣita. Below, I add my own voice to this cacophonous chorus.

While the merits of individual interpretations may be debated, the fact that there *are* so many, and exhibiting such a disparate range of opinion, demonstrates something more fundamental: that the *Mahābhārata* is what might cautiously be termed a pluralist text, that engages a variety of religious doctrines and explicitly or tacitly permits them to coexist, without insisting on dogmatic uniformity. The text thus lends itself to multiple interpretations, and this may be telling of the historical period in which it was composed, as well as of the relatively ecumenical spirit of the text itself. Any analysis of the religious ethos of the text therefore must be at least somewhat subjective, emphasizing some currents of discourse and treating others as secondary.

Recent scholarship has tended to give weight to the theist strains in the text, as exemplified, for example in the Nārāyaṇīya portion of the Anuśāsanaparva.[12] For various reasons I am disinclined to follow this trend. No doubt all scholars aspire in their work to "let the text speak for itself." This is, however, a special problem for a text like the *Mahābhārata*, which is garrulous in the extreme. It expatiates on religion in so many different ways that it's entirely possible for two scholars to "let the text speak" and arrive at quite different conclusions. I have chosen to take my cue on this subject from those areas of the text that directly confront questions of religion, namely, the *mokṣadharma* section of the Śāntiparva. I believe this is a defensible selection for two reasons. The first is that in this section, the text itself acknowledges the plurality of religious doctrines. It sifts and weighs them, and self-reflexively attempts to articulate them in some systematic synthetic form. The second is that, notwithstanding the apparent discrepancies between the "didactic" and the "narrative,"[13] there is considerable congruence to be found between the conclusions reached in these sections, and the assumptions underlying the text as a whole. The philosophical outlook expounded in the *mokṣadharma* section reverberates through the entire text. Echoes of it may be found in the philosophy of the *Gītā*, as well as in other segments of the text that address the questions directly. I will therefore focus on the *mokṣadharma* as detailing most succinctly the *Mahābhārata*'s self-consciously and reflectively formulated opinions about religion, with the caveat, however, that the categories developed are not absolute but to be employed heuristically.

In the *mokṣadharma* section of the *Śāntiparva*, the twelfth and largest volume of the text, the *Mahābhārata* explicates its own views on the nature, aims, and purpose of religion (*dharma*).[14] The section forms part of a larger education imparted in three phases to the victorious Pāṇḍava elder Yudhiṣṭhira by the dying grandsire Bhīṣma. In this third and final section on *dharma*, Bhīṣma's lessons are augmented by numerous anecdotes about sages and deities. Several exalted characters appear in person to tutor Yudhiṣṭhira, Vyāsa and Kṛṣṇa among them, underscoring the wisdom and maturity of Bhīṣma's comments.

Broadly conceived, in the *mokṣadharma* section, religious activity is said to be of two basic types. These are *pravṛtti dharma* and *nivṛtti dharma*;[15] "these are the two paths upon which the Vedas are established" (XII.233.6).[16] *Pravṛtti* and *nivṛtti* are offered as the most embracing categories for understanding the diversity of religious thought and practice in classical India. They are not new; *pravṛtti* and *nivṛtti* represent the *pitṛyana* ("way of the fathers") and the *devayana* ("way of the gods") respectively, a categorization already found in texts such as the Jaiminīya Brāhmaṇa, and the Bṛhadāraṇyaka and Chāndogya Upaniṣads.[17]

Taken in sum, *pravṛtti* and *nivṛtti* are a commodious device employed by the writers to claim knowledge of the plurality of religious practices and to assign them relative value. Thus, the variety of extant beliefs and practices are typologized and hierarchalized. The hierarchy itself is of interest, and tells us something about the ultimate religious predilections of the writers. On the other hand, the fact that they sought to retain the multiplicity and to synthesize it, tells us that they found value in divergent forms of religious practice and the ruminations of the *mokṣadharma* section are a way to rationalize them. The final product is a powerfully coherent picture of the religious values embraced by the composers of the epic, in which the diversity of religious phenomena is retained, but the value assigned them is reassessed. Thus both orthodoxy and change are accommodated. Orthodoxy is preserved in principle, but its preservation is partly illusory in that the nomenclature of *pravṛtti/nivṛtti* necessitates a two-tier system of values, in which the orthodox position is displaced of priority, ultimately relegated to a supportive position rather than the primary one.

Let us look at the details.

Pravṛtti and *nivṛtti* are conceptualized as two types of religion that are fundamentally antithetical to each other. They are, however, sought to be reconciled at nodal points in their theologies. They might heuristically be analyzed as being distinct from each other on four counts: (1) they attract different types of practitioners, (2) they avow different goals, (3) they practice different ethics, and (4) they utilize different methods of achieving their goals. As we shall see in more detail, *pravṛtti* connotes acts of ritual engagement with the world, while *nivṛtti* implies a turning away from the concerns of the world, a thorough and cultivated disregard for the values on which the world is structured.

Pravṛtti Dharma

Pravṛtti dharma is an evolute of what the *Gītā* occasionally disdains as "the religion of the Vedas" (BG II.43–45). The word is derived from the suffix *pra* attached to the root *vṛt*. The combination has a broad semantic range, meaning "to commence, increase, grow, act, prevail, happen." One meaning is "active life; taking an active part in worldly affairs."[18] In the *mokṣadharma* section of the Śāntiparva, the term *pravṛtti* refers to that level of religion that is practiced by ordinary people, immersed in the ordinary activities of living ordinary lives. It is the level at which the vast majority of humanity functions. *Pravṛtti dharma* is this-worldly and pragmatic, and is characterized by an active immersion in life. This involvement in life is neither arbitrary nor personal, however. It is envisioned as being studied and ritualized, consciously enacted, contained within carefully demarcated constraints of time, space, and multiple hierarchies.

If *dharma* were bipedal, *pravṛtti dharma* would be one sturdy limb. It offers all that one might need to live a productive life in society: a vertical orientation that situates humanity in relation to the cosmos, a lateral orientation that locates one in relation to others in the world, and a somewhat underdeveloped inner anchoring that facilitates a reflective appreciation of the rest. In its vertical inclination, *pravṛtti dharma* offers a highly refined analysis of the relationship of human beings with the cosmos. This is what we know as the sacrificial religion of the Vedas. *Pravṛtti dharma* visualizes this relationship as a reciprocal exchange between human beings and the various divinities that regulate the functions of the cosmos. It also prescribes the attitudes that are appropriate for human beings to this relationship—reverence, honor, methodically precise worship. The laborious systems of Vedic sacrifice are based on this analysis. Human beings maintain their commitment to the divine by executing with scrupulous care the rituals of the sacrifice. In return, the *devas*, supported by these ritual activities, are obligated to assist humans with their diverse agendas.

Pravṛtti dharma implies more than just the Vedic tradition, however—and in this sense is not the old Vedic religion at all, but something quite new; *pravṛtti* dharma is the Vedic tradition reconstituted and redefined, so that while it embraces the religious vocabulary of the Vedas and the symbology of the sacrifice, it extends, prolongs, and modifies it. For example, *pravṛtti dharma* extends the precision of Vedic ritual into social terrain to achieve a more refined typology of social relationships than was the case in Vedic literature. Thus in its "lateral" dimension, *pravṛtti dharma* is concerned with assigning each element its proper place and method of living. The correct relationships between human beings and other elements (nature, animals) are suggested. Also implied is the manner in which human beings should conduct themselves in relation to them. Some animals deserve affection, reverence, and protection (cows), while others are considered unclean and loathsome (dogs). In general, humans are privileged over the animal world, but this privilege is not unambiguous, because animals can have powers that supersede those of humans. Nature, in its myriad forms as earth, water, and food, is seen as being organically connected with the human world. Humans are extensions and modifications of the same elemental matter that composes nature; this attitude is an extension of the insight captured in the famous *Upaniṣadic* proclamation: "I am food! I am food! I am food! I am the eater of food! I am the eater of food! I am the eater of food!" (*Taittirīya Upaniṣad* 3.10.6).

Relationships among human beings are more specifically itemized at this lateral level, and the norms by which they are to be conducted are ritualized. This is what we recognize as the formula *varṇāśramadharma*. The Vedic world, of course, was already familiar with the classifications of *varṇa* as famously evident in the *puruṣasukta* (Rg.10.90), and the Brāhmaṇas developed an analysis of *varṇadharma*. In the *pravṛtta* strands of *Mahābhārata* religious discourse, these discussions are amplified. The fine details of *varṇadharma* are drawn out, in maneuvers anticipating the taxonomical labors of the *Dharmaśāstras*. The duties and privileges of the various *varṇa*s are elaborated at length, and several sections of the postwar books are devoted to assigning social value to embryonic subclass groups. Class hierarchies, therefore, are a crucial element of *pravṛttidharma*, of increasing consequence in determining a person's duty. (More on this in Chapter Three).

Varṇa represents one axis of social ordering; another is achieved by the device of *āśrama*. Whereas the Vedic tradition was fundamentally the religion of a householder, the concept of *āśrama* was designed to acknowledge and accommodate divergent lifestyles that were gaining popular sway, in particular the lifestyle of celibate mendicancy.[19] In the *pravṛtta* sections of the *Mahābhārata*, *āśrama* is increasingly a point of reference in assessing one's social obligations. The signification of the word *āśrama*, however, is still fluid, connoting sometimes a *stage* in the larger life cycle of an individual, and sometimes a permanent *lifestyle* chosen by the individual.

To the evolving orthodoxies of *varṇa* and *āśrama* should be added the less heralded but equally trenchant hierarchies of sex and seniority. In actuality, more primary than either *varṇa* or *āśrama* in determining one's *dharma* in a situation is the variable of sex. As we shall see, the *dharma* of a man is almost always differentiated from the *dharma* of a woman, in each *varṇa* and *āśrama*. It is the tacit, but most fundamental ordering principle of *pravṛtti dharma*. Finally, in a classification that often passes unremarked, one's obligations may also be inferred from one's position within a familial hierarchy. Classical Hinduism had a systematization of relationships almost as elaborate and refined as that of classical Confucianism; thus, the younger member of any partnership was deemed to have different responsibilities from an elder; a younger brother, for example, had different privileges and responsibilities from his older sibling. In formulations very much reminiscent of classical Confucian thought, the younger owed the elder unquestioning filial obedience and respect. The elder owed the younger guidance, protection, and support.

The lateral level of *pravṛtti dharma* thus embraces all aspects of a person's social relationships, both domestic and public. It contextualizes individuals, situates them relationally on the interlocking matrices of sex, age, occupation, and binary relationship. All of these factors are crucial reference points in determining one's duty.

A universal ethics is decidedly absent in *pravṛtti* dharma. As far as one can determine, there is no Kantian universal person with categorical ethical obligations; while one can find the odd statement implying a universal ethics, a closer examination reveals a hoax. Ethics in *pravṛtti* dharma are almost always sex or class-differentiated. Thus, "universal duties" (*dharmān śāśvatān*) are enumerated in *Śāntiparva* XII:60.7–8, and are explicitly stated to apply to all classes: "freedom from anger, truthfulness of speech, an agreeable nature, forgiveness, fathering children upon one's own wives, purity, avoidance of quarrel, sincerity, and maintenance of dependants"[20] (XII.60.7–8). The reference to wives, however, immediately betrays the limited audience addressed; *pravṛtti* ethics are always contingent on the social location of the moral agent.

All of the above factors lead to the conclusion that ethics in *pravṛtti dharma* are of necessity *situational* rather than categorical; there are no deontological obligations incumbent on all beings. In the act of ascertaining one's duty, one must weigh in balance one's numerous obligations, the "*śāśvatān*" as well as those of sex, *varṇa*, *āśrama*, and seniority. Thus one arrives at one's *svadharma*, one's own peculiar and distinctive *dharma*.

The personal, individual dimension is somewhat neglected in *pravṛtti dharma*. Fundamentallly, it is a system of social ethics. To the limited extent that we can speak of individual personal goals in the *pravṛtta* context, we might allude to what the text calls the *trivarga*, also known as the *puruṣārtha*s. Later Hinduism codifies these as the "purposes, aims, or goals of a human being," but in the *Mahābhārata*, this theology is tentative and evolving. In several passages, the *puruṣārtha*s are cited more as the hallmarks of a truly cultured and sophisticated man; that is to say, one who is educated, urbane, and worldly-wise, is one who is schooled in the *trivarga*, the triad of *dharma*, *artha*, *kāma*. It is in this sense that we can understand the deer's admonition to Pāṇḍu in Ādiparva. The deer contends that Pāṇḍu should not have shot him while he was engaged in the act of mating; "You who understand the pleasures of women, and the truths of the scriptures and *dharma* and *artha*; such an unholy act is unbecoming of a god-like person like yourself"[21] (I.109.21). The deer's assertion is that a man of cultivation and refinement would not have committed so barbaric an act as to injure a being in the process of enjoying *kāma*; he would have understood the delicacy of the moment. *Artha* and *kāma* are pursuits natural to the human condition; tempered with study of scripture and *dharma*, they should be indulged with refinement, consideration, and taste.

In other passages, the *puruṣārtha*s are ordered according to class. Thus, while one may generalize that *dharma* is the duty of all people of all *varṇa*s, it is especially so of male *brāhmaṇa*s, who are the custodians and interpreters of *dharma* for the rest of society. *Artha* is approved for all classes of male householders, but for *kṣatriya*s and *vaiśya*s more than for *brāhmaṇa*s.[22] The quest for *kāma* is similarly legitimated for all classes, but a crude and hedonistic pursuit of *kāma* is characteristic only of the lowest classes and *asuras*. The *puruṣārtha*s in the *Mahābhārata* are about personal moral and aesthetic refinement, so that one's base human proclivities are tempered with cultivated restraint. It is to this limited extent that we can speak of a personal dimension to *pravṛtti dharma*; for the most part, it is outwardly oriented, toward a social and communitarian ethics. A theology of the individual is decidedly underdeveloped.

The primary concern of *pravṛtti dharma* is the twice-born male householder, and his interrelationships with all other elements of his universe. *Pravṛtti dharma* elucidates his duties and responsibilities in every sphere of life, and in so doing also sketches out the duties of other groups. As in the Vedic tradition, wives and children are understood not as separate entities in themselves, but as adjuncts who enable and facilitate the religious life of the male householder. *Pravṛtti dharma* prolongs this tendency into classical Hinduism. The paternalist bent of Vedic religion is taken to its logical extension, so that the lives of women are inextricably entwined with that of their husbands, past, present, or future. An extensive theology is articulated, enjoining the devotion of women to their husbands. These trends coalesce in the evolution of the ideology of the *pativratā* woman, the woman "avowed to her husband/lord." The *pativratā* woman is the dominant paradigm for ideal female behavior in *pravṛtti dharma*.

In this tri-dimensional way, *pravṛtti dharma* paves the way for the theologizing systemizations of classical Hinduism, and addresses every aspect of lived ordinary life. Its "method" of practice, therefore, is faithful and ritualized adherence to all the regulations and guidelines set in place by the Vedic tradition: participation in the Vedic sacrifice for those to whom it is permitted, in the capacity in which they are permitted to participate; compliance with boundaries in all social relations; heedfulness of all varieties of *dharmas* in the pursuit of goals appropriate to one's station. It is preeminently the religion of the householder: "The *dharma* characteristic of *pravṛtti* is prescribed for householders"[23] (XIII.129.16). While embedded in the concept of the *āśrama*s is the recognition of lifestyles other than that of the householder, renunciation still remains a distant fourth lifestyle/stage in most *pravṛtti* formulations, and is given little emphasis.[24] The twice-born male householder is the locus of the theologizing activities of the text.

The spiritual goals of *pravṛtti dharma* are modest, compared with those of *nivṛtti dharma*. As in Vedic religion, optimal religious engagement yields a period of residence in heaven (*svargaloka/devaloka*). *Pravṛtti dharma* is a little different from Vedic religion, however. Whereas death and heaven, with the supportive ritual activities of one's descendants represented the end of existence in the Vedic scheme, in *pravṛtti dharma*, the *karma*-and-rebirth worldview of the *Upaniṣads*[25] has forged some pathways. *Pravṛtti dharma*, therefore, operates on the understanding that when the merit from one's works (*karma*) is exhausted, one will return again from heaven to live as a creature on earth. One will pick up again the trajectory of life interrupted with one's death, and continue in a new existence. Implicit in the theorizing of *pravṛtti dharma* is that it is a *temporary* path, a point of waiting and holding until one is mentally and spiritually ready for the true religious path. *Pravṛtti* is the domain of busy-ness, activity, and ritual worldliness, and is geared toward the ephemeral: temporary goals and temporary rewards. When one tires of its repetitive transience and begins to seek some manner of permanence, one will turn to the *uttamadharma*, the "true or ideal religion," that is, *nivṛtti dharma*. In *Mahābhārata* shorthand, *pravṛtti dharma* is therefore called the religion of acts (*karma*), and the religion that is "rebirth-oriented" (*pravṛttiḥ punarāvṛttiḥ* XII.210.4).

Nivṛtti Dharma

Nivṛtti dharma is envisioned as the structural opposite of *pravṛtti dharma*. It represents an emphatic departure from all of the preoccupations of *pravṛtti dharma*, and is geared radically toward the achievement of personal spiritual ends. The word *nivṛtti* is derived from the suffix *ni* added to the root *vṛt*. Together, the word connotes disappearance, cessation, abstinence from work, inactivity, resignation, discontinuance of worldly acts or emotions, separation from the world.[26] Its idiomatic use in the *Mahābhārata* suggests renunciation, a decisive rejection of worldly life, its overarching worldview, the various systems and hierarchies that support that worldview and its many social and ritual monuments. It diagnoses this life as fundamentally flawed, a wholly unsatisfactory place of entrapment, and earnestly seeks release from it.[27] *Nivṛtti dharma*, therefore, is vitally premised on *Upaniṣadic* views of existence. The world (*saṃsāra*) is seen as a place of suffering and anxiety that are perpetuated by one's actions (*karma*, both of a moral and a ritual nature). One's participation in this realm of pleasurable distraction is endlessly rehearsed through rebirth. The only worthy goal of human striving is to emancipate oneself from the shackles of birth and death (*punarjanma*), and achieve lasting peace, permanent happiness (*mokṣa*). In defiance and repudiation of all social convention, *nivṛtti* directs itself to the goal of *mokṣa*, which also represents freedom from the cyclical enclosures of birth and death. *Nivṛtti dharma*, therefore, is frequently used as a synonym for *mokṣadharma*, "the religion of freedom."

While *pravṛtti dharma* is the religion of the ordinary—practiced by ordinary folk in society, using the familiar method of sacrificial religion, aimed at the modest goal of worldly prosperity, *nivṛtti dharma* is by definition the religion of the extraordinary, requiring exceptional effort. "The wise say that birth, death, and other afflictions rule over and are beyond [the control] of human beings"[28] (XII.306.106). If one hopes to control one's life, therefore, instead of being controlled by it, one must engage in uncommonly arduous work. In contrast to the communal leanings of *pravṛtti dharma*, the goals of *nivṛtti dharma* are ambitious and squarely soteriological; it aims for nothing short of absolute liberation from the cycle of deaths and rebirths intuited in the philosophy of the *Upaniṣad*s. It therefore refers to itself as "the highest path" (*nivṛttiḥ paramā gatiḥ* XII.210.4). Its method of practice is correspondingly extreme and rigorous, and intended only for the exceptionally focused, hardy few.

Mokṣa is unequivocally articulated as the final goal of *nivṛtti dharma*, but the *Mahābhārata*'s views of the content of *mokṣa* are still under construction. Is it achievable while still living? Where does one's body go when one achieves *mokṣa*? Should it be visualized as a physical space, or as a mental or emotional realm?[29] Who has the *adhikāra* to *mokṣa*? What are the duties of the renouncer, or should he or she have any? These details have not been worked out in the text, although it anticipates some of the directions in which classical Hinduism evolved.

It would seem that the composers of the text were open to the proposition that *mokṣa* may be achieved in a variety of ways. These are most famously indicated in the *Gītā*, whose theology of the "three paths" came ultimately to represent the core of Hinduism. Although the *Gītā* never formally speaks of three paths, it discusses the possibility of liberating oneself through the modes of *jñāna* (contemplation of one's true identity), of *karma* (the path of a peculiar type of disciplined action), and ultimately of *bhakti* (earnest devotion to God, in the *Gītā* conceptualized as Kṛṣṇa, elsewhere accommodating Śiva). It would seem that trodden with earnestness, any and all of these pursuits might bring one to the desired destination of *mokṣa*. In the *mokṣadharma* section, the path most privileged is that of *jñāna*, of immersing oneself in the contemplation of one's true identity as the Self (*ātman*/*puruṣa*). While later Hinduism expands on the techniques of *bhakti* and *karmayoga*, in the *Mahābhārata* I would argue the archetype of the *nivṛtti* practitioner is the ascetic, the *tapasvin* characterized by acts of extreme asceticism, involving the deprivation, chastisement, and ultimate mastery over the body.

Through the denial of all bodily comforts, through dire and extreme acts of self-torture, the *nivṛtti* practitioner symbolizes his or her understanding of the temporality of the body and of the enchantments of *saṃsāra*, and rejects them, often torturing them out of existence. The activities of *tapasvins* generate *tapas*, a burning, dangerous fund of heat that is both literal and metaphorical. It can destroy those who transgress them, or alternatively it can be used to scorch the seeds of attachment to the world[30] (XII.204.16). Through acts of asceticism, therefore, *tapasvins* combat the attractions of the world, accruing a psycho-spiritual power that paradoxically rivals and surpasses the powers of the temporal world.

According to many passages in the *mokṣadharma* section, success in *nivṛtti* engagements is crucially linked to the extent to which one identifies oneself with other beings, and cares for their suffering. "When one sees all beings in oneself and oneself in all beings, then one has realized the individual soul that is *Brahman*"[31] (XII.231.21). The ideal person is "one who [sees the identity] of all beings with himself, and the welfare of all beings [with his own]"[32] (XII.321.23). Kṛṣṇa echoes this philosophy to Arjuna in the *Gītā*, "Through [true knowledge] you will see all creatures without exception within yourself and then within me"[33] (BG.IV.35). The goal, then, is wisdom. This is particularly so in the *mokṣadharma* section of the *Śāntiparva*, and is evident in statements such as "Man has only one enemy, o king, and no second. This enemy is known as ignorance. Impelled by it, one is led to perform terrible and pitiless acts"[34] (XII.286.28).

The natural logical corollary of intuiting deeply one's identity with other beings is treating beings with gentleness and compassion. The ethics professed by *nivṛtti dharma* therefore are demanding. At once simpler and sterner than those of *pravṛtti dharma*, the values of rigorous self-discipline take precedence over the goals of social harmony. *Nivṛtti dharma* defines *dharma* as "that which strives for the benefit of creatures; *dharma* is so called because it is wedded to *ahiṃsā*"[35] (XII.110.10). It removes *dharma* from the obfuscations of social relationships and renders it a simple dictum: "People know that the eternal *dharma* is that which is ancient, which is friendliness, and [which works for] the welfare of all"[36] (XII.254.5). *Dharma* is not about calibrating one's social obligations, weighing one's social position in relation to others. *Dharma* enjoins care of all beings, irrespective of social standing or even species: "*Dharma* is so called because it supports [all creatures]. Creatures are protected by *dharma*. Because it is inalienable from its support [of beings], it is called *dharma*" (XII.110.11).[37] A person devoted to *nivṛtti* ethics, therefore, is identified by his or her solicitude and kindness towards others.

Ideal *nivṛtti* adherents are described by their calmness, their patience, their perfect balance of mind. Pāṇḍu captures the archetype in a passage from the *Ādiparva*, where he determines briefly to adopt *nivṛtti* practices. "If one man chops my arm off, and another anoints it with sandalpaste, I shall wish neither good upon one, nor ill upon the other. I shall do nothing out of a will to live, or a will to die; and neither rejoice at life nor hate death"[38] (I.110.14–15). Yudhiṣṭhira hankers after this ideal on the various occasions when he tries to opt out of *pravṛtti dharma* after the war. The *nivṛtti* sage is described in the *Śāntiparva*: "He is one into whom words enter like frightened elephants into a well and never come out. He hears no evil of others. He remembers no evil. When dispraised, he is silent" (*tūṣṇīmāsīt nindāyāṃ* XII.237.10). The same passage continues, "He can make a spot teeming with people seem perfectly still[39] (XII.237.11) . . . [Such a person] is never glad when honoured, never angry when insulted, assures all creatures of his compassion"[40] (XII.237.14). One who practises *nivṛtti* is one "whose life is the practice of *dharma* (*jīvitaṃ yasya dharmārthaṃ* XII.237.23), who feels distressed at causing grief to others, and who embraces noninjurious conduct (*ahiṃsā pratipadyate* XII.237.19). Such a person is "the refuge of all creatures"[41] (*śaraṇaḥ sarvabhūtānāṃ* XII.237.20). His cardinal ethic is that of nonharmfulness, of avoiding injury to other beings. As one *nivṛtti* practitioner challenges a *pravṛtti* one: "If there is any ethic evident that is superior to *ahiṃsā*, that is rooted in righteousness instead of the *āgamas* or *śāstras*, if you see it, do explain it"[42] (XII.260.19).

Contrasted with *pravṛtti, nivṛtti* ethics may therefore be characterized as personal, self-cultivational, and mystical. While *pravṛtti* values are oriented to the social and pragmatic, *nivṛtti* ethics typically concern themselves with the care of other beings, with truthfulness, charity, patience, self-restraint, and compassion. At least in theory, *nivṛtti dharma* therefore refuses to recognize social differences as in any way authoritative. "If these [high qualities] are evident in a *śūdra*, but are not found in a *brāhmaṇa*, then the *śūdra* is not a *śūdra*, and the *brāhmaṇa* is not a *brāhmaṇa*"[43] (XII.182.8). While limited to the exceptionally gifted few, *nivṛtti dharma* is in this sense paradoxically more egalitarian than *pravṛtti dharma*. "My scale" says Tulandhara, one *nivṛtti* adherent, to his adversary Jajali, "is evenly balanced for all creatures"[44] (XII.254.12). "A wise man is one who looks equally upon a *brāhmaṇa* who has disciples and wisdom, a cow, an elephant, a dog and a dog-eater"[45] (XII.231.19). *Nivṛtti dharma* insists that true worth is to be measured by conduct, not by birth: "The birth of great souls, who have purified themselves is through austerities. [Such people] are unaffected by low birth. Those learned in the Vedas hold a virtuous *śūdra* to be equal to a *brāh-*

maṇa. I myself look upon such a one as Viṣṇu, who pervades and supports the whole universe"[46] (XII.285.28). Liberation (*mokṣa*) is an achievement of one's mental rectitude, one's personal effort, and is divorced from consideration of one's social station. It is achievable by all who undertake the proper *yoga*, or means: "Whether a person is of low caste or a woman who is attached to *dharma*, both, by following this path [of *yoga*] may achieve the highest end"[47] (XII.232.32). Ignorance is the only obstacle to liberation. To obliterate ignorance, one should with reverence accept instruction from whomever has the wisdom: "Acquiring knowledge from a *brāhmaṇa* or *kṣatriya* or *vaiśya* or even a *śūdra* of low birth imparted graciously, one should accept it with confidence . . . All *varṇa*s are *brāhmaṇa*s. All are born of *Brahman*, and all constantly utter *Brahman*. With the knowledge of *Brahman*, of truth and of the *śāstra*s, I say this whole universe is pervaded by *Brahman*"[48] (XII.306.85–86).

Nivṛtti dharma is therefore pursued by the uncommonly tenacious and spiritually rugged few who, the ideal holds, may come from any walk of society. Its goal is radical and immoderate. Its primary method of accomplishment is ascetic renunciation of the world. It is accompanied by a stringent code of ethics whose most compelling injunction is that of nonharmfulness to other beings (*ahiṃsā*). The primary orientation of *nivṛtti dharma*, therefore, is vertical, toward *mokṣa*, toward release from the cycles of death and rebirth. Whereas *pravṛtti dharma* is geared toward a more harmonious existence within the cyclic world (*saṃsāra*), *nivṛtti dharma* aims to transcend the limitations of *saṃsāra* forever, and entails a renunciation of interest in the values of *pravṛtti*.

Nivṛtti dharma may also be understood as being tri-dimensional. The difference is that its other dimensions are conceived more as aids or adjuncts to the primary spiritual pursuit than as ends in themselves. Thus, in its personal dimension, *nivṛtti dharma* is deeply and intensely introspective, and calls for a psychological transformation in the individual. It calls on a person to reorient his or her physical, mental, and emotional patterns toward the achievement of equanimity. While the practice of *nivṛtti dharma* must begin with this earnest internal transformation, however, the underlying soteriological objective is paramount; it is the crucial inspiration for one's efforts. Similarly, the lateral dimension of *nivṛtti dharma* also emerges out of its more fundamental spiritual striving: care of other beings is at once the prerequisite and the outcome of one's *nivṛtti* directedness. In order to achieve true equanimity, one must learn to conduct oneself in nonharmful ways. Conversely, in the seeking after the highest end, one is of necessity altered into a more sympathetic human being, full of compassion and generosity for the suffering of others.[49]

Reconciling Domestic and Ascetic Ideals

These are the two basic impulses of religion described by the *Mahābhārata*. In the *Śāntiparva*, the two are contrasted. Scholars of Hinduism have often talked about the tension at the heart of Hinduism, the tension between the world-denying and the world-affirming elements of the tradition.[50] Some have argued that this tension was never resolved.[51] The basic ambiguity in attitudes to "the world," physically, socially, and theologically construed, is as evident in the *Mahābhārata* as in other strands of Hindu literature. In the *mokṣadharma* section of the text, however, the superiority of the *nivṛtti* path over *pravṛtti* is strenuously asserted, both in terms of its goals and in terms of its ethics. "In this, all the three worlds, with their animate and inanimate elements are established. *Nivṛtti dharma* [leads to] the unmanifest eternal *Brahman* . . . *Pravṛtti* is [the path of] rebirth. *Nivṛtti* is the highest end"[52] (XII.210.3–4). *Pravṛtti* is explicitly connected with worldly and temporal concerns, while *nivṛtti* is associated with the highest objectives of humanity. In parallel constructions encountered repeatedly in the section, *nivṛtti dharma* is elevated above *pravṛtti dharma* in value. As Bhīṣma summarizes, for example: "The ascetic who discriminates between good and evil, who is always intent upon achieving the highest knowledge, who observes *nivṛtti dharma*, achieves that high end"[53] (XII.210.5).

The *nivṛtti* critique of *pravṛtti* follows various avenues. The intelligence of *pravṛtti* followers, immersed in their pretensions of culture and ritual observance, is held to be inferior. For example, one section, comparing the types of people engaged in both activities, concludes: "Of the two, the intelligent tread the higher path [of *nivṛtti*]"[54] (XII.205.3). The ritual supports of *pravṛtti dharma* are also questioned. The *devas* to whom worship is addressed in sacrificial culture are dispensed with as being of little use, and as sharing the fortunes of all other beings; they must return from age to age to enjoy the fruits of their *pravṛtti* orientation, hence are not much different from human beings[55] (XII.327.43–60). They are said to have departed from the *nivṛtti* path because it was too difficult to practice, and to have become enjoyers of sacrificial libations for their own gratification (XII.327.7). The sacrificial world and its theology of prosperity and progeny are held in contempt: Medhavin says, "How can one like me worship with animal sacrifices involving cruelty? . . . I am born of *Brahman* through *Brahman*. I am established in the Self, though I am childless. In the Self alone shall I be. I do not require a son to rescue me"[56] (XII.169.31, 34).

Vyāsa, reputed author of the Great Epic, reinforces these judgments in his instruction to his son Śuka. Having discussed the two paths of *pravṛtti* and *nivṛtti*, the one characterized by Vedic acts, and the other by knowledge, he says: "By acts, a being is bound. By knowledge, however, he is freed. For this reason, *yogī*s who see the other shore never engage in acts"[57] (XII.233.7). The renunciation of (ritual) acts, the very hallmark of *nivṛtti dharma*, is stated to be the highest penance (*tapa uttamaṃ* XII.214.4).

The unrivalled excellence of *nivṛtti* is thus repeatedly affirmed in the *mokṣadharma* section. Yet, the activities associated with *pravṛtti* religion are not discarded altogether. They are recast instead as lower-order values. This process is tackled with the help of myth. The origins of both types of religion are located in a myth that we find in the *Śāntiparva*. In this myth, the great ascetic sage deity Nārāyaṇa calls together the seven *ṛṣi*s, and asks them to produce an authoritative treatise on the two types of religion, *nivṛtti* and *pravṛtti* (XII.322.26ff.). Nārāyaṇa then allocates each to different beings in the universe. He himself remains avowed to *nivṛtti*, thus reinforcing it as the religion of the enlightened, but he makes the deities, including Brahmā, share in the sacrifice, which is the very essence of *pravṛtti*. The divergent ideals of the two traditions are thus sought to be reconciled in this way. The famous *saptārṣi* (seven sages, also called here the *citraśikhaṇḍins*) of Vedic lore are cast as the progenitors of the religion of *pravṛtti*. A parallel seven *ṛṣi*s are said to have been created for *nivṛtti*. These are: Sana, Sanatsujāta, Sanaka, Sanandana, Sanatkumāra, Kapila, and Sanātana (XII.327.64). These *ṛṣi*s are envisaged as eternal *brahmacārin*s, who have never been involved in the tumultuous confusion of the world. They appear periodically to offer didactic support to those in need.[58]

The above myth accommodates *pravṛtti* within *nivṛtti* by proposing that different creatures are created for different ends—some for *pravṛtti*, some for *nivṛtti*. While there is no doubt as to the precedence of *nivṛtti*, the existence of *pravṛtti* may be tolerated, and in some instances, may be accepted as being necessary for some people, who are spiritually less evolved. This allows for a hierarchalization of values, in which the values of *nivṛtti* supersede those of *pravṛtti*. *Pravṛtti* is recognized, but cast as a pedestrian householder religion. *Nivṛtti* in the same stroke is hailed as the acme of religious understanding. The *mokṣadharma* continues its intimations that "Acts cleanse the body.

Wisdom, however, is the highest end"[59] (XII.262.36); "He who surrenders himself to penance [*nivṛtti*] for a long time avoids birth and death"[60] (XII.307.7). *Nivṛtti* is paid unambiguous ideological deference. It alone targets the critical malaise of existence, and it alone treats it.

In later Hindu tradition, the thesis of two religions is regroomed so that *pravṛtti* and *nivṛtti* no longer represent two alternatives for religious practice, as proposed earlier, but two levels of rehearsal of the same basic *dharma*. This tendency is visible even in the above-quoted passages of the *Mahābhārata*. Later tradition refines and institutionalizes this in its elaboration of the *āśrama* system. An ordinary man may thus immerse himself in *pravṛtti* engagements until the fourth *āśrama*, *saṃnyāsa*, now interpreted as a consecutive stage of life. After he has lived a rich and productive domestic life, contributing to society, in *saṃnyāsa* a man may soak himself in *nivṛtti* practices to the fullest extent that he desires. The *saṃnyāsa āśrama* thus works as one of the points of interlude between the two traditions.[61] In the *mokṣadharma* section of the *Mahābhārata*, however, these niceties are still in the process of refinement, and *pravṛtti* and *nivṛtti* are understood as two options of religion, albeit not of equal spiritual worth.[62]

Historical Antecedents

The sharp philosophical differences between the two "religions" may be better understood by examining their different historical antecedents. As suggested, *pravṛtti dharma* is a direct descendant of the rewards-oriented sacrificial religion practiced by the Vedic Aryans.[63] The religion of the ancient Vedas was primarily this-worldly, aimed at gaining health, material prosperity, and success. It aimed for the acquisition of heaven—a space where one could enjoy all of the pleasures of material existence, without encountering any of the difficulties. At its higher levels, it was based on an intuition that there was an intrinsic and natural harmony to the universe (*ṛta*). Vedic religion was geared at cherishing and supporting this harmony through scrupulously correct behaviour in every arena of life—ritual, social, and personal. *Nivṛtti dharma*, on the other hand, is inspired by the varieties of *śramaṇa* and *yogic* traditions that had been operating for centuries on the fringes of the Aryan *madhyadeśa*, "heartland." These traditions are thought to go as far back in their practices as Indus Valley religion. They had always been critical of the ritualistic and exclusionary aspects of Vedic sacrificial religion. In particular, the use of animals in Vedic sacrifice invited repeated and sharp criticism. In some cases, the critiques of these groups found expression in protestant anti-Vedic movements, some of which eventually coalesced to form the religions of Jainism and Buddhism.[64]

The *Mahābhārata* is the beneficiary of this dual heritage of religious practice. In its religious discourses, we see it grappling with the divergent ideals and merits of these two legacies, finding both valuable in different aspects, and trying to assimilate them into a common practice, without giving up either one. The main points of controversy are precisely those that irked the first Jains and Buddhists, namely, the use of animals in sacrifice, the worldly orientation of the sacrificial religion, and the abuse of privileges by the *brāhmaṇas*.[65] The cruelty involved in animal sacrifice and the alleged superficiality of Vedic religion are particular sources of disquiet. From time to time, the Vedic religion is ridiculed as being shallow and insubstantial. Kṛṣṇa himself, in the *Gītā*, is heard castigating the religion of the Vedas as being for "the unenlightened" (*avipaścitaḥ* BG.II.42). He describes it as "inspired by desires, set upon heaven, bringing on rebirth, and abounding in rituals aimed at the acquisition of pleasures and power"[66] (BG.II.42–43). He advises Arjuna that this religion "robs those addicted to pleasures and power of their minds"[67] (BG.II.44), and that it should be transcended (*nistraiguṇayo bhava arjuna* BG.II.45). Similarly, there are numerous debates in the text on the use of animals in sacrifice. In one very famous instance, the seven sages, this time curiously representing the *nivṛtti* position, argue with the gods about the correct meaning of the word *ajaḥ* in the context of the sacrifice. The gods maintain that the word means "goat," connoting that a goat is a crucial ingredient of the sacrifice. The sages, however, interpret the word as "seed," and insist that it is a seed that is required, and not a goat. The celebrated king Vasu is implored to settle the argument. When he, out of fear of the gods, decides incorrectly in their favor, saying that the word means "goat," and not "seed," he falls from his seat in heaven directly into hell, as a result of his dishonesty. The correct use of the word, it is maintained, is "seed" (XII.324.2ff.). This story is cited twice in the text. Significantly, we see that the gods have been toppled from their position of power by the sages, who now possess not only great power on account of their austerities, but also wisdom. In another occurrence, the eminent sage Kapila (one of the seven *nivṛtti* sages; also the founder of Sāṃkhya?[68]), espying a cow being prepared for the sacrifice, is heard to exclaim in disgust, "Oh, the Vedas!" (XII.260.8). This comment generates a discussion between the presiding priest Syūmaraśmi and Kapila. Kapila insists that no law can be higher than that of nonharmfulness (*ahiṃsā*)[69] (XII.260.17), and that if it were truly the case that the animal benefits from being sacrificed, as is argued, then it should logically be the family of the animal who brings it forward for slaughter[70] (XIV.28.11–12). When Syūmaraśmi energetically argues in favour of Vedic religion, Kapila informs him tersely that if sacrifices are indeed necessary for the proper functioning of the universe, then there are many sacrifices that do not require cruelty to animals. He lists off five such sacrifices in support of his argument (XII.261.19).[71]

Numerous other devices are also used by the text to relativize the necessity of sacrifice. In one passage, for example, a hierarchy of sacrifice is enumerated, in which the *Brāhmaṇas* perform the sacrifice of penances, and *kṣatriyas* perform the traditional sacrifices that involve the slaughter of animals (XII.224.60–61). In this passage sacrifice is recognized, but is implied to be a lower form of religious practice. A similar move is accomplished in another passage, which states that, "In the *Kṛta* age, the performance of sacrifices was not necessary. Such performance became necessary in the *Tretā* age"[72] (XII.224.62). Thus in the optimal of times, sacrifice was never practiced. It is only as the age degenerated that sacrifice came into being. These devices, like the above, deny the absolute necessity of sacrifice and relegate it to lower forms of religious practice.

In these exchanges, we can see the tensions generated by the attempts to assimilate the two discordant traditions into one. This tension is for the most part creative, however, rather than acrimonious. The *Mahābhārata* uses these dialogues to argue both positions back and forth. Eventually, they stimulate a synthesis that is highly original, and quite successful in its resolution of the two discordant systems. While the text betrays a strong attachment to its Vedic heritage, the ethics of the *yogic* traditions are compelling. In the synthesized religion we find in the *Mahābhārata*, the higher ethics and the otherworldly objectives of the *yogic* traditions prevail over the this-worldly orientation of Vedic religion, but the Vedic religion is still affirmed. This resolution is achieved in two ways: (1) by a prioritization of values, and (2) by a reinterpretation of the meaning of sacrifice. Through the first technique, the values of the *yogic* tradition are elevated above those of the sacrificial religion.[73] This high tradition, with its stern ascetic and ethical ideals comes to be called the religion of *nivṛtti*. It comes to represent the highest aspirations of the tradition. Because of its demanding and rigorous nature, however, and its otherworldly direction, it is not for the vast majority of human beings, at least not yet. Therefore, the values of the Vedic religion, softened somewhat by the ethical concerns of the higher tradition, are endorsed for the varieties of ordinary human beings. This comes to be called *pravṛtti dharma*. Through the second technique, the very concept of sacrifice becomes re-defined,[74] so that sacrifice in the renunciant tradition is no longer a literal sacrifice involving animals and other accoutrements, but a sacrifice of the breath, to the eternal constancy of the Self.[75]

In pointed and conscious contrast to Jainism and Buddhism,[76] which are similarly inspired by ascetic and otherworldly ideals, the *Mahābhārata* retains a high value for household religion. Even where it fully valorizes the ideals of the high religion, it insists that the household religion is the basis, support, and sustenance of all society. *Gṛhasthāśrama* is what makes the asceticism of students, elders, and radical renunciants possible; it is the refuge of all these seekers. Society could not function without household religion, and household religion must therefore be respected and maintained. So it is that Yudhiṣṭhira, the eldest of the Pāṇḍava brothers, is lectured repeatedly on these issues at the end of the war. When, Aśoka-like, he is repulsed by his crucial role in precipitating the war, and seeks to flee toward life in the forest, he is reminded time and again of his duties as a householder, and his responsibilities as a king.[77] A full quarter of the *Mahābhārata* is directed at educating Yudhiṣṭhira in these matters, at describing to him what is the proper place for religious and secular duties, and what is the proper place for the pursuit of personal salvation. The enormously lengthy books of the *Śānti* and *Anuśāsana parva*s serve precisely this purpose. When, at the end of this very detailed instruction, Yudhiṣṭhira still seeks escape to the forest, the great sage Vyāsa, hitherto patient and accommodating, finally loses his temper. He gives Yudhiṣṭhira a thorough dressing-down, calling him thick-headed and foolish, and storms that all the sages summoned to instruct Yudhiṣṭhira over the last six months had been wasting their time (XIV.3.1–10). Chastened by these vituperative words, Yudhiṣṭhira reluctantly discards yearnings for escape to the forest, and commits himself to life as a householder king. In strains of the text, *pravṛtti dharma* is strongly advocated for the majority of human beings. People should continue to perform their social functions and duties, but with the significant difference from Vedic religion that now their daily works should be imbued with the consciousness that these are not ultimate goals. The correct and faithful performance of tasks will still yield a period of residence in heaven. But heaven is a short-term respite, not to be considered one's highest aspiration. A person in heaven must inevitably return to rebirth and the difficulties of the world. If one desires complete freedom from the world, one should aim higher, toward *nivṛtti*, toward pursuit of the ultimate path.

This is the broad context for the religion of the *Mahābhārata*. At the time that a reader enters into the text, the above stage has already been set.

The religious ideals of the *śramaṇa* and *yogic* traditions have already been acknowledged as preeminent, and become enshrined as the *nivṛtti* level of religious practice. The ideals of the erstwhile Vedic religion have suffered some displacement in rank, but are still strongly retained as the *pravṛtti* level of religious practice, and are urged on the majority of the population. One problem persists, however, and much of *Mahābhārata* religious discourse is engrossed with this problem. In the above schema, we have the values of an essentially world-negating religion, being superimposed on that of a domestic religion. How compatible are they? Is it even possible for them to harmoniously merge? Or are they fundamentally logically incongruent with each other?

Nivṛtti and *Pravṛtti*: The Trouble with Ethics

The crucial difficulty in assimilating the two traditions lies not in accepting the values of the higher religion. The *Mahābhārata* does this with no serious display of angst. It fully accepts the superior claims of the *yogic* traditions, and supports them with enthusiasm. The difficulty lies in synthesizing their ethics. This is best illustrated by a review of the ethics of each tradition. *Nivṛtti* represents an ascetic religion whose ethics are best suited to the life of a renouncer. In list after list, these are, not always in the same order, *ahiṃsā*, *satya*, *asteya*, *brahmacarya*, *dama*, *kṣamā*, *aparigraha*: noninjuriousness, truthfulness, nonstealing, celibacy, self-restraint, forgiveness, nongrasping, and so forth. The majority of these ethical ideals present no dilemmas for a domestic religion; truthfulness, nonstealing, self-restraint, forgiveness, nongrasping, may be practiced in any context at any time, without intruding on social agendas. They are not, in fact, significantly different from the ideals of the Vedic religion itself. The ideals of *ahiṃsā* and *brahmacarya*, however, require closer scrutiny. For *nivṛtti*, as we have noted, one of the cardinal ethical precepts is that of *ahiṃsā*, of living without the exploitation of, and injury to, other beings. Causing injury to beings produces *karma* (now interpreted as a subtle psychic quality that binds one to the world) and as long as one is still producing *karma*, it is impossible to escape *saṃsāra*, which is the overarching goal of *nivṛtti* practice. This, however, is a major complication for a householder's religion, for even in the passages extolling *nivṛtti*, *ahiṃsā* is recognized as an impossible ideal. "I do not see any creature in this world that supports its life without doing any act of injury to others. Animals live upon animals, the strong upon the weak"[78] (XII.15.20). There is a frank recognition that it is not possible to live without injuring beings. As one passage argues, even ascetics, with their minimalist food intake, cause injury to beings, for "there are many creatures in water, in soil, and in fruit"[79] (XII.15.25). The same passage reasons: hundreds of beings are killed in our breathing, eating, and sleeping, even when we are exercising the most scrupulous care. In fact, "there are many creatures that are so minute that their existence can only be inferred. With the falling of the eyelids alone, they are destroyed"[80] (XII.15.26). How, then, is it possible to live without injuring beings? How can we continue to live in the world without causing some form of injury to some being, however unwittingly?

This is a particularly pertinent question from the *pravṛtti* side. As a householder's religion must pragmatically view it, *hiṃsā*, or injury, is a gross necessity of living in the world. Without *hiṃsā*, one could not eat, because beings are injured in the act of producing food. Without *hiṃsā*, one could have no order in the world, because beings are injured when they are disciplined by the king.[81] Without *hiṃsā*, one could possess nothing, because beings are injured in the process of protecting one's property from others.[82] Battles, even the most self-defensive and righteous ones, necessitate *hiṃsa*.[83] Even to eat necessitates *hiṃsā*. Is it at all possible to live in the world without causing harm? This is the predicament faced by a householder's religion.

A similar complication is represented by the ascetic ideal of *brahmacarya*. Even in its most orthodox formulations, the word *brahmacarya* connotes "celibacy," and this meaning has clung to the term from its earliest times.[84] *Brahmacarya*, moreover, is an inalienable component of the search for the Highest; its very etymology signifies it as "the path that leads to *Brahman*." Celibacy, therefore, is crucial to the path that leads to *Brahman*, an incontrovertible credential of the ascetic life. Yet, this is an obvious and significant problem for household religion. How does society continue, if all religious people are enjoined to be celibate? To live in the world, it is necessary to procreate, for without procreation, the world cannot go on. Notwithstanding its *nivṛtti* overlay, in the *Mahābhārata*, the perpetuation of the world is one *pravṛtti* value that will not be compromised. In the ancient Vedic religion, the world was a good thing, a place of many blessings and comforts. Its end is still not seriously to be desired. Moreover, "sexual activity and the procreation of children are . . . sacred acts and duties."[85] Procreation is one of the three debts of life that one owes to one's forbears, a weighty obligation that contributes to a man's wholeness as a religious being. How is it possible to reconcile that, with the high emphasis placed on celibacy by an ascetic tradition?

The fundamental preoccupation of religion in the *Mahābhārata*, in my view, is mediating between the divergent values of *pravṛtti* and *nivṛtti*. The text must find a way to balance the ethical demands of an essentially ascetic, world-denying tradition, with the necessities of living in the world. Most particularly, the convergence of the two systems is problematized by the twin issues of sex and violence. The *Mahābhārata* must determine how to permit people to live lives that necessitate violence, necessitate sex, while still honoring the ascetic ideals of noninjuriousness and celibacy. Having already accepted the ultimate priority of the *nivṛtti* path, it must now determine how to align the values and practices of *pravṛtti* so that they are logically consistent with the higher aims of the tradition, so as to imbue life-in-the-world with the consciousness of its soteriological goals. In my view, this is the primary challenge faced by *Mahābhārata* religion.

The *Mahābhārata* formulates at least two significant responses to this challenge, one pragmatic, and one philosophical. Sex and violence cannot be eliminated while one is still living in the world; this much is a given. What it is possible to do, however, is to curb their most destructive potential. Thus, sex and violence may continue to exist in society, but in a highly regulated, refined, even ritualized kind of way.

At the pragmatic level, the *Mahābhārata* attempts to physically control sex and violence. To anticipate some of the analysis offered in succeeding chapters of this work, sexual activity is limited to certain uses, certain times, certain places, and certain people. Within these set perimeters, sex is conscionable and decent, and may be accepted. Violence is prevented from random expression in the same way. It is held in check by being limited to particular uses, particular people, at particular places, during particular times. Any serious departure from these guidelines is considered reprehensible, and subject to reproof.

Let us look at some of these issues briefly.

1. To begin with, sex and violence are confined to particular uses. Taking the example of sex, we may notice that although the text has a considerable tolerance for the sexual misdemeanors of people, and there is some variance in views, the *Śānti* and *Anuśāsana parva*s lean toward the position that sexual activity should ideally be limited to the purpose of procreation. A man should approach his wife during her "season" (*ṛtu*), and *only* during her season: "a *brāhmaṇa* becomes a *brahmacārin* by going to his wife only in her season and never at other times"[86] (XII.214.10). To approach her at any other time is a regrettable fault of virtue. While there are some ambiguities, the predominant view

of the *Mahābhārata* is that sex is least offensive when limited to the purpose of procreation.

Similarly, violence is designated only for set purposes. It is an obvious necessity of war, and war is indispensable to the maintenance of *dharma*. Kṛṣṇa says in the *Gītā* that when *adharma* waxes despotic and tyrannical, God himself descends to earth to destroy it. The role of a warrior, fighting a righteous war, is imagined in the same way. Through righteous war, a warrior replicates the role of God on the battlefield. More precisely, a warrior acts as an instrument of God, performing God's work. Violence is also essential to the disciplining of criminals, for the maintenance of order in the social world. It is necessary for the protection of the weak from the strong. Violence is also unavoidable in acts aimed at the acquisition of food, either through agriculture, or through hunting. Finally—and this is a point of considerable debate—violence may be a vital requirement of the sacrifice. In all of these venues, the use of violence is accepted and sanctioned. Violence may not be put to wrongful uses—for example, in hedonistic pursuit of personal desires, or when motivated by hatred or revenge. The *kṣatriyas'* wanton abuse of their power to victimize the *brāhmaṇas*, as reflected in several of the frame stories of the epic, is, for example, offered as one of the rationales for the *Mahābhārata* war itself. Violence may be used only for the reinforcement of socially recognized *dharma*.

2. In another technique of management, sex and violence are spatially confined. Thus, the violence associated with warfare is relegated to the battlefield, in open confrontation with an equal. The violence associated with the disciplining of criminals is confined to the king's domain. The violence associated with sacrifice is contained within the sacrificial arena, while that of producing food is localized to agricultural fields, forests, and slaughterhouses. In these contexts, violence is admissible. Outside of these delineated boundaries, apparently, it is not.[87]

Similarly, sex is confined to particular spaces. For ordinary people, it is limited to the home. For a wealthy nobleman, it is permissible in the private space of his concubinage. For all men of means, it is also permissible in brothels. This is not to say that one does not encounter mating couples elsewhere—in forests, in boats, in the bushes, in the guise of deer—but there is an explicit demand that sex acts should be performed in private spaces.

3. Sex and violence are also limited in their duration. Thus, violence is acceptable at certain periods of one's life, but not at others. Violence is not acceptable as a student, when one is living with one's guru as a *brahmacārin*. It is not acceptable as an aged *vanaprasthin*, when one leaves behind all of the preoccupations of social and communal life (unless one is absorbed with *vanaprastha* as a lifestyle, in which the rules are different). It is not acceptable as a *saṃnyāsin*, when one wanders radically alone in the pursuit of truth, living as a mendicant. In all of these periods of life, it is discouraged. It is, however, acceptable while one is practicing *gṛhasthāśrama*, and indeed, necessary. For example, it is necessary for a male *gṛhasthin brāhmaṇa* to perform sacrifices, for that is his function in the world. It is necessary for a male *gṛhasthin* warrior to engage in battle, for battle is the calling of the warrior. It is necessary for a male *gṛhasthin* hunter to slay animals and provide for his family. It is necessary for a male *gṛhasthin vaiśya* to engage in agricultural activity, and produce food. Any violence that may be unavoidable in this pursuit, is therefore necessary and defensible. In all of these cases, violence is acceptable.

Similarly, sex also is restricted to certain periods. It is not acceptable as a student, for, as already noted, abstinence is expected of *brahmacārin*s. It is not acceptable as an aged *vanaprasthin*, because one is expected then to direct oneself to knowledge of the spirit (the case of those engrossed in *vanaprastha* as a lifestyle is again different). And it is certainly not acceptable as a *saṃnyāsin*. It is, however, acceptable, and obligatory, for a householder. It is in fact the duty of a male *gṛhasthin* of any variety to procreate and repay his debt to his ancestors. And it is the duty of his wife, as his partner in the practice of *dharma*, to help him procreate and repay that debt. In *gṛhasthāśrama*, men and women are expected to be sexually active and productive. Sex, therefore, is an indispensable feature of householder life. It is not, however, tolerable in other phases of life.

4. Finally, sex and violence are delimited to particular classes of people. So, for example, the violence associated with sacrifice is appropriate for a male *gṛhasthin brāhmaṇa* within a sanctified ritual space. The violence associated with growing food is acceptable for a male *gṛhasthin vaiśya* in the context of his agricultural activities. The violence associated with war, hunting, and the disciplining of criminals is acceptable for a male *kṣatriya* in the appropriate arenas—on the battlefield, in the forest, or in court. It is not, however, appropriate for

anyone else. For example, it is not acceptable for a *brāhmaṇa* of any hue to hunt or bear arms in battle.[88] It is not appropriate for a *vaiśya* to slaughter animals for a sacrifice. And it is not appropriate for a *kṣatriya* to engage in the violence associated with agriculture. Thus, specific varieties of violence are distributed among particular classes of people. They cannot be shared by people of other classes, and the varieties of violence are not interchangeable.

In the same way, sex also is circumscribed to certain classes of people. *Gṛhasthin* men and women of all castes and classes may engage in sex with their married partners within their homes. In addition, *gṛhasthin* men of means and courtesans may engage in sex with each other either in harems or in brothels. *Gṛhasthin* men might also be permitted to engage in sex with their slave girls in their homes, although this is contested (see Chapter Four). These categories are not interchangeable. As already noted, it is not permissible for a non-*gṛhasthin* man to engage in sex with anybody at all. It is also not permissible for a woman of any caste or age to be sexually involved with her slaves.

In this way, the potential excesses of sex and violence are sought to be curbed through management. They are conceded to be vital to the proper functioning of society, but in need of governance. Through a highly evolved process of legitimation, sex and violence are regulated and contained within set spatial, temporal, and social confines. These are some of the pragmatic techniques that the *Mahābhārata* evolves to deal with the troublesome topics of sex and violence.

These matters are also the source of considerable *intellectual* ferment in the *Mahābhārata*, where the text takes a more reflective approach to coming to terms with them. One of the primary philosophical methods that emerges from grappling with this problem is the teaching of *karma yoga*. The doctrine of *karma yoga* is enunciated with conciseness by Kṛṣṇa in the early chapters of the *Gītā*, but it forms much of the philosophical backdrop of the *Mahābhārata*. Its core teachings of maintaining equanimity and steadiness in the midst of all strife recur with regularity in practically every religious discourse of the text, and the *Mahābhārata* brings it to creatively bear on the problem of mediating the ethics of *pravṛtti* and *nivṛtti*.

The teaching of *karma yoga* says that at a philosophical level, it is possible to ameliorate the *karmic* damage done by sex and violence by changing how we think about them. The case of violence is instructive. From the discourse of the *Gītā*, it would seem that once one has satisfied one's conscience that one is fighting in favor of a righteous cause, one should set aside one's lingering qualms and engage in battle to the best of one's ability. Kṛṣṇa, for example, emphasizes to Arjuna that the *Mahābhārata* war is a *dharmayuddha*, a just war, a war that is condoned by, and for the purpose of *dharma*. It is therefore proper to fight such a war. Second, even where the cause may be righteous and just, it would seem that one should make all efforts to ensure that violence is only ever a last resort and that alternatives have been exhausted. In the *Udyogaparva*, for example, Kṛṣṇa describes the measures he used to prevent the war. He says that to begin with, he attempted conciliation. He lowered the Pāṇḍavas's demands, and tried to compromise, using pacifying and gentle language. When that failed, he attempted to create divisions in the Kaurava camp (*bheda*). He attempted, that is, to alienate Duryodhana, by winning all of Duryodhana's supporters to the side of *dharma*.[89] When that also failed, he attempted bribery (*dāna*). He tried to woo away Duryodhana's mainstay, Karṇa, the one ally on whose prowess Duryodhana explicitly relied, with promises of kingship and family. When that also was of no avail, he attempted threats of punishment (*daṇḍa*). He warned that the war to come was going to be a war to surpass all wars in its carnage. He described its gore and horror in grim detail, and presaged the violent deaths of Karṇa, his friends, and his family. He even exposed to Karṇa his identity as God, and revealed to him his plans for the destruction of the universe. When all these ruses to prevent the war failed, however, he knew that the war was inevitable. He had made every attempt to negotiate with the Kauravas, and to compromise with them, but their greed and hostility were insurmountable. The only solution now was war, and it was a just war, a war sanctioned by *dharma* (V.7–19).[90]

Having assured oneself that one has made every attempt to avoid violence, therefore, one should approach the issue with a serene mind. At such a point, the violence of war should be viewed simply as a necessity. It should not be motivated by hatred, or anger, or desire to cause injury. Nor should it be occasioned by thoughts of revenge, or thoughts of personal gain—wealth, kingship, fame. The only way to remain sinless is to be completely detached from either embankment of emotionality. With one's thoughts fastidiously innocent of any personal purpose, one should engage in the violence of war strictly as a duty. With this kind of dispassion, says Kṛṣṇa in the *Gītā*, one incurs no *karma*, no guilt.

This is Kṛṣṇa's teaching to Arjuna on the battlefield of Kurukṣetra, the teaching of *niṣkāma karma*. The violence of battle thus becomes a ritualized act that contributes to maintaining the harmony of the world, rather than taking away from it. It becomes a sacralized, blessed event, complementing the act of God in his periodic destruction of the world.

So much for the case of war; how adaptable is the teaching of *karma yoga* to other forms of violence? The story of the hunter, recounted to the Pāṇḍavas in the *Āraṇyakaparva*, may prove a good case study. The hunter is introduced to the *brāhmaṇa* Kauśika as a great sage, wise in the highest truths of the universe. Kauśika is bemused at how a hunter, performing such foul and contemptible work, surely highly sinful, could possibly be a great sage? So he proceeds with some curiosity to meet the hunter. Arriving there, he finds that the hunter has already divined the purpose of his visit. He invites Kauśika into his home, and discourses with him at some length on the content of *karmayoga*. The hunter explains to Kauśika that he is not affected by the dirty and polluting nature of his work. His mind is serene. He does the work not because he derives any personal satisfaction from it—for he himself is vegetarian! Neither does he do it out of greed for money. He is not impelled by taste, or cruelty, or the love of the chase. He is also, however, not dissuaded from his work by any personal aversion. The fear of pollution, the low social status ascribed to the work, disgust for the actual work of slaughter: none of these factors discourage him. He does it simply as his assigned task in life, with calm detachment, his conscience undisturbed, his mind disciplined. In this way, he attracts no sin to himself. He functions in the world with perfect equanimity, swayed by sensations of neither pleasure nor disgust.[91]

In this context also, the violence associated with hunting is relieved by the mental purity of the individual. Because the person is not prompted by any personal desires, his act is rendered blameless, and does not accrue *karma*.

The same understanding may be mobilized to revise the way that a person thinks about sex. Sex, like violence, is an incontrovertible necessity of living in the world; this much may be acknowledged. What remains to be admitted, however, is that indulgence in sex may keep one interminably bound to this world, because sex acts, perhaps more than others, tend to generate strong *karmic* attachments. If one follows the *karma yoga* path, however, it is possible to envision a way out of this cycle. It can be done if one can disengage one's personal desires from sex. As in anything else, one should not be driven by desire and lustfulness, even in sex. It should be done in a proper, sacrificial, ritualized kind of way, with alertness, with the close consciousness that it is one's proper duty. Moreover, while one should not be activated by desire in sex, one should also not be deterred from it by revulsion for one's partner, or other kinds of distaste. It is one's proper *gṛhasthin* duty to engage in sex; therefore, one must do it with a quiet and chaste mind.

A whole host of lesser injunctions then regulate the function of sex. Sex must be limited to one's own married partner. It must not be motivated by lust. It should therefore be restricted to the purpose of procreation only. A man should approach his partner only during her productive season. During that season, however, he *must* approach her; it is his imperative duty to do so. This kind of mental discipline negates the *karma* that would normally accrue from sexual activity. Having conducted oneself not according to one's desire, nor having desisted from right conduct out of aversion; having conducted oneself, in other words, strictly out of one's sense of what is right, and what needs to be done, one accrues no *karmic* outcome from it.

This *karmayoga* understanding of sex is extremely pertinent to the examination of female sexuality in the *Mahābhārata*. It may, for example, be the only way to interpret the exceptionally rigorous fidelity practiced by the *pativratā* woman, the only way that does full justice to her agency, her [illegible]ity, and her spiritual aspirations. These linkages are drawn in greater detail in Chapter Five.

In summation, what is unique, innovative, even revolutionary about Kṛṣṇa's discourse in the *Gītā* is that he interprets *nivṛtti* as a mental, rather than a physical act. Faced with the choice of uninhibited indulgence in spiritually damaging acts (*pravṛtti*), and abandoning those acts altogether (*nivṛtti*), Kṛṣṇa says that one could certainly run away from action. That, however, would be an inferior act; more than that, it would be an act of hypocrisy, because one would be physically abandoning activity, while remaining moved by it mentally. Authentic renunciation is of the mind (BG.V.2, VI.1). This is the kind of renunciation achieved by true *yogī*s. Mentally, one should yield all interest and purpose in the world, and turn one's mind toward *mokṣa*. Physically, however, one should assiduously and scrupulously perform the duties that are assigned to one.

The doctrine of *karma yoga* is proposed as a creative resolution of a perennial religious problem. It is proffered by the *Gītā* as a "middle way."[92] It responds to the extraworldly yearnings of the individual without denying his or her worldly responsibilities. Neither reality is sacrificed to the other. Worldly existence is not sacrificed to otherworldly goals, nor are otherworldly goals compromised. It seems very clear that the doctrine of *karma yoga* was conceived precisely to obviate the necessity of leaving society physically, in order to pursue *nivṛtti* goals. By disentangling one's acts from all personal feelings of desire or aversion, one may achieve the kind of mastery over oneself sought through years of harsh austerity by forest sages. The *karmayoga* philosophy is thus the critical innovation of the Hinduism of the *Mahābhārata*, its response to the renunciant leanings of the heterodox schools. "The Great Bhārata," as one scholars notes, "is ideologically centered in the *karmayoga* theme."[93]

Conclusion

What I have attempted to do in the above discussion is to create a space for a discussion of female sexuality in the *Mahābhārata*. Using the text's own nomenclature, I have focused on the paths of *pravṛtti* and *nivṛtti*. It seems to me that this emic typology, used heuristically, can be of profound use in unpacking the text's attitudes toward women and sexuality. It is obvious to me that the authors' simultaneous avowal of both *pravṛtti* and *nivṛtti* values, notwithstanding the palpable tension between them, is the key to unlocking the apparent inconsistencies we encounter in the attitudes toward women and sexuality in the text. This is because, depending on which level of religion a narrative seeks to evoke, radically contradictory ideologies may be put forth. To see this, we need to understand the levels at which the text operates, and the subterranean dialogues that continue between them.

Chapter Two

Nivṛtti Dharma
The Search for the Highest

In the previous chapter, we sketched in broad strokes the general framework of religion in the *Mahābhārata*. We proposed that the *Mahābhārata* is jointly inspired by two separate traditions of religious practice, one ascetic and one domestic, and argued that the text consciously tries to synthesize the values of the two. We noted that while for the most part this synthesis is quite successful, the differences between the two traditions appear irreconcilable at two nodal points: the issues of sex and violence. We argued then that much of *Mahābhārata* religion is engrossed with discovering a median path between extremes of violence and sex. Finally, we suggested that the *Mahābhārata* is able to integrate the values of the two traditions in two thoughtful ways, one through rigorous management, and the other through a philosophical adjustment in our methods of thinking about them.

In this chapter, I would like to initiate the analysis of sexuality by bringing into convergence two streams of dialogue—the *Mahābhārata*'s ideas and assumptions about women, and the *Mahābhārata*'s thinking on religion. We will begin with the soteriological orientation of *nivṛtti dharma*. As we will see, the analysis of the gender ideology of *nivṛtti dharma* is by no means simple; it is intertwined with the discourses of *yoga*, asceticism, and renunciation and it is within these discourses that we must locate our discussion of female sexuality. For while the place of women in *nivṛtti* ideology may appear straightforward, to get some sense of the practical and material aspects of women's engagement in *nivṛtti* practices it is necessary to detour through a typology of the varieties of ascetic and renunciant traditions. It then becomes possible to investigate the place of sexuality in each stream, and to examine the ways in which women participated in ascetic and/or world-renouncing endeavors, both as objects of the male gaze and as practicing subjects in their own right.

Nivṛtti Dharma: The Soteriological Orientation

Hinduism is typically thought to teach a theology of liberation accessible through various "paths" (*jñāna, bhakti,* and *karmayogas*), and the *Gītā* overall supports this analysis, outlining *karmayoga* (chapters three and four), *bhaktiyoga* (chapters nine through eighteen, particularly eleven), and *jñānayoga* (dispersed through the entire discourse) and weighing them against each other. In the *Mahābhārata* as a whole, however, these paths are not so discretely defined. For the most part, the *nivṛtta*, or soteriological strand of the tradition is characterized by a technique that is an amorphous composite of several types of religious practice. This technique is most commonly called *yoga*. The late Vedic period saw the emergence of numerous religious groups, both Brahminical and heterodox, and a shift in focus from the community to the individual. These trends generated something of a "discourse of *yoga*"[1] and "*yoga*" may be said to be the quintessential religious practice associated with the *nivṛtta* form of *Mahābhārata* religion.

Yoga

The exact use of the term *yoga*, however, is notoriously difficult to pin down. As van Buitenen notes, the word and its cognates occur almost 150 times in the *Gītā* alone (1981, 17). Its basic root is *yuj*, meaning "to yoke" "harness," or "attach," but this refers to such a complex of ideas that the term has a broad semantic range. At the least, *yoga* "always refers to a strenuous effort to which a person has committed himself" (17).

In the epic, the word *yoga* is associated with identifiable beliefs and practices. First, it assumes a weltanschauung in which the world is an eternally preexistent place of inevitable and endless suffering.[2] Worldly engagements are futile and transient and hence (ritual) action is of no efficacy. The only worthwhile goal is to seek something constant within oneself, beyond the interminable vacillations of the world. In *yoga* therefore one is urged to cultivate a liberating knowledge (*vidyā, jñāna*) "that would lift one permanently and absolutely beyond the vicious circle of action, death, rebirth, and action again."[3] This *jñāna* implies the intuition of a permanent, unchanging reality at the core of the person, and the *Mahābhārata* seems to use the language of dualism and nondualism somewhat idiosyncratically, referring one moment to the resplendent *puruṣa* that inheres in the body but remains unbesmirched by the wranglings of the world; and another moment to the blissful, pervasive vitality of *Brahman* (XII.262.45). *Yoga* may also be adapted to a *bhakti* worldview, in that the *parampuruṣa* of Sāṃkhya may be viewed as the *īśvara*, or the *yogeśvara*, the "lord of *yoga*."[4] Thus philosophically *yoga* employs both theistic and nontheistic language,[5] dualist and nondualist frames.[6] The exact formulation of ontology seems to be secondary to its primary interest: that of proposing a way of conducting oneself in the world, through the transcendence of attachment, hatred, and desire (*rāgadveṣamoha*, III.2.34, V.42.8–12).

In addition to the above, *yoga* is also associated with certain mental attitudes. The most frequently mentioned quality is that of equanimity, of being unruffled in the face of both pleasant and unpleasant experience. *Yoga* involves a hardy mental stoicism, a sternness with oneself to remain resolutely balanced regardless of what one encounters. The ascetic Gautamī, for example, remains stalwart even through the death of her son (XIII.1). *Yoga* also involves an ethical care and concern for others. Thus, Pāṇḍu in undertaking *yoga*, declares his intention to live "never ridiculing anyone, never frowning at anything, always gently-spoken, delighting in the welfare of all creatures . . . always equal-minded to all breathing creatures, as though they were my children"[7] (I.110.10–11). Finally, *yoga* involves meditation (XII.232), a withdrawal of the senses, inhalation, and exhalation combined with concentration (XII.192), and the recitation of *mantras* (XII.189).[8]

How does one locate women in the practice of this *yoga*, which is the inseparable companion to the pursuit of *mokṣa*? This is not an easy question to answer, given that the *Mahābhārata* is a patriarchal work not entirely cooperative with feminist projects. One must therefore look for other avenues into a discussion of this material, and the most obvious one is that of asceticism.

The most ubiquitous adjunct of *yogic* practice is asceticism.[9] Asceticism is the stock solution to a life of worldly misery; whenever people are distraught with grief, fear, or anxiety, they are counseled in ascetic values, ascetic perspectives. Thus, when in *Ādiparva*, Pāṇḍu learns of his inability to father children, it is to asceticism that he turns (I.110). When an insomniac Dhṛtarāṣṭra frets on the eve of the great war, the *nivṛtta* sage Sanatsujāta instructs him on ascetic values (V.42–45). The renouncer Medhavin repeatedly harangues his father on the futility and transience of worldly life, and enumerates to him the consciousness-altering, liberative virtues of the ascetic life (XII.169). Ascetic repudiation of the world is the primary technique for achieving *nivṛtti* goals in the *Mahābhārata*. This element of physical trial is stressed in numerous passages describing *yoga* (XII.188, XII.289, XII.294, XII.304).

As with much else in the *Mahābhārata*, however, asceticism is an inchoate jumble of practices, a complicated and heterogeneous affair not easily summarized. That it is a major preoccupation is obvious even from a casual perusal of the text. Ascetics peer out of every other page of the epic and are highly idealized figures, exalted, esteemed, feared for their paranormal powers, and generally held in awe. In spite of the occasional stabs against it, asceticism is roundly revered, encouraged, and valorized throughout the text.

It is not necessary here to enter into the lengthy debate over the origins of Indian asceticism, with its highly vexed question of whether later Hindu ascetic and yogic practices evolved from the Vedic tradition itself, or whether there were other influences that shaped Hindu practices. It is certainly clear from the earliest strands of Vedic literature that some form of asceticism was practiced in Vedic times,[10] but whether this was the precursor of the varieties of asceticism we see in later literature is the subject of tremendous disagreement.[11] For our purposes, these questions should sensitize us to the fact that there is likely to be a multiplicity of ascetic forms and styles practiced in the *Mahābhārata*.

Varieties of Asceticism in the *Mahābhārata*

It would seem that the most obvious principle for distinguishing between varieties of ascetic practice is by way of identifying the goals of ascetic practice. This, however, presents another complication, because, as an overview of the material reveals, goals are not always obvious. While sometimes austerities are very clearly directed toward one goal or another, others are more difficult to read. It is clear that ancient India held a high nostalgic value for a life of simplicity, frugality, and mental and physical stoicism, a life that admitted the conquest and stern disciplining of the body—hence asceticism is widely practiced. However, even though asceticism is the most common instrument of the *nivṛtti* orientation, not all ascetics in the *Mahābhārata* are soteriologically motivated. Some practice asceticism as an extension of a broader eremitic lifestyle framed by adherence to Vedic tradition. Others practice asceticism for the purpose of attaining very worldly objectives. In what follows, we will look, briefly, at the varieties of ascetics mentioned in the text and summarize the goals to which they seem to be devoted. Following that, we will search another route into a discussion of women's participation in ascetic practice.

There are eleven major terms employed for ascetics in the text; together, they encompass the range of ascetic activity we encounter. Prima facie, it would seem that five are descriptive of a renunciant orientation: *yati, bhikṣu, yogin, parivrajaka,* and *samnyasin*; and six are descriptive of a Vedic one: *ṛṣi* (and various grades of *ṛṣi—brahmārṣi, jarārṣi, mahārṣi, devārṣi, viprārṣi, paramārsi*); *muni, valakhilya, vaikhānasa, siddha*. The term *tapasvin* appears to be used adjectivally, to refer to all varieties of ascetics. We also find reference to ascetic activities associated with the terms *brahmacarya, vānaprasthya,* and *saṃnyāsa*. This categorization, however, is by no means absolute; indeed, it can only be provisional and heuristic because many of the terms share commonalities. Some terms are used interchangeably with others—but not consistently; some appear to be committed to soteriological pursuits, while others seem to engage in austerities idiosyncratically. The challenge, then, is to disentangle *nivṛtti* varieties of asceticism from the *pravṛtta*, or "worldly."

Let us look at brief descriptions of these figures.

Ṛṣi	Numerous characters are called *ṛṣis* in the text—e.g., Vyāsa, Nārada, Agastya, Dadhīci, Lomaśa, Cyavana, Atri, Bharadvaja, Bhṛgu, Utaṅka, Kaśyapa, Kaṇva, Vasiṣṭha and others; at other times, several of these are also known as *munis*. As a rule, *ṛṣis* are *brāhmaṇas*, and seem committed to upholding the Vedic tradition. They study the Vedas. They are also said to propound philosophical theories. Thus, in the Anuśāsanaparva, the doctrine of *karma* is said to be expounded by them. There are two groups of *ṛṣis*: The first type takes a vow of perpetual celibacy (*urdhvaretas*): for example, Kaṇva. The second group is married but at least for periods practices celibacy. They have children of their own or sometimes they adopt children exposed to the elements, for example, Kaṇva, Sthūlakeśa. They observe rigid vows. They perform rituals and *saṃskāras*. They attend sacrifices. *Ṛṣis* are usually described as merciful, high-souled, truthful, illustrious, self-restrained, and contemplative. The relations between *devas* and *ṛṣis* are marked with tension. Indra, the chief of the *devas* lives in constant fear that the *ṛṣis* might usurp his position by virtue of their ascetic power. Hence he sends *apsarās* down to earth to disrupt their penance.

Vaikhānasa	*Vaikhānasas* are forest dwellers. Like the *Vālakhilyas* and other ascetics, they are said to be in control of their senses (*jitendriya*), always engaged in *dharma* (*dharmapara*). They avoid sensual pleasures, enjoy the fruits of their penance immediately, and finally ascend to heaven (XII. 236.20). They subsist on roots, fruits, and flowers and observe stern vows (XII. 236.15). They are followers of the Vedic *dharma* as are the *Vanaprasthins*, and the *Vālakhilyas* (XII. 160.24). The hermitage of *Vaikhānasas* is situated in the Himalayas in the northern region (V.109.9). The *Vaikhānasas* are described as devotees of Nārāyaṇa (XII. 360.14).
Siddha	*Siddhas* are heavenly/semidivine beings (XII 284.17). Usually they are paired with other semidivine beings: Caraṇa (I.92.25, IV.26.10; [in this case, the word appears to be used to describe both renouncers and forest-dwellers] V.179.4, V.187.23, XII.175.23, XII.193.12), *Gandharva*, *Yakṣa* (I.111.1, [in this instance again, the word is used for both renouncers and forest-dwellers] V.62.22, XII.145.13), *devas* (IV.51.13) and also with sages (*ṛṣis*) (I.111.9, I.117.33, IV.51.13, XII.54.4, XII.260.35). *Siddhas* are said to be sons of Bṛhaspati and well-versed in the Vedas (I.60.6). They are very successful ascetics (III.2.71, I.4.10, XII.155.3, XII.160.23, XII.274.12). They observe celibacy (I.57.57, XII.290.71). They are also engaged in *japa* and *homa* (I.64.38). They have a *yoga śarīra* (II.8.26). They live in the woods (3.25.20).
Munis	*Munis* are of cleansed souls (*bhavitātmānam*), and residents of forests (*vane nivasatam*) who subsist on bulbs, fruits and roots (*kanda mūla phalāśinām* XIII.14.82)—cannot obtain food prepared with milk XIII.17.04 Upamanyu says that the names of Mahādeva were given by *munis* who were seers (*tattva darśibhiḥ*). XIII.17.26 Mahādeva is said to be the best among *munis*. (*munīnām api yo muniḥ*) (XV.15.17) Vyāsa is referred to as *muni* by Vaiśaṃpāyana. XV.35.10 Vyāsa tells Yudhiṣṭhira that he should not feel pity that one has taken up residence in the forest (*vanavāsa*), that he eats wild rice (*svadate vanyam annam*) and wears the dress of *muni* (*munivāsāṃsi*). XVI.5.22 Kṛṣṇa ascends heaven and is received by *munis* (*pratyudyayuḥ munayaḥ)* XV.45.12 After the Pāṇḍavas returned, Dhṛtarāṣṭra with Gāndhārī, Kuntī and Saṃjaya retires to Gaṅgādvāram. He performed severe penance (*atasthe tapastīvram*), subsisted on air, and is referred to as *muni* in this verse.

The above varieties of ascetics appear to engage in austerities in conjunction with an eremitic lifestyle, and would seem to represent the ideal of Vedic tradition: men of self-restraint and contemplative practice, who nevertheless remain committed to the norm of Vedic practice, participate in Vedic ritual, learning, and teaching, and expect to achieve the goal of heaven. The following, however, would appear to be varieties of ascetics who, to a greater or lesser extent, shun Vedic sacrifice, and are committed to goals beyond heaven, to the deathlessness of *mokṣa*.

Parivrajaka	This word occurs only in the Śāntiparva, and functions as a synonym for *saṃnyāsin* (a renouncer) (XII.184.10, XII.185.3, XII.269.16). Carvaka, a demon and a friend of Duryodhana, visits Yudhiṣṭhira in the guise of *parivrajaka*, with a *tridaṇḍī* in his hand and a tuft of hair on his head. The words *bhikṣu* and *parivrajaka* are used interchangeably in these verses (XII.39.23, XII.39.33).
Yati	*Yati* also practices renunciation, but not as a stage of life. Unlike a *ṛṣi* he is opposed to the Vedic tradition of sacrifices. The Śāntiparva speaks of *yatidharma* in several places (XII.38.13, XII.226.5, XII.294.36, XII.306.94, XII.336.5, XV.33.32). The aim of *yatidharma* is to attain freedom (*mokṣa*) (XII.262.29). He fears birth and death (XIII.16.15). He is engaged in *dhyānayoga*. He is able to see the *ātman* through the power of meditation and penance (*tapas*) as one sees his own image reflected in the mirror. Since he possesses a knowledge of the Self—is an *ātmavedi*—(XII.335.85), he can attain *brahmanirvāṇam* (VI.27.26) (I.1.197). He is in control of his senses, free of passions and patient (III.145.30) (I.38.9). Anger destroys his penance (I.38.8). He practices celibacy (*urdhvaretas*) (II.11.34), (II.48.40), (III.222.42). He does not have a permanent abode, wanders throughout the country (III.28.16), and leads a secluded existence (XII.308.168). He has his head shaven and carries a *kamaṇḍala* and *tridaṇḍa*. (III.262.16). He is close to Nārāyaṇa (V.69.5). The Āśramavāsikaparva contains a discussion between a sacrificial priest and a *yati* concerning animal sacrifice. The *yati* does not approve of animal sacrifice and practices *ahiṃsā*. The *yati* says that abstinence from cruelty to all creatures is justified simply on the basis of what is perceptible to the five senses and that any means beyond sensory perception is not necessary (XIV.28.18).

Yogin	Humans as well as gods are referred to as *yogis*. Vidura is a *mahāyogin* (XV.35.12). Vyāsa and Sanatkumāra are also referred to as *yogins*. (XIII.18.1, XIII.14.159). Śiva and Viṣṇu are called *yogins* (XIII.14.155, XIII.135.104). Śiva is the best among *yogins* (XIII.14. 155). He is also known as *kālayogin* (XIII.17.48). The Pāṇḍavas are said to be observers of *yoga dharma* (XVII.1.44, XVII.2.1). *Yogins* have access to esoteric knowledge (XII.225.15); *yogins* who practice *dhyāna* achieve *nirvāṇam* XII.188.22. The one who has no fixed abode (*aniketa*), who takes shelter under the foot of a tree (*vṛkṣa mūla āśraya*), who does not cook for himself (*apacaka*) (in other words leads a life of mendicancy) is a *muni*, an eternal *yogin* (*sadā yogi*), a renouncer (*tyāgi*), and a mendicant (*bhikṣuka*, or *saṃnyāsin*) XII.12.09; Vyāsa says all beings go back to the *Brahman* and this knowledge is only accessible to *yogins* (*yogibhiḥ paramātmabhiḥ dṛṣṭvā*) (XII.225.15).
Bhikṣuka	The *bhikṣuka (samnyasin)* renounces all action. He is a refuge (*abhayam*) to all creatures. He is friendly and benevolent to all creatures. He controls his senses. He is free of all attachments and passions. He subsists on food obtained without asking. He eats as much as needed to keep him alive. He must obtain only as much as he requires. He has to go begging when the smoke in the houses ceases, and the fire in the hearths are put out and people in the houses take their food. He neither rejoices when he gets something nor feels sad if he could not get anything. He seeks food just enough to keep him alive. In this process he should not deprive anybody of his or her food. He has to go begging alone, not in groups. He treats a clod of earth and a lump of gold equally. He does not save anything for his own use. He has neither friends nor foes. He does not care if anyone praises or blames him. He should not be ostentatious in his acts of piety. He must lead a solitary life. In the rainy season he lives in one place but in the summer he spends only one night at an inhabitable place. He takes shelter in an empty house, a forest, a cave, a river or at the root of a tree (XII.9.22 ff., XII.237.36 ff, XIV.45.17 ff). He should practice the following eight virtues: non-violence (*ahiṃsā*); celibacy (*brahmacaryam*); truthfulness (*satyam*); honesty (*arjavam*); freedom from anger (*akrodha*); jealousy (*anasūya*); and slander (*apaiśunam*); and self-restraint (*dama*) (XIV.46.35).

Returning now to the question of gender, where does one locate women among this variety of ascetics? Can we speak of female *yatis* and *munis*, *brahmārṣis*, *yogin*s, and *parivrajakas*? Searching the material, one finds that there are no overt references to female *ṛṣis* or *munis* or *yatis*, but we have the occasional reference to *siddhās*, *bhikṣukīs,* and *parivrajakās*. To conclude from this that some forms of asceticism were ideologically supported for women and others barred would, however, be a hasty and unwarranted extrapolation. Our data are simply too sparse to support generalizations that are tenable.

I propose, therefore, another avenue of entry into the topic, to speak not of types of *ascetics*, but types of *asceticisms*. In what follows, I identify four broad types of *asceticisms*, distinguished from each other by their goals as well as by their methods and forms. In analyzing these, we can clear some of the hedges to see where sexuality figures in ascetic practice, and in the pursuit of *mokṣa* in particular.

Broadly speaking, some measure of ascetic practice is required of four *ways of being in the world*: *brahmacarya*, *vanaprasthya*, *parivrajya* (or *saṃnyāsa*), and being in observance of a *vrata* (vow). The first three terms, *brahmacarya*, *vanaprasthya*, *parivrajya* (or *saṃnyāsa*), are inherently ambiguous and it is often unclear what precisely each signifies outside of its immediate context. Patrick Olivelle makes this point in his 1993 work, *The Āsrama System*. As he notes, there are both ancient and classical understandings of concepts such as *brahmacarya*, *vanaprasthya*, and *saṃnyāsa*. In the older formulation, these three categories, which along with that of *garhasthya* are collectively known as the *āśramas*, signify *vocations* or *choices of lifestyle* that a twice-born man may pursue on completion of his basic theological education. In the classical formulation, however, and in subsequent Hinduism, the *āśramas* are taken to be not vocational alternatives, but *successive stages of life*, signifying the ideal life span of a twice-born man. This distinction is important for interpreting sexuality because the older sense of these terms evokes *nivṛtti* resonances while the classical evokes *pravṛtti* ones, and the ideology of sex in *nivṛtti* and *pravṛtti* is decidedly at variance. Whereas *nivṛtti* involves an absolute *negation* of sexuality (a negation that paradoxically generates greater sexual power, as Doniger has pointed out[12]), *pravṛtti* involves the close *regulation* and management of sex. Hence, the term *brahmacarya* in *nivṛtti* has significantly different connotations from what it carries in *pravṛtti*. An overview of the ways in which these terms are used in each tradition will clarify the issue.

We have noted that asceticism is a characteristic of both, world renunciation, and worldly engagement. Thus the *pitṛyana* (the "path of the ancestors") of *pravṛtti* dharma also accommodates and valorizes asceticism without, however, giving it highest priority. In much the same way as we observed *pravṛtti dharma* rationalize sex and violence, acknowledging their necessity but limiting their power, it takes the radical, antinomian tendencies of asceticism and domesticates them. Through the theological innovation of the *āśrama* system, a modified form of asceticism is accommodated in every phase of this life cycle. In the student stage, the youth guards his chastity carefully, lives simply, serves his guru with selfless regard, and studies. His life is defined by its austerity, its sternness and rigor—qualities that are typical of ascetic life in general. Following the student stage of life, he abandons all overt ascetic engagements and immerses himself in domestic existence. The symbolic rite of passage into this stage is marriage. Domesticity is not to be a hedonist adventure, however, for even in marriage and worldly life, some memory of his collegian orientation toward asceticism is retained in the elaborate rules governing his sexual life. As Jamison notes, the purpose of these rules is to imbue sexual and procreative life with the solemn spirit of celibacy: "Thus, sexual abstinence can be regularly reaffirmed as a goal in the midst of a busy procreative life."[13] In following the rules for sexual engagement in *pravṛtti dharma*, the householder lives an attenuated kind of sexual life, not only recalling the abstemious self-discipline of his student days, but also anticipating the pursuits of his future life, when he will devote himself to higher spiritual pursuits.

With *vanaprasthya*, the individual comes closer to that goal. He leaves behind sexual life again and adopts a moderate course of ascetic activity, living in the forest on roots and fruit, still engaged in the *pravṛtti* exercise of maintaining the householder fires, but increasingly distancing himself from the concerns of that world. Finally, in *saṃnyāsa*, he is permitted to shed all ties to society and the world, and to pick up again with seriousness the thread of ascetic practice that he had held in his student days (though never entirely dropped). The consciousness of a future soteriological purpose thus grounds the structural course of a man's entire life in *pravṛtti dharma*. But whereas the *nivṛtti* practitioner undertakes the pursuit of *mokṣa* immediately, seeing no value in the world outside of it, the *pravṛtti* practitioner pursues it modestly and moderately. He gets a foretaste of the methods to the achievement of *mokṣa* in his student days,[14] but he postpones the focused search for most of his life, until he has fulfilled the demands of the social world in which he is implicated.

Through the device of the *āśrama* system, *pravṛtti dharma* takes the radical asceticism of the *nivṛtti dharma* and distributes it into stages of an otherwise domestic and socially productive life. The antistructural, world-negating edge of *nivṛtti dharma* is blunted, and the individual's spiritual aspirations are accommodated through the absorption of *nivṛtti* practices in moderate and manageable doses. The ideology of renunciation is thus appropriated in such a way that it presents no serious threat to worldly life. Only those who have fulfilled their obligations by the world are suited to engage in it. The social world can in this way continue to function with all its preoccupations, and individuals are still promised *mokṣa* within one lifetime.

The point of the above overview is to alert us to the hazards of interpreting terms such as *brahmacarya*, *vanaprasthya*, and *saṃnyāsa*. This is because in any instance, ascetic activity may be supporting either a *pravṛtti* orientation or a *nivṛtti* one, and one needs to be awake to the different goals, methods, and assumptions of both traditions in order to avoid generalizing the traits of one to the other. The *Mahābhārata*, which typically defers to the ancient vocabulary even while anticipating its classical semantic reformulations, evokes both understandings of these terms at different times, and one is left to infer entirely from context what each term signifies in each instance. While some varieties of *brahmacarya* or *vanaprasthya* are directed at the *devāyana* of *mokṣa*, liberation, desiring release from the cycles of *saṃsāra*, a large part is very clearly inspired by more pedestrian worldly goals, the highest of which is heaven (*svarga, devalokam, brahmalokam, or somalokam* (XIII.130.18).[15]

Brahmacarya

It is now time to take account of these differences in more detail. *Brahmacarya*, according to the classical formulations of the *āśrama* system, refers to the period of celibate discipleship that constitutes the twice-born boy's first ritual stage of life. *Brahmacarya*, however, is also undertaken as a vocational lifestyle and where this is the case, it seems to serve both the old Vedic ideology geared at heaven and the new ascetic ideology geared at liberation. Celibacy is the most distinctive trait of *brahmacarya* pursued as a lifestyle. Where it is geared toward the goal of heaven, it is accompanied by the performance of strenuous austerities. In the *nivṛtti* soteriological orientation, it would seem that the entire meaning complex of the term *brahmacarya* is evoked: *brahmacarya* is the path that leads to *Brahman* (hence *mokṣa*). The individual thus shuns marriage and domesticity on *ideological* grounds, as inimical to the goals of a focused religious life. In both of the latter cases, the word *brahmacārin* connotes lifelong celibacy rather than discipleship[16] and in this sense is in *direct opposition* to what *brahmacarya* signifies in the *pravṛtti* stream: a *preparation* for conjugal householder life. The celibacy of the *nivṛtti brahmacārin* in particular represents a conscious rejection of the world-sustaining values of the *pravṛtti* path, of marriage and the domesticity that sex inevitably prefigures, with the understanding that *nivṛtti brahmacārins* are focused on a higher path of self-realization.

We have examples of all of these forms in the *Mahābhārata*. *Brahmacarya* as a stage of life, indicative of a *pravṛtti* orientation, is followed, for example, by four of Vyāsa's students who, on completion of their studies, disperse to marry and take up their ritual duties as *brāhmaṇas* (XII.315.9). Others, such as the itinerant sage Nārada are reputed to be *brahmacārins* by vocation, though not explicitly directed to the goal of liberation.[17] In addition, we find many references to individuals who continue as *brahmacārins*, avowing themselves to lives of celibate self-denial in a *nivṛtti* mode. Vyāsa's son and disciple Śuka is one example of this. One hears also of Jaigiśavya, the mendicant guest of Asita Devala, who achieves *mokṣa* through silence (IX.49.5 ff.). Asita Devala, inspired by his example, vacillates between *pravṛtti* and *nivṛtti* paths, and finally determining on *nivṛtti*, follows suit (IX.49.59–61). In these cases, *brahmacarya* serves *nivṛtti* ideals. The term *brahmacarya* thus can refer to different things in different contexts; in all cases it connotes celibacy, but celibacy is in the service of differing ideals in each case. In *nivṛtti*, celibacy supports the ideal of world renunciation, in *pravṛtti* it supports discipleship, and in the liminal case of characters such as Nārada, who pursue it neither as a stage of life nor in the interests of *mokṣa*, celibacy forms part of the repertoire of asceticism that is geared at achieving higher worldly goals, such as heaven and the proximity of the gods.

Vanaprasthya

The second type of asceticism evident in the text is that of the *vanaprasthin* ascetic, and the *vanaprasthin* is perhaps the most contested figure in discussions of asceticism in the ancient Indic world. As the name suggests, *vanaprasthins* reside in forest hermitages, and live reclusive lives of unadorned simplicity. The critical question, however, is: to what end? Is the *vanaprasthin* the model of the *pravṛtti* actor, who is conscious of his dues to society and its ritual world, but is mentally and spiritually attuned to soteriological goals? There's vast disagreement on these points, but as we have seen, there are several varieties of *vanaprasthins* operating within the text, exhibiting a range of motives. The *Āpastamba* Dharmasūtra describes two basic types of *vanaprasthins*, one who retires alone to the forest and successively reduces his dependence on food and nourishment, and the other who lives a simple domestic life with wife and children on the margins of society (II.9.22.1–9). In the *Mahābhārata*, one description of life as a *vanaprasthin* is found in XII.236.

> The *vanaprasthin* is one who gradually abandons the stage of being a householder and enters the next stage of life as a forest recluse. He undertakes this after much deliberation, after the birth of grandchildren, the appearance of wrinkles on his body, and the greying of his hair. In the forest he continues to perform the fire sacrifice and worship the deities he revered while being a householder. For the purpose of sacrifice he tends some cows. The offerings to the fire constitute clarified butter. He observes vows and eats only once. He subsists on rice and wild grain. He worships his guests. He eats what is left after feeding his guests. In order to perform the fire sacrifice and worship his guests, he is allowed to store grain and other items for a day or a month or twelve years. Throughout the year he exposes himself to the elements. In the rainy season he gets drenched and in summer he sits in the sun surrounded by fires on all sides. No luxuries are permitted. He sleeps on the bare earth and may use small mats of grass for sitting. He is supposed to stand on his toes. He bathes three times a day before he performs the sacrifice. He is forbidden to use any implements. He uses his teeth or stones to clean grains. If his vows are rigid, he will subsist on roots, fruits and flowers like the Vaikhānasas. Sometimes he will survive on a liquid diet, taking gruel either in the bright fortnight or dark fortnight. His wife or wives also observe similar austerities. (XII.236)

Is the *vanaprasthin* geared toward *nivṛtti* goals, or *pravṛtti* ones? From the above description, it would seem that *vanaprasthin*s should be understood as supporting *pravṛtti* ideals, as is apparent from their maintenance of the minimal accoutrements of the Vedic tradition—the household fire, veneration of *devas* and *pitṛs*, and some household rituals. This conclusion is not without ambiguity, however, for in spite of their ritual practices, *vanaprasthins* often espouse radical *nivṛtti* ideals. A good case in point is Vyāsa. A forest-dwelling sage and *guru*, who, though unorthodox in not possessing a wife, lives in an *āśrama* with his attenuated family of one son, maintains the household fire and performs the Vedic rituals of the *agnihotra* and so forth. Even sans femme, Vyāsa may rightly be taken to epitomize the *pravṛtti* tradition. He offers priestly services to people (for instance, at Yudhiṣṭhira's *rājasūya* and later, at his *aśvamedha*), and later, admonishes Yudhiṣṭhira sternly on his worldly duties. As Bruce Sullivan has pointed out in his work on Vyāsa,[18] the sage replicates the priestly role of Brahmā in the world, where Brahmā is archetypally a Vedic deity, epitomizing *pravṛtti* functions.

The story cannot end there, however, because on the other hand, the philosophies espoused by Vyāsa address soteriological aspirations, and thus contain quintessentially *nivṛtti* content. Thus when, on the eve of the war, Dhṛtarāṣṭra pleads for spiritual counsel to allay his anxieties, Vyāsa refers him to the sage Sanatsujāta. Sanatsujāta is one of the seven sages recognized in the origin myth of the *pravṛtti* and *nivṛtti* traditions, and is acknowledged as one of the progenitors of the *nivṛtti* tradition. The discourse that Sanatsujāta offers directly enunciates the high objectives of the *nivṛtti* tradition. Similarly, in training his own son, Śuka, Vyāsa discloses only *nivṛtti* ambitions. It is his advice that "Family, children, wife, the body itself, one's exertions, and all one's possessions acquired with difficulty are insubstantial and useless in the next world. Your interest does not lie in excessive attachment to them"[19] (XII.316.32–33). One should, therefore, detach oneself from them and be resolutely alone, for "the desire for living in a village is like a binding cord"[20] (XII.316.37). He exhorts Śuka to "abandon both virtue and vice, truth and falsehood. Having abandoned truth and falsehood, abandon that by which these are cast off"[21] (XII.316.40). Śuka will achieve wisdom and peace by setting aside all partiality for friends and intimates, and conducting himself with humility before all (XII.317.29). It is only in taking his father's advice seriously that Śuka embraces the *nivṛtti* path, holding himself resolutely aloof of worldly involvements (XII.320.19).

Vyāsa may thus be regarded as one archetype of the forest sages to be found in the *Mahābhārata*. Although they themselves do participate in certain Vedic functions, and thus cannot be considered antistructural in the same way as the ideals of *nivṛtti* hold, at the level of ideas, they espouse the philosophies and ethics of *nivṛtti*, explicitly denouncing the ritual and social preoccupations of *pravṛtti* and advocating the radical ethics and teleology of *nivṛtti*. This kind of *vanaprasthin* represents the inherent religious ambivalence of the text as a whole, intensely inspired by renunciant ideals yet also dialectically committed to maintaining order in the world. One way to read them may be as figures rehearsing toward liberation and counseling others on *nivṛtti* ideals, but not yet accomplished enough to achieve it themselves. This would seem to be the case with Vyāsa, who coaches his son Śuka on *nivṛtti* ideals but later, lamenting his loss and seeking to follow his itinerary through the high heavens, discovers to his embarrassment that he is not advanced enough to replicate Śuka's success (XII.320.29–30).[22]

A second archetypal *vanaprasthin* is the *brāhmaṇa* who marries and then sets up a home away from the presses of the village. He is thus both householder and *vanaprasthin* simultaneously. This is the most common variety of *vanaprasthin* encountered in the MBh. The famous seven sages of Vedic lore might be said to represent this type: all the Bhārgavas, Agastya, Vasiṣṭha, Viśvamitra, and others make their homes in the forest, living a simple eremitic existence while engaging in their duties as priests and Vedic teachers. Intimately involved in the intrigues of the gods and the *asuras*, they often operate as advisers or counselors to one or the other side in the battle for universal sovereignty. These figures are most obviously modeled on the *ṛṣis* of ancient Vedic lore. Most often, they reinforce Vedic paradigms rather than *śramāṇika* ones[23] and are cited as the progenitors of the *pravṛtti* tradition, exemplifying Vedic values. They are idealized as forest-dwelling creatures, eking subsistence out of the simple fare of the forest, often suffering pecuniary hardship.

A third archetype of the *vanaprasthin* is the one who retires to the forest in the third stage of life, after having lived a rich life in society. This *vanaprasthin* is almost always aged, and almost always *kṣatriya*; Dhṛtarāṣṭra, Bṛhadaśva, Yayāti, Śibi, and various other kings all retire to the forest in the twilight of their royal careers. *Brāhmaṇas* in the *Mahābhārata* are most often *originally* forest-dwellers and do not undertake *vanaprasthya* as a stage of life. Exceptions are those who serve as ministers and advisers to kings, figures such as Kṛpa or Dhaumya, who accompany their lieges wherever they go.

There are thus at least three distinct types of *vanaprasthins* operating in the forest, if we do not include all the figures whose presence is clearly anomalous—such as kings deprived of their kingdoms, exiled heirs, and disenchanted others: figures such as Nala, Satyavat, and the Pāṇḍavas themselves are almost always *kṣatriya*. Only one of these types, the third, undertakes *vanaprasthya* as a stage of life, and this appears to be a *kṣatriya* pursuit. Otherwise, the forests are clearly the turf of *brāhmaṇas* who reside there permanently. Among these, some raise families and are actively engaged in ritual activities. Others, in the first category, engage in ritual but are mentally and spiritually inclined toward *nivṛtti* goals. Hence they occupy a liminal and uneasy space between Vedic and *śramaṇa* worlds.

All of these types, however, engage in asceticism to varying degrees, and asceticism always involves a negotiation of sexuality. More on this below.

Saṃnyāsa

The third form of asceticism is that of the *parivrajaka*, also known as the *saṃnyāsin*.[24] He is the one who renounces familial ties and social values and undertakes a radical pursuit of individual soteriological goals.[25] The defining features of the world renouncer in ancient and medieval Indian asceticism may be summarized as follows: (1) cutting social and kinship ties; (2) living an itinerant life without a fixed home; (3) mendicancy associated with the abandonment of socially recognized economic activities and the ownership of property, especially of food; (4) abandoning ritual activities customary within society; and (5) celibacy.[26]

Pāṇḍu provides us with a good description of *saṃnyāsa*, before he, at the persuasion of his wives, forsakes it as an option.

> I shall unflinchingly yoke myself to harsh austerities. Ever alone, each single day under a different tree, I shall beg my food. A shaven mendicant, covered with dirt, sheltering in empty spaces, or sleeping at the foot of a tree, I shall traverse this earth. I shall renounce all that is dear and hateful, I shall neither grieve nor rejoice, I shall remain balanced before praise and abuse, without blessings, without greetings, without choices, without possessions. I shall make fun of no one, frown at nothing, always sweet-spoken, delighting in the welfare of all creatures. I shall never offend any of the four orders of moving and unmoving beings, remaining always equal-minded to all breathing creatures, as though they were my children.
>
> I shall beg my food one time a day of seven families. If there are no alms to be had when they themselves go hungry, I shall take whatever food they offer, a little every time, whatever I receive first. When the seven are done, I shall never beg more, whether I received anything or not. If a man hacks off my arm with a hatchet, and another anoints the other arm with sandalpaste, I shall neither think well of one, or ill of

> the other. I shall do nothing out of a will to live, or a will to die; I shall neither welcome life, nor turn away death. All the rites for prosperity that the living can perform, I shall pass them all by, when I come to their instants and dates. At all times, I shall forsake all that makes the senses work, give up duties and cleanse all the grime of my soul. (I.110.7–18, van Buitenen's translation)

The Śāntiparva describes further the life of the *saṃnyāsin*. His life of renunciation is based on the Upaniṣads. He undertakes renunciation when, as a *vanaprasthin*, he is weak from old age and physical ailments. He enters the next stage of life by removing his hair and nails and purifying himself with various acts. Being detached from every object of the senses he meditates on the *ātman* and performs the *ātmayajña*. He takes five or six morsels of food, after offering them to the vital breaths (*prāṇas*) while reciting the *mantras* from the Yajurveda. He lives alone. He does not have a permanent residence. He enters the villages only for begging food. The *saṃnyāsin* is a refuge to all creatures. He is of virtuous conduct. He has realized the *ātman*. He is freed from all sins, and feelings of anger and delusion. He is not interested in action for the sake of this world or the next world. He has neither friends nor enemies. He has subdued his senses. He lives in this world unconcerned about anything. Eventually he attains eternity (XII.236).

In *saṃnyāsa*, individuals formally renounce the world and practice *nivṛtti* ethics in a focused and serious way. In the *pravṛtti* tradition, where *saṃnyāsa* is conceived as the fourth and final stage of life, *saṃnyāsa* is limited to males of the upper three castes, and has a sacrament that marks its beginning. In the *nivṛtti* tradition, where *saṃnyāsa* is undertaken as a vocation, the rules are hazy. It is unclear, for example, what qualifies one for *saṃnyāsa* (*adhikāra*), or what rituals, if any, mark the entry into the life of a *saṃnyāsin*. Some narratives would suggest that *saṃnyāsa* may be undertaken without formal ritual—as, for example, in the case of Vyāsa's son, Śuka, whose progress toward *mokṣa* is described in several chapters of the Śāntiparva.[27] Others, however, show *saṃnyāsin*s with the formal appurtenances of renouncers, such as begging bowl, robes, and staff. This is the case with Sulabhā (see below).

Saṃnyāsa also is treated both as a stage of life and as a vocation. The Kaurava minister Vidura undertakes *saṃnyāsa* toward the end of his life. When the Pāṇḍavas visit their elders in the forest, they are informed that Vidura has wandered off into radical homelessness. He is also described as being naked (*digvāsā*) and covered with dirt (XV:33.15–29). Since wandering without clothing, the last vestige of civilizational life, was a practice of certain sects, Brahminical and Jain, it is possible to suppose that Vidura had become initiated into a particular sect during his last years of life. In other contexts, *saṃnyāsa* appears to have been undertaken as a vocation. The perpetually wrathful Durvāsas appears to be some variety of unclad *saṃnyāsin*. Śeṣa, "the eldest and best of snakes," is said to have devoted himself to *nivṛtti* practices from the very beginning (I.32.2ff); and Devāpi, Śaṃtanu's elder brother, "while still a child, entered the forest" (I.90.48). In the *nivṛtti* interpretation of *saṃnyāsa*, the word *saṃnyāsin* implies not an elderly person who abandoned householder life after having raised children and ensconced them into their own families; it denotes simply somebody who has renounced the world, and yields no information about age, children, family, and so forth.

Mahāvrata

The fourth form of asceticism is more squarely teleological, aimed at the achievement of particular ends, such as children, power, and sovereignty. This type of asceticism is apparently preceded by the declaration of a vow (*vrata*) that binds the individual to certain rules, necessitating certain conduct while barring others. We might therefore refer to it as the asceticism of a *mahāvratin*, one who is formally undertaking a course of action for a limited period of time. This is by far the most extreme form of asceticism practiced in the *Mahābhārata*. These ascetics appeal to the deity, and then perform superhuman feats of asceticism, involving hyperbolic acts of self-mortification, such as standing on one toe with one's hands raised high amid five blazing fires in the roaring heat of summer. Through these acts of self-mortification, ascetics hope to impress the deity and win his or her favor. The deity will then grant them their desired boons. Perhaps surprisingly, this type of asceticism is very common in the *Mahābhārata* and is practiced by every variety of being: *rākṣasas*, *dānavas*, *asuras* of all kinds; human beings, animals, birds. Kṛṣṇa is seen to practice it, for the birth of a son (XIII.15.4–6); Arjuna practices it for the acquisition of weapons (III.39.10ff.); Viśvāmitra practices it to become a *brahmārṣi* (I.165.40ff.), and Mataṅga practices it to become a *brāhmaṇa* (XIII.129.1–16). Different sages routinely practice it, as do the *asuras*. This kind of *mahāvrata*-based asceticism is therefore extremely common.

Such asceticism is most often a *pravṛtti* pursuit, involving an initiation and a period of practice that ends on acquisition of the desired goal.[28] It may also be a *nivṛtti* activity, however, depending on the goals that one aims to achieve. For example, while this kind of asceticism is generally practiced for the attainment of worldly goals, it may also be practiced in the spirit of *bhakti*, seeking not a temporal end but a spiritual one. This is suggested, for example, in the lengthy *Śāntiparva* hymn offered to the god Śiva.

Differences Between *Pravṛtti* and *Nivṛtti* Uses of Asceticism

One significant difference between the asceticism of *pravṛtti dharma* and the asceticism of *nivṛtti dharma* is that in addition to the other ways in which ascetic activity is routinized, regulated, and moderated in *pravṛtti dharma*, there are numerous rules pertaining to qualification, or *adhikāra*, for ascetic activity. In *pravṛtti dharma*, asceticism, and the *āśrama* scheme into which it is interjected, are both explicitly limited to males of the three upper castes. Women and *śūdra*s do not qualify for ascetic activity, particularly in its more pristine forms during the *brahmacarya* stage of life and the *saṃnyāsa* stage of life. Women are sacramentally inducted into the system through marriage, but their role is supportive rather than primary. They assist their husbands in the fulfillment of their domestic duties, and may be permitted to accompany their husbands in the *vanaprasthya* stage, at the latter's prerogative.[29] They are not acknowledged in any independent way within the *āśrama* scheme.[30] *Śūdra*s do not participate in the *āśrama* system at all, since they do not receive any of the sacraments. Their claim to the system is summarily dismissed, as illustrated in a story of the *Anuśāsanaparva*. A *śūdra*, seeking learning, approaches one guru after another for instruction, but is rejected by all. Finally, one *brāhmaṇa* accepts him as a disciple. The *śūdra* thus acquires an education in the sacred texts, and as a result is reborn into more promising circumstances in his next life. The *brāhmaṇa* who instructed him, however, suffers negative *karmic* consequences in his next life, and is significantly demoted in status (XIII.10.3ff.). A more brutal story is recounted in the Uttarakāṇḍa of the *Rāmāyaṇa*. The *śūdra* youth *Śāmbūka* offends against the natural order by practicing austerities. Through his transgressive activities, he is alleged to have caused the premature death of a *brāhmaṇa*'s son. For his temerity, he is summarily executed by Rāma, and the world is thus said to be restored to order (*Rām.*, VII.76, MBh.XII.149.62). The moral of the story is the same in both instances: *śūdras* (and women) do not have the *adhikāra* to pursue traditional ascetic activities. These are the exclusive privilege of twice-born manhood. The renunciant orders of later Hinduism instituted similar restrictions. The majority of the lineages of the Daśanāmis, for example, to this day observe sex and caste restrictions.[31]

In the relatively unregulated asceticism found in the *nivṛtti* tradition of the *Mahābhārata*, however, no such restrictions are apparent. Both women and *śūdra*s are found among *nivṛtti* renouncers in the text. Some of these characters are discussed below.

Male Ascetics and Sexual Transgression

One final note about male asceticism in the *Mahābhārata*. From the context, we can determine that much of the advice alerting men to the hazards of dealing with women is directed at novice *saṃnyāsins* such as Śuka, renouncers who are about to undertake the goal of *mokṣa* with earnestness. In the text, however, it is not *saṃnyāsin*s who are most in need of this advice. Accounts of *saṃnyāsin*s, in fact, are highly idealized. At the point that Śuka departs the world, for example, he has no interest in women. He is not at all tempted, even though he is surrounded by a veritable bevy of beauties in Janaka's court (XII.312.35 ff.). Similarly, there is no question of Mudgala becoming tempted by the charms of women. He has a clear sense of what is permanent and what is impermanent, and does not hesitate to dismiss even the pleasures of heaven as being unworthy of his exertions (III:247.1–44).[32] Accounts of *saṃnyāsin*s, therefore, are more idealistic than realistic and do not give us a good sense of what the real challenges may have been for male ascetics. The only subgroup of ascetics we see seriously challenged by sexual desires is that of the *vanaprasthin*s. Moreover, it is not that of the *kṣatriya vanaprasthin*s who adopt forest life as a stage after concluding *garhasthya* responsibilities. Dhṛtarāṣṭra, Śibi, and others, for example, are never seen in sexual encounters after their retirement to the forest; they are depicted as being elderly, and beyond such concerns at their time of life. The ascetics who find themselves in sexual situations, and often, are the *brāhmaṇa vanaprasthin*s of the first and second categories, who reside in the forest as a vocational lifestyle. There are many, many occasions of male *vanaprasthin* ascetics, traveling through the forest, being stimulated by the sight of a woman sporting in the water, or an *apsarā* passing by, with her skirt blown aside by the wind. Vyāsa is very obviously excited (*kāmamohita*) by the image of the *apsarā* Ghṛtācī while he was performing the offices of a *hotṛ*, and he suffers some embarrassment for this (XII.311.1–8). Droṇa is the result of his father Bharadvāja's excitement over the *apsarā* Ghṛtācī; he ejaculated on a reed (I.121.3–4). Kṛpa and Kṛpī were born by the same means. Their father, Gautama, became aroused at the sight of the *apsarā* Jalapādi, who had been sent to distract him (I.120.7–14). The *vanaprasthin* sage Parāśara became stimulated at the sight of Satyavatī rowing across the river (I.57.56–64). Ṛśyaśṛṅga was born when his father, Vibhandaka Kaśyapa, was titillated by the sight of the *apsarā* Urvaśī (III.110.14). Śruvavatī was born when *ṛṣi* Bharadvāja's passions were stirred at seeing Ghṛtācī (IX.47.57); Sarasvat was born when *ṛṣi* Daḍhīci ejaculated into the Sarasvatī, after becoming excited on seeing Alambuṣā (IX.50.5–9). In the heavens, even the priestly god Brahmā, who represents the idealized form of *vanaprasthin* sages, is said to have been aroused by the sight of Dīkṣā and her sisters, to the extent that he discharged his semen into the fire[33] (XIII.85.8). The group, therefore, that appears to be most susceptible to sexual interludes are the *vanaprasthin*s who have lived in the forest for generations.

Sexuality in *Nivṛtti Dharma*

One element common to all varieties of asceticism is the control of sexuality; as noted in the previous chapter, this is the single most fundamental credential of the ascetic life. In this context, women represent a special challenge. This is either stated outright, or implied in many of the passages of the text. One such passage states, "Women lead [men], ignorant or wise, again and again down the wrong path, in the control of lust and anger. The nature of women is such that it is harmful to men. Therefore, the wise do not delight in women"[34] (XIII.48.36–37). In another passage, we hear that "they are demons who go about with wondrously beautiful forms. They are incomparably beautiful and very cruel, and always connive to destroy austerities"[35] (III.113.1). Yet another advises that for a man who practices *brahmacarya*, "the stories of women are not to be heard. Nor are they to be seen naked. At any time, from the very sight of them," it is explained, "the weak are afflicted with passion"[36] (XII.207.12). The negative link between women and asceticism thus seems firmly established. Women are "terrifying magical illusions," the text tells us. "They confound the ignorant"[37] (XII.206.9).

These statements are relatively common in the text, and capture well the sense of caution that teachers hope to instill in male ascetics toward women. It is further evident that the problem with women hinges exclusively on sexual provenance. It is not simply that women are a disturbance; it is that women exercise enough sexual appeal to derange men and fill them with passion. This is why men are advised specifically not to look at undressed, sexually exposed women. The fear is of their power to attract men to them sexually. It is female sexual attractiveness that is threatening, that represents peril to male ascetics.

Male Perceptions of Female Sexuality in *Nivṛtti Dharma*

Female sexuality is a menace to male ascetics for a variety of reasons, and these are pondered at various points in the text. The most obvious reason is that desire for a woman may distract a man from his ascetic engagements. Celibacy is crucial to ascetic practice, and *brahmacarya* of either variety is "difficult to practice" (*suduskaram brahmacaryam* XII.207.11). Enticed by desire for a woman, a man may become diverted from his ascetic purpose, and yield to his bodily wants. While the occasional lapse may not appear to be a serious problem, there is the danger that a man's attraction for a woman may pull him into a full-scale reimmersion into worldly life. That would be a much bigger calamity. A man may become seduced again into the pleasures of worldly life, and without being cognizant of it, slide into the rhythms of domesticity. Trapped again in the sinewy snares of children and dependents, a man may find himself out of the running for *nirvāṇam* for yet another lifetime. One passage in the text analyzes this process. It says: "Because of the keen desire men have for women, children are born from them." Children are a special danger, because once one becomes entwined in their affections, one may lose conviction in the self-denial necessary for the *nivṛtti* path. A wise man is advised, therefore, to "Cast off those vermin born of one's body, made as if of one's limbs and one's consciousness. Cast off those leeches whom one regards as one's children, born of oneself and one's mind" (XII.206.9–10). "Sons, family, community life all lead one to the realm of rebirth"[38] (XII.290.67). One should steer studiously clear of them. It is a commonplace assurance that, "When one is freed of the many strong nooses created by children and [worship of] gods, one abandons happiness and sorrow and is free, having attained the highest end"[39] (XII.212.45). One of the reasons to avoid sexual contact with woman, therefore, is to avoid a relapse into domesticity.

Sexual intimacy with a woman also has more subtle and adverse consequences for a male ascetic. This is because of the theory of *tapas*. In the

Mahābhārata, as in most Indian texts, the fundamental logic of ascetic pursuit is that by performing stern austerities, beginning with the rigid restraint of one's sexual urges, one generates a heat, or energy, called *tapas*, which can be harnessed and manipulated. This internal heat is a by-product of one's ascetic practice, and grows steadily with the consistency and severity of one's austerities. Although it is only a by-product, it is nevertheless quite crucial, for it is this energy that then can scorch the seeds of *karma* so that they no longer sprout into life. With this energy, visualized as an intense and potent blast of heat, one can burn through the *karma* that keeps one captive in *saṃsāra*, and catapult oneself to the other side, the side of *mokṣa*, where there is no more rebirth. *Tapas*, therefore, is a precious and coveted bank of energy. When not being employed for burning up one's *karmic* bonds, it translates into a power to perform outstanding feats—incinerate offenders to ashes, transform them into reptiles, raise people from the dead, and so forth. This is why the curse of *ṛṣi*s and long-time ascetics is so dreaded, because through the course of many years of rigorous observance, ascetics have such an accumulation of *tapas* that they can radically alter people's lives.

It is important to note that the practice of *nivṛtti dharma* demands restraint of *all* of one's raw emotional impulses. This is a fact that often goes unappreciated; *any* form of intense self-discipline generates *tapas*, and conversely, any departure from self-discipline results in a depletion of *tapas*. The *Gītā*, for example, identifies three key areas where self-control is imperative, in the combination *rāgadveśakrodha* (BG III.34, 37). In this formula are found the three most persistent sources of *karmic* bondage: *rāga*, "love/attachment/passion/lust"; *dveśa*, "hatred/animosity/resentment/vengefulness"; and *krodha*, "anger." Mastery over *rāga* seems to get the most emphasis in the epic, perhaps because it makes for colorful stories, and because it is the most obvious source of challenge to ascetics. It is easy therefore to forget that *dveśa* and *krodha* are just as pernicious, both from the point-of-view of personal self-cultivation and from that of accumulating the *tapas* necessary to "scorch the seeds of bondage." Wrath is as futile as lust; both deplete *tapas* and implicate one in the world. The mastery of all of these is vital for the *nivṛtti* path. All of them, if controlled, harnessed, disciplined, yield energy and vigour (*tapas*). Conversely, all of them—lust, hatred, anger—if indulged, sap one's vitality and strength, diminishing both one's power of clear discernment and one's ability to perform extraordinary feats (such as that of leaping from *saṃsāra* to *mokṣa*). By yielding to the seductive temptations of anger or hatred, one destroys one's *tapas* just as quickly as by yielding to sexual desire.[40]

That said, however, the most ready technique for accumulating *tapas* is through the control of one's sexual desires. The more formidable one's mastery over sexual urges, the more spectacular one's power. Conversely, the simplest means for sabotaging *tapas* is indulgence in sexual activity. This is why the gods spend so much time engineering sexual situations for ascetics. They lure the ascetics into sexual involvement with women, in the hope of expending the sages' cache of *tapas*. When the sages' energy is thus depleted through sexual activity, the sages no longer represent a threat to the gods, having lost their power.

For a male ascetic, sex is a particular hazard, because the physical loss of fluid experienced by a man in ejaculation most tangibly represents his diminution of ascetic energy. One statement in the *Śāntiparva* voices this concern: "Even in dreams, passion so churns the mind and thoughts [of men] that even without contact [with women], their sperm spills out of them"[41] (XII.207.22). The squandering of semen is a senseless dissipation of the man's vital energy. This is why one of the explanations for the former prosperity of the Dānavas is that "they never took pleasure in the emission of their semen into empty space, into animals, into inappropriate wombs, or on sacred days"[42] (XII.221.44). When they forsook these good habits, their sovereignty came to an end. Since women are invariably represented as the source of male sexual fantasy, they are easily targeted as culprits in causing this expenditure of semen; hence, in many narratives, women come to be condemned. In these ascetic narratives, women are simply sexual objects, and sex implies bondage to the world. "One who regards repeated births to be only due to sexual union with women is free"[43] (XII.277.28).

Female Personality in Male Ascetic Discourse

The above, then, is one angle on the relation of female sexuality to *nivṛtti dharma*. It represents male apprehensions of women's sexual power, and points to the fact that the female body is a rich source of sexual fantasy and stimulation for male ascetics. This is a sexuality that is externally ascribed to women. Women in this stream of dialogue are objectified as sexual beings, and male fears of female sexuality coalesce into a characterization of women that is primarily sexual.

The fact that female bodies are sexually objectified in male ascetic discourse is hardly surprising; feminist research on all ascetic traditions should lead us to anticipate precisely this development. Ascetics in all traditions must overcome their sexual urges and learn to restrain their desire. The difficulties are two. One is that these statements assume a heterosexual male audience, leading one to conclude that all ascetics in the *Mahābhārata* are heterosexual men. This assumption is not borne out by the evidence of the text (see below). The other is that, typically, the problem is located not in male desire, but in woman herself. "According to *śruti*, women are frail and infirm. They are without rites and unrighteous"[44] (XIII.40.11); women are "intrinsically full of passion"; they are, in fact, "the eternal embodiment of the senses" [45](XII.206.9). Male ascetic antipathy for women is projected without reflection on women, so that it becomes not male desire for women that is the source of consternation, but women themselves. Women come to be viewed as being willfully seductive, willfully deceitful, bent on foiling the penances of men.[46]

These male biases obtain a special boost from the Sāṃkhyan presuppositions of the text. The *Mahābhārata* borrows much of its religious vocabulary from Sāṃkhya philosophy. This philosophy, as encountered in the *Mahābhārata*, proposes a set of dichotomies in which the masculine is identified with *puruṣa*, the indwelling eternal self of an individual. This *puruṣa* is envisaged as being submerged in the playfully enticing, mutating femininity of *prakṛti*. Woman symbolizes *kṣetra*, the world, the field of multiplicity and action, while man symbolizes *kṣetrajña*, the knower of the field, whose intrinsic wisdom penetrates through the diverse charms of *prakṛti* (XII.206.8). Being *kṣetra*, hence worldly and material, woman represents all that *saṃsāra* represents: pleasure, enjoyment, amusement, attraction; sense-addiction, passion, indiscipline, lust. She is naturally identified with the senses and the seductive lure of the world. The male ascetic, therefore, in order to achieve freedom from the world, must replicate in his own acts the clarity of the ancient *puruṣa*; he must disengage himself from the sinuous coils of womanhood, just as *puruṣa* must disengage from *prakṛti*. Just as the *puruṣa* shines through the—willfully?—obscuring fogs of *prakṛti* and emerges serene and distinct from her, the male ascetic must resist being overcome by womanhood, and divine himself to be the *kṣetrajña* that he intrinsically is. This constitutes his *śānti*, his final liberation.

The link between woman and the world in Sāṃkhya is so tenacious as to seem organic. As one ecstatic soul, newly enlightened, joyously exclaims of *prakṛti*, "I will no longer live in the company of that which has for so long deceived me. Deceived by it, I, who am without transformation, considered myself to be constantly changing"[47] (XII.295.32). In the same manner, the male ascetic aspires to no longer be duped by womankind. In order to achieve the cosmic aloofness of *puruṣa* from *prakṛti*, he must cultivate a worldly aloofness from the daughter of *prakṛti*, namely woman. Since the primary dichotomy of *puruṣa* and *prakṛti* is expressed within Sāṃkhya itself in gendered language, it is readily exploited to legitimate the prejudices of male ascetics. Thus, women are easily identified with the attractions of the phenomenal world, from the absorbing enclosures of which men must escape. "For this reason," the poet concludes, "wise men should especially avoid [women]" (XII.206.8). This characterization of womanhood is taken for granted in the *nivṛtti*-inspired portions of the text.

It would be easy to assume from these reflections that asceticism in the *Mahābhārata* is a male-dominated business. A cursory reading of the text could certainly give this impression, because at first glance, the names of male ascetics far outnumber those of female. On closer examination, however, one finds that this is not the case. Both male and female ascetics inhabit the text. To demonstrate this, it is necessary to recall our detour through the nature of asceticism in the *Mahābhārata*. The point that we are now ready to make is that every one of these forms of asceticism is practiced by women as well as by men.

Women and Asceticism

That a tradition of female asceticism existed in ancient India has been noted by scholars. "There is overwhelming evidence . . . for the existence even within the Brahmanical tradition of independent female ascetics"; "Early Sanskrit grammatical literature records several names for female ascetics."[48] Similarly, "We have ample evidence that there were female ascetics in India in the past, and anyone acquainted with this country knows that there are still such persons today."[49] These contentions are borne out by a methodical survey of women's participation in the varieties of asceticism identified above.

Women as Brahmacāriṇīs

Beginning with *brahmacarya*, *brahmacarya* as an *āśrama* was by definition only open to boys of the upper three castes, and while there apparently were parallel rituals for girls in the past, they are not mentioned in the *Mahābhārata*.[50] The daughters of gurus may, however, have received some education, and may have been allowed to participate in the same activities as the boys.[51] In *Ādiparva*, for example, Devayānī seems to spend all her time with Kaca, a student and an ascetic (*sa brahmacārī ca tapodhanaśca* I.71.38). Śakuntalā, who grew up in her adoptive father Kaṇva's *āśrama* similarly appears in Duḥṣanta's court in the garb of an ascetic, and is termed an "evil ascetic" (*duṣṭatāpasī*) by Duḥṣanta. Later, she is said to have "controlled the heat that she had accumulated with her austerities" (I.68.18, 22). In the *Ādiparva*, we are told that "Bṛhaspati's sister, the best of women, was a *brahmacāriṇī*, an adept in *yoga*, who, unattached, roamed the entire world"[52] (I.60.26). She eventually married Prabhāṣa, the eighth *vasu*, and became the mother of Viśvakarman (I.60.26). Uddālaka's daughter Sujātā, similarly, grew up in the *āśrama* of her father, and married his pupil Kāhoḍa (III.132.7–20). These women grew up in forest hermitages, and may well have fallen into the life-patterns of male students, although they cannot be said to have practiced *brahmacarya* as a formal *āśrama*.

We do however, find unambiguous references to women who practiced *brahmacarya* as a vocation right from childhood. This includes Diśā, the aged ascetic whom Aṣṭāvakra encounters in the *Anuśāsanaparva*. She calls herself a *brahmacāriṇī* (*kaumāraṃ brahmacaryaṃ me* XIII.21.20), and is described as "an old and highly blessed ascetic, who lives in observance of a *dīkṣā*";[53] Aṣṭāvakra is advised to pay his respects to her on seeing her (XIII.19.24). Balarāma, on his pilgrimage, comes across a hermitage where lived a *brāhmaṇa* woman, "an adept, who had from youth led the life of *brahmacarya*. That ascetic, disciplined with *yoga* and perfect in austerities, went to heaven"[54] (IX.53.6). The same passage alludes to another woman, the daughter of Śāṇḍilya. "There was once a lady, a renouncer, the daughter of the great-spirited Śāṇḍilya. She was a self-restrained *brahmacāriṇī* of formidable vows. Having earned in her *āśrama* fruits equivalent to those of an *aśvamedha*, the radiant and blessed woman, possessed of the fruit of her efforts, went to heaven and was worshipped by the self-restrained high-souled ones"[55] (IX.53.8). There is also the daughter of the celebrated ascetic Kuṇigarga. "There was one auspicious and beautiful woman renouncer. Through the practice of tremendous and difficult austerities, she lived in her *āśrama* without fear. She, without father, disciplined, did not wish for a husband, but was unconcerned, never having seen a husband worthy of herself. So she continued with her strenuous ascetic activities, which caused pain to her body. She worshiped the gods and the *pitṛs*, and lived in the unpeopled forest"[56] (IX.51.5, IX.51.7–8). Śāṇḍilī, whom Gālava meets in the *Udyogaparva*, was apparently a *vanaprasthin* ascetic living by herself and practicing austerities on Mt. Ṛṣabha (V.111.1ff). One may conclude, therefore, that while some privileged young women may have enjoyed some of the benefits of *brahmacarya āśrama* as a stage of life, a period of discipleship directed at their fathers, most of the *brahmacāriṇīs* found in the text practiced sexual abstinence as a lifestyle, in conjunction in some cases with *nivṛtti* goals (see Sulabhā below).

Women as Vanaprasthinīs

In *vanaprasthya*-style asceticism, although the formal injunction to male householders is that they may proceed to the forest either with or without their wives (*sadāro vāpyadāro* XII.61.4), it seems that in most cases women *did* accompany their husbands, and sometimes, so did other women. While most texts on *vanaprasthya* suggest that in this stage a man abandons his wife, as in the *Upaniṣadic* paradigm of Yājñavalkya and Maitreyī, where the former gives his wives the choice of whether or not to accompany him, the MBh. says of *vanaprasthya* that "It is the mode in which wives emaciate themselves" (XII.236.2). Gāndhārī and Kuntī, for example, both accompany Dhṛtarāṣṭra in his retreat to the forest. In some cases, it appears that elderly widowed women retreated into the forest even on their own, without spouses. This is the case with the generation of Kaurava women preceding Kuntī and Gāndhārī. Satyavatī, Ambikā, and Ambālikā all set out together to retire to the forest. "They performed extraordinary austerities, and at last the ladies gave up their bodies, and went the chosen path"[57] (I.119.12). This appears to be a commonplace occurrence, because they are advised to do this by the sage Vyāsa himself: "Go now; leave everything. Yoke yourself and live in the forest of austerities . . ."[58] (I.119.7). Earlier, Kuntī and Mādrī had persuaded Pāṇḍu not to undertake *saṃnyāsa*, so that they might accompany him in *vanaprasthya*-style eremitism, which they did (I.110.25–28). In other cases, widowed women appear to have lived as ascetics in the forest, with their children. Kuntī, for example, after the Vāranāvata episode, assumes the guise of an ascetic (I.144.3). She could only have done this if there were enough of a tradition of female asceticism already established to make her disguise plausible. Similarly, the widow Gautamī appears to have lived with her young son in the forest (XIII.1.9ff.). Vasiṣṭha's daughter-in-law Adṛṣyantī, left widowed and alone when Vasiṣṭha ventured off to kill himself in grief, continues by herself in the forest, and gives birth to her son, Parāśara (I.167.10ff.). In the same way, Mādhavī, the daughter of Yayāti, is said to "choose the forest as her husband" (V.118.5), and ventures forth into the forest completely by herself. Moreover, nobody attempts to dissuade her from her choice. After Kṛṣṇa's death, his wives depart to the forest (16.8.72). Four of Vasudeva's wives Devakī, Bhadrā, Rohinī, and Madirā prepare to mount his pyre and die with him (16.8.18.24), but Akrūra's wives go forth as wanderers (16.8.70). Rukminī and other named wives enter fire, but Satyabhāmā and others enter the forest (16.8.71–72).

It is in *vanaprasthya* practiced as a vocation, however, that we see the largest numbers of women. Their presence is not always obvious, but may be inferred from the fact that practically all of the sages and gurus were married. Viśvamitra alludes to his wife in the *Śāntiparva* (XII.139.27). Vasiṣṭha, in the *Ādiparva*, is seen with his wife and family (I.166–67). Various Gautamas are seen with their wives. The epic itself opens with the student Utaṅka striving to obtain earrings for his guru's wife, the Gautamī Ahalyā. All of the Bhārgavas are seen with their wives: Bhṛgu with Pulomā, Cyavana with Sukanyā, Ṛcīka with Satyavatī, Jamadagni with Renukā. These wives live and work with the men in the forest, and in some cases, engage in the same kind of ascetic activities. Arundhatī is praised by Mahādeva with the words: "The supreme perfection that has been acquired by the pure-minded Arundhatī, what this auspicious and committed one has achieved is greater than what has been achieved by you great ones, who also have bound yourselves to vows for my sake, over here"[59] (IX.47.47–49). Without food or water, she cooked food for Śiva, listening to his discourses, for twelve years, unperturbed even when the fire consumed her toes. Lopamudrā is similarly praised as an exemplary *vanaprasthya* wife, living in unembellished simplicity. The wives of the seven sages are depicted in various activities in the text. The princess Śāntā is said to have married Ṛśyaśṛṅga and lived with him in spartan modesty.

Not only wives, but entire families are seen with the male ascetics. Vasiṣṭha is shown in a *vanaprasthin* domestic scenario, with his widowed daughter-in-law and her child (I.166–67ff.). Uddālaka is seen in another scenario with his infant son and grandson (III.132.6–20). Kaṇva lives in the forest with his adopted daughter, Śakuntalā (I.65.1ff.). Śukra is a devoted and indulgent *vanaprasthin* father to his daughter, Devayānī (I.71.21ff.). Sthūlakeśa shares his hermitage with his adopted daughter, Pramadvarā (I.8.5ff.). Thus, the forest in the *Mahābhārata* is peopled with comparable numbers of men and women, practicing *vanaprasthya*-style modest asceticism as a vocation. The existence of women is not especially acknowledged, but is evident to anyone who takes a closer look.

Women in Saṃnyāsa

In the case of *saṃnyāsa* asceticism, it is worth making the point with some emphasis that women did renounce the world, and were apparently permitted and recognized as doing so.[60] This is evident in statements such as the following, which stipulates the kind of women who are not suitable for marriage. Among the types listed are women who have a renounced the world (*pravrajitā* (XIII.107.124). Women clearly did involve themselves in *nivṛtti* practices. In these engagements, they are acknowledged as achieving success and perfection.

We have several examples of such women. The most obvious one is the *bhikṣuṇī* Sulabhā, found in the *Śāntiparva*. She is seen in the garb of an ascetic, and is said to be an itinerant *yoga*-practicing mendicant. Several other *saṃnyāsinīs* are mentioned in the *Śalyaparva*, along the *tīrtha*s (pilgrimage sites) visited by Balarāma. In the *Rāmāyaṇa*, we encounter the *tapasvinī* Svayamprabhā (IV.52–53). (In the *Rāmopākhyāna* of the MBh., she is called Prabhāvatī III.266.41–42). In the *Uttarakāṇḍa* of the *Rāmāyaṇa*, moreover, the sage Vālmīki informs Sītā that "Not far from my hermitage, there are many female ascetics established in pious practices" (VII.49). Mādhavī, in the *Udyogaparva* of the MBh. appears to have wandered into homelessness (V.118.5). Although we have fewer details here, Piṅgalā, the fallen woman who gains true realization upon the death of her lover, appears to have wandered off into homelessness.

Women as Occasional Ascetics

Finally, there are many examples of women undertaking *mahāvratas* or extreme ascetic practices directed toward finite goals. Umā undergoes exacting rigors to obtain Śiva for her husband. Ambā displays dogged determination in her austerities, undertaken to accomplish the death of Bhīṣma (V:170–97). Draupadī, in a previous birth, emaciates herself in *tapas* to acquire a good husband (I:157.6–10), Śruvavatī lives as a *brahmacāriṇī* and conducts penances to obtain Indra for her husband (IX.47.1–55).

Women thus dot the pages of asceticism as much as do men. They are given less importance, and this may be for various reasons. Men traveled more, providing ritual services for patrons, and had more prominent roles to play even in ascetic life, as gurus and teachers and priests. Women tended the household, and supported their husbands in the simplicity in which they lived, when they were not independently practicing austerities themselves.

The fact of female asceticism should not in fact surprise us, because there is a well-established tradition of female asceticism recalled in classical Hindu mythology. The goddess Pārvatī is the mythic paradigm of the woman ascetic whose austerities were so fierce as to terrify the gods. The reverence inspired by her formidable powers seems to reverberate in the text in the accounts of *tapasvinīs*. Not only is women's capacity for asceticism, and their ability to unpack the lofty subtleties of the most rarefied truths valorized at the conceptual level, but asceticism is treated as the fair domain of women. Women who do enter into ascetic activities, even though they may be vastly outnumbered by men, are admitted and inducted into ascetic practice, and trained by male gurus. Moreover, their prerogative to engage in these activities, their *adhikāra*, is supported by their male colleagues, at least as far as we can gather from the narratives. The ferocious ambitions of Ambā, for example, are supported by the sages of the forest, even though they are explicitly geared toward the negative end of wreaking revenge on Bhīṣma. Ambā is mentored by the forest sages, said to formally renounce the world (*pravraja*), and is instructed in the methods of renunciation (V:176–88).

The point of the above demonstration is to illustrate that, at least in the imagination of the author(s) of the *Mahābhārata*, the forests were populated by both men and women. Both men and women were engaged in practicing moderate and extreme degrees of ascetic life. Yet, it is only women who are held up as hindrances to ascetic practice, reflecting the male perspective that characterizes the text. The sexual challenges facing women ascetics are neither seriously imagined nor treated. But what of women's sexual desires? Did women ascetics not face the challenges of sexual temptation? Do male bodies play a parallel part in the endeavors of women ascetics, as female bodies play for men?

Women Ascetics and Sexual Desire

There is no shortage of didactic injunctions to women, exhorting them to protect their chastity. These are commonplace in the text. For the most part, however, these statements are directed at maintaining the sanctity of *pravṛtti dharma*. There are very few directions addressing women occupied with *nivṛtti* contemplations. As Lynn Teskey Denton remarks about contemporary female ascetics, "If we know little about the spirituality of the average householder woman, we know even less about women who are not householders but whose lives are fully religious."[61] What information we can glean about the lives of women ascetics, therefore, we must infer from the general ascetic norms that seem to be in existence, and from particular events. A preliminary overview of the accounts of female ascetics and sexuality suggests that women replicated the patterns of male ascetics. The accounts of *saṃnyāsinīs* and what I have dubbed *mahāvrata* women ascetics, like those of men, tend to be highly idealistic. Therefore, we rarely find a *saṃnyāsinī* or occasional *tapasvinī* deterred from her focus by sexual desires. It is only among *vanaprasthin* women, and young *brahmacāriṇīs* that we find sexual challenges and slips. Even there, it is only *vanaprasthin*s who live out their lives in the forest, rather than *vanaprasthin*s by *āśrama* who experience sexual temptation.

From what we can gather about *saṃnyāsinī* women ascetics from the few who are mentioned by name, we can surmise that women only embarked on ascetic practice once they had achieved a level of conviction about their domestic or sexual lives. We can look at four short vignettes to understand this better. The first is that of Piṅgalā.

Piṅgalā

Piṅgalā is said to be a courtesan whose lover dies tragically in an accident. "At that time of great anguish, she achieved wisdom and tranquility" (XII.168.47). Realizing in those moments of grief that the only enduring love is that of the Self within her, she resolved to hone her insight with further knowledge.

> I am free of desire. [Human lovers], who are really embodied forms of hell, destroy one with their desirable appearances. They will never again deceive me! I am awake, restored to consciousness. I am endowed with true wisdom, I am without purpose, I am unmoved by worldly objects. Happiness and sadness have gone; being without hopes is the highest happiness. Having driven off hope and discouragement, Piṅgalā sleeps in tranquility.[62] (XII.168.50–52)

In this song, Piṅgalā recounts her encounter with the divine. She experiences the liberating insight of what is true reality, and as a consequence, all of her earthly desires naturally fall away from her. Thus, where she had been caught in the trap of sexual and emotional attachments before, they no longer affect her, for she has moved beyond them. Now she sees human lovers as "hell personified," and refuses to be "deceived" by them any longer.

Piṅgalā's language describing male lovers wholly parallels the statements about women lovers in the discourses of male ascetics. Just as women lovers are represented as being deceitful and lustful in male discourses, male lovers are here represented as hellish beings, deceitful and lascivious, diversions from the true reality. Desire for them must be overcome in order for a woman to become free.

Interestingly, in Piṅgalā's song, the supreme soul is described in masculine terms, as a lover, a woman's "dear lord" (*kāntam*), by the side of whom a woman has always lain. He is the one lord worthy of love, whom most women do not, unfortunately, recognize: "What woman is there who holds this [the Supreme Soul] as her lover and loves it, even when it comes near?"[63] (XII.168.49). Piṅgalā regrets that she, too, had been in that state of error: "I have for a long time lived, agitated, beside this dear love, in whom there is nothing but calm tranquility, but unable to reach him"[64] (XII.168.48). Now she has awoken, and identified her true love. The sexual motifs of her *pravṛtti* life are carried over into *nivṛtti* to characterize her relationship with the divine. The Supreme Soul is thus visualized as her male lover. The obverse is not true in the confessionals of male ascetics. There, the Supreme Self continues to be described as masculine, but the imagery is nonsexual. This is congruent with the gendered language of Sāṃkhya, in which *puruṣa* is always associated with the masculine.

Kuṇigārgyā

The story of Kuṇigārgyā is related in the *Śalyaparva*. After the death of her father, this young woman remained in the forest, undergoing strenuous acts of *tapas*. She never married, because she could never find a man who was worthy of her. Yet, we are told, she was happy! (IX.51.9). She practiced austerities for a long time, until she was so old that she could no longer get about on her own. When she prepared to cast off her body, however, she was asked by the sage Nārada "how can a girl who has never cultured herself [through marriage] enter heaven?" (IX.51.11).[65] Not to be deterred, Kuṇigārgyā offered half her austerities to any man who would marry her. One man, Śṛṅgavān, agreed, on the condition that she only live with him for one night. Much to his consternation, however, on their wedding night, she transformed herself through her *tapas* into a beautiful young woman, making him instantly regret the condition that he had placed on their marriage. The next morning, she shed her body and proceeded to heaven, leaving her husband so distraught that he, in an extraordinary reversal of the *satī* paradigm, cast off his own body and followed her to heaven (IX.51.3–23).

In this anecdote, we see the woman ascetic in a position of spiritual power. She yields to the worldly prejudices of both Nārada and her husband, but in such a way as to illustrate their hollowness. She agrees without argument to marry, but marries only to observe the formal letter of the rule. Then, she overturns her husband's prejudices about her age by appearing as a beautiful young woman on their wedding night. She is so beautiful, in fact, that Śṛṅgavān is led to abandoning his own life, to join her in heaven. Both men in this narrative are depicted as being held captive to *saṃsārika* values. Kuṇigārgyā foils the biases of both, and emerges as the most enlightened of the three.

Śāṇḍilī

Śāṇḍilī is a character who makes a brief appearance in the *Udyogaparva*. She is cast as a *brāhmaṇa* woman who lives alone on a peak of Mount Ṛṣabha, doing solitary acts of *tapas*. One day, when the *brāhmaṇa* Gālava and his friend, the mighty bird Garuḍa, stop there for the night, she greets them hospitably, and offers them food. Before falling asleep, Garuḍa considers the idea of abducting the "sorceress" (*siddhā*) for her magic powers. On awaking, he finds that his wings have fallen off. Reflecting that this is the result of the injurious thought harbored the night before, he apologizes to Śāṇḍilī, and she forgives him. "Innocent of any blemishes and blameless in my ways, I have embraced strict conduct, and thus achieved the highest perfection,"[66] she tells him (V.111.14). She restores the bird's wings to even greater grandeur, and sends the two off with the parting words: "Never despise a woman, even if she is despicable"[67] (V.111.16). This is a very minor episode in the larger body of the text, but it is an interesting one. Śāṇḍilī is depicted as a hermit recluse, engaged in acts of self-mortification. She is said to be an accomplished and enlightened sage. But when men attempt to trifle with her, assuming her to be a woman and therefore quaint and not to be taken seriously, she reveals her powers to them. Garuḍa is grounded from flight, and must beg forgiveness before he can continue his journey. The question of sexual desire simply does not arise. Śāṇḍilī, like others of her stripe, has moved beyond the sway of sexual temptation, and is instead at the point of observing that the sex of the *nivṛtti* striver is of no consequence. In these narratives, the women demonstrate that sex is no criterion of ascetic worth. Far from being befuddled in sensual preoccupations, as the stereotypes of women in the *Mahābhārata* would have it, these women illustrate that prejudices of gender are markers of spiritual naïveté in the *nivṛtti* path. A truly enlightened being will have transcended them.

Sulabhā

Possibly, the most relevant female figure to this discussion is the *tapasvinī* Sulabhā. Sulabhā is explicitly described as a *bhikṣuṇī*, a renouncer: "In the age of *dharma*, there was a mendicant woman named Sulabhā, who wandered over the whole earth practicing *yogadharma*"[68] (XII.308.7). Having heard much in her travels about the sagacity of the king of Mithilā, she decides to test him. "Doubting whether [Janaka] had been freed into *dharma*, Sulabhā, endowed with *yoga*-power, entered his mind with her own"[69] (XII.308.16). Through her *yogic* powers, she enters into his body. The king senses her presence, and objects. Amid much high-flung discourse, he berates her for the impropriety of her conduct as an ascetic: "The triple stick is not for one who is attached to desire; it is for one who is devoted to *mokṣa*. It is not protected by you. Fair one, you are not liberated"[70] (XII.308.56). He goes on to advise her that, "You are a *brāhmaṇa* woman, belonging to the highest caste. I am a *kṣatriya*. There can be no union for us. One should not cause an intermixture of classes"[71] (XII.308.59). He calls her actions sinful. Sulabhā responds with discourse on the metaphysical truths of the universe. Gārgī-like, she asks him a series of pointed questions. If, she says, as the religion holds, all beings are essentially one, their souls being of the same stuff, how is it possible for him to distinguish himself from her? What is his body, and what is hers? "If you see your body in your own body, and your soul in your own soul, why is it that you do not see your own body and your own soul in the bodies and souls of others?"[72] (XII.308.126). How, therefore, can he ask the question: Who is she? What, after all, is the difference between him and her? His prejudices about gender and sexual conduct reveal that he is yet a novice, and far from wise in *nivṛtti dharma*. "What mark of freedom is there in one who fails to cast an equal eye on the agreeable and the disagreeable, on the weak, and the strong?"[73] (XII.308.130).

In this passage, Sulabhā is already an adept. She has excelled beyond the stage of sexual temptation, and is unconfounded by the riddles of sexual ethics. In her lengthy discourse with the king, moreover, she pronounces what may be the last word on sexuality in the ideals of the *nivṛtti* tradition: that the differences between genders exist only at the level of lower, worldly knowledge. A truly enlightened person knows that there is no essential basis for prejudice between male and female, for both are of the same stuff. Only one uninitiated in the higher truths would be confused by it. In this kind of resolute self-confidence and deep insightfulness, Sulabhā is typical of *Mahābhārata saṃnyāsinī* ascetics. By the time that we meet them, issues of sexual temptation have long been resolved.

In these episodes, we see women ascetics speaking not to issues of sexual temptation, but to those of sexual prejudice and stereotyping. They themselves personally are beyond being lured into sexual involvement. What we do see them doing, however, is tackling the sexual chauvinism of men. In these vignettes, women are positioned as the instructors of the men. They reveal to the men their sexual preconceptions, which are incompatible with the practice of *nivṛtti dharma*, and which represent lower levels of knowledge. At the highest level of knowledge, differences of gender are inconsequential. In all of these situations, the women emerge as the more enlightened and adept of the two.

So much for *saṃnyāsinī* ascetics; where we do see women struggling with their sexual desires is in the accounts of *vanaprasthin*s. In this, they parallel the trend for male ascetics. The majority of both men and women who succumb to sexual temptation are *vanaprasthin*s. Moreover, they are *vanaprasthin*s by vocation, not by life stage. Thus, while older men who retire to the forest at the end of a long career are not shown to be sexually stimulated, neither are women. There is no question of Kuntī, Gāndhārī, Satyavatī, and others of their ilk being tempted to engage in sexual activity. There is a clear understanding that for both men and women, their sexual lives are over, and that they are now in the forest in pursuit only of their personal salvation. For both, it is only among ascetics who live *vanaprasthin* lifestyles as a vocation that we encounter occasions of sexual temptation.

It is in this light, I believe, that we should read the narratives of forest women who err sexually. We have the infamous story of Ahalyā, who willfully or innocently committed adultery with Indra (XII.258). We have Renukā, who became aroused at the sight of the king Citraratha sporting in the water with his wives, and thus committed adultery in thought (III.116.5–10). We have Ruci, the wife of Gautama, who apparently was tempted by the offers of Indra, but was restrained from acting on them. Among supernatural beings, we have Svāhā, who fornicated with Agni, after impersonating the wives of seven seers. The primary difference between the indiscretions of male and female *vanaprasthin* ascetics is that whereas male sexual indiscretions are taken in stride, being at most the subject of amusement, female indiscretions amount to actual crimes. Thus, even though we know that the majority of the *vanaprasthin* sages are married, their sexual misadventures with other women are looked on with indulgence. Parāśara, Vyāsa, Gautama, and others suffer no disopprobrium for yielding to their sexual temptations, even to the point of fathering children. Women *vanaprasthin* ascetics, on the other hand, are sometimes treated quite harshly. Ahalyā earns herself unending notoriety in Hindu tradition, and is ordered by her husband to be killed (XII.258). In the *Rāmāyaṇa* account, she is turned into a stone. Renukā, for becoming momentarily aroused by the sight of the king Citraratha, is actually punished with death. She is killed by her own son, Rāma Jāmadagni, at the behest of his father. (She is later restored to life at the plea of the same son III.116.10–19.) Svāhā in her sexual escapades is accorded an uncommon indulgence for her impersonation of the sages' wives, but the wives are summarily abandoned by their husbands. Even when they are cleared of all suspicion, the sages refuse to reconcile with them (III.215.13).

Children?

While sexual desire is thus not a particular impediment for *tapasvinī*s, one is tempted to hypothesize that the pull of children may have been more compelling. Do children inhibit the ascetic labors of women, as enduring stereotypes would prompt? The narratives of women in the forests do not support this conclusion. In the *Āśramavāsikaparva*, Yudhiṣṭhira pleads with his mother Kuntī not to embark into the forest with Dhṛtarāṣṭra and Gāndhārī. He, along with his brothers, begs her to stay, even threatening to use his royal privilege to forbid her from going. Kuntī, however, is undeterred. She had, she says, done her motherly duty by seeing them through to their final victory in the war. Now it was her time to devote herself to her own spiritual work: to prepare herself for death. She insists on entering the forest (XV.24). In another vignette, the loss of her only child could have distracted the elderly Gautamī from her ascetic practices. When her beloved son succumbs to death after being bitten by a snake, the hunter Arjunaka, anticipating the grief of Gautamī, offers to kill the murderous snake. With steely self-control, however, Gautamī resists. Insisting that the death of the snake will not bring her son back, she urges the hunter to refrain from harming the snake, saying she will not act out of anger or revenge (XIII.1.9ff.). In these tellings, women display a moral and spiritual resolve that is characteristic of accomplished sages. They function here as exemplary figures, imparting instruction to others through their personal fortitude.

Conclusions

In concluding, it is necessary to entertain the question of what such data ultimately mean. If we have references to characters and narratives about women, to what extent can we take them as literary hyperbole, and to what extent should we assume they reflect historical reality? Isn't the very fact that we can enumerate them at all a testament that even if they reflect historical truth, they were exceptions among exceptions, served literary purposes rather than real, and no historical mileage should be drawn from literature, which by its very nature artfully bends reality and weaves fiction with fact? Olivelle seems to respond to this question: "These literary references do not necessarily demonstrate the historical reality of such female ascetics. What they do demonstrate is that in at least some segments of the Brahmanical tradition female asceticism was recognized as both legitimate and praiseworthy and that such women could choose to become ascetics on their own and not at the behest of their husbands."[74] As Khandelwal points out in another context, moreover, the conceptual importance of such images "far exceeds their statistical presence because of the way they problematize standard representations of both religious renunciation and gender in Hindu India."[75] Images have symbolic power. If nothing else, tales of women ascetics and renouncers represent paradigms of the independent religious practice of women, paradigms that generations of real women may draw on as resources to forge their own religious paths.

Thus what the above survey reveals is that in the imagined world of the *Mahābhārata*, there were numerous women active in *nivṛtti* preoccupations, if not always as radical renouncers, as ascetics of varying grades of ambition. If one were to draw some generalizations about women in the *nivṛtti* stream, one might say that in male ascetic discourse, women are sometimes cast in the role of temptresses, immersed in the sensual enjoyments of the material world. These discourses furnish us with some harsh statements belittling women's intelligence, their aptitudes, and their moral sense. There is, however, another trajectory of thought that may be recovered from the text, and it evaluates women's aptitudes in a positive and balanced way. The text states unambiguously, for example, that "*Brahman* has no sex—it is not male, female, or neuter"[76] (XII.242.22). Women's aptitude for freedom is recognized in other statements, such as: "Whatever one's sex, male or female, the person who gains knowledge of *Brahman* has never to undergo rebirth"[77] (XII.242.23). In the chronicles of Sulabhā, Kuṇigārgyā, and others, women's full competence for assimilating the highest truths is affirmed. What's more, in these accounts, women are treated with a liberality and deference that is at marked odds with the condescension that characterizes attitudes to women in other parts of the text. Their moral direction is valued. In various instances, for example, women's guidance is actively sought. Gāndhārī is famously sought out by her husband and others in the Kaurava court for her quiet sagacity. The *brāhmaṇa* Satya's wife Puṣkaradhāriṇī disapproves of her husband being addicted to cruel sacrifices, and admonishes him on the true meaning of *dharmic* ordinances. She is described as "pure-minded" (*śuciḥ*) and emaciated from *tapas* (*vratakṛśā*) (XII.264.6). These assertions reinforce the conclusions that may be reached from pondering some of the parables of *tapasvinī*s. The exchange between Sulabhā and Janaka, for example, is transparently a narrative device to emphasize the point that as long as one still discriminates between self and other, and responds with prejudice to superficial attributes such as sex, one exhibits one's paucity of knowledge. True liberating knowledge is distinguished by its ability to transcend such differences. "By wisdom alone are the high and low among beings distinguished. By wisdom . . . was the creation of the universe. Wisdom alone is the highest end"[78] (XII.229.10). Wisdom is the only recognized determinant of accomplishment, and the narratives of women on the *nivṛtti* path attest that wisdom is not the preserve of one sex. Women's qualification and aptitude for liberation is affirmed in the ascetic strains of *nivṛtti* discourse.

This perspective is reinforced by the other methods of *nivṛtti* practice. The *karma yoga* path, for example, reiterates the point that liberation is available equally to men and women. "Whether a person belongs to a low caste, or is a woman who desires to follow *dharma*, by following the path [of *yogic* equanimity], they will certainly achieve the final goal"[79] (XII.232.32). Similarly, we have the *bhakti yoga* endorsement from the *Gītā* where Kṛṣṇa declares, "Even people of low origins, women, *vaiśya*s, nay *śūdra*s, go the highest course if they rely on me"[80] (BG.IX.32). In all varieties of *nivṛtti dharma*, issues of sex, caste, and other markers of social consequence are of no account. Beings qualify for *mokṣa* in all of these methods by the earnestness of their efforts, not by birth.

Chapter Three

Wedding and Bedding in *Pravṛtti Dharma*

In the previous chapter, we unpacked the ways in which female sexuality is understood in the *nivṛtti* stream of the *Mahābhārata*. In this chapter, we will take a closer look at the *pravṛtti* stream.

Pravṛtti dharma is the strain of Hindu tradition focused on life-in-the-world. As observed in Chapter One, life-in-the-world necessarily entails the negotiation of practices—such as sex and violence—that present inherent dangers to civic order. For, while *saṃsāra* cannot logically function without either of these, left uncontrolled and unregulated, they are volatile qualities and pose the threat of disorder to society. Thus, whereas renunciant traditions may at least ideologically and rhetorically repudiate sex and violence altogether, civil societies must perforce contend with them. The management of sexual relations, therefore, is a major concern for life-in-the-world. Society must determine how to allow sexual practices to exist, without having them overwhelm or undermine its foundations.

All societies are invested in ordering human activity, and typically, they govern sexual practice in two overarching ways:

> 1. They stipulate general rules for sexual behavior, rules that are applicable to all members of a society. For example, the taboo against incest is common to most societies. Many societies also prohibit homosexuality, and until quite recently, fornication and adultery. Modern societies also disallow sexual assault and rape. These might be considered *legal* strictures circumscribing and containing sexual conduct. In addition to these formal regulatory measures, societies also evolve ethical codes that through social pressure define and shape sexual behavior. Thus, most societies have norms of sexual "decency" cautioning against coveting other people's spouses, and in general articulate the niceties of interactions between sexual agents.

2. In addition to these general principles, societies also define boundaries between specific classes of individuals. Modern Western society thus has extensive codes of conduct regulating the behavior of health care providers vis-á-vis their patients, of teachers vis-á-vis their wards, of lawyers vis-á-vis their clients, and of others in positions of power. In older times, it also circumscribed sexual behaviour by linking it with class identity; thus, aristocrats were expected to maintain endogamy, and serfs were similarly expected to marry within their class. These kinds of defining and regulatory labours, some formal and others less so, undergird the sexual life of civil societies; the particular norms, however, naturally, vary from one culture to another.

The Hindu tradition has a typology of sex that reaches back to its hoary beginnings. Sex was a preoccupation within Vedic religion itself, which dictated when and under what circumstances a couple should be sexually active. Sexual imagery played a signal role in the structure and symbolism of the Vedic sacrifice, with some rituals explicitly involving quasi-sexual acts. The sexuality of the couple was of great consequence to the rhythms of the cosmos. Hence a man ritually engaged was expected to be abstinent, and a woman's sexuality was sought to be harnessed and channeled into the mysterium of the sacrifice.[1] Vedic society thus was concerned to control, regulate, and maximize sexual energy for its highest uses. In the process of doing so, it evolved an elaborate corpus of rules that distinguished sacred from profane, useful sexuality from wasted varieties of it, and a general code of sexual ethics.

As part of its larger work of ordering all aspects of life-in-the-world, the *pravṛtta* strain of the epic concerns itself with these sexual ethics. It retains many Vedic strictures and elaborates them further; there is, however, a major shift in focus. Thus, while Vedic society's preoccupation was with the sacrifice, and the control of sexuality was ancillary to that, classical Hinduism is much more concerned with society as a whole. In the *pravṛtta* strain of the epic we see an overwhelming preoccupation with defining boundaries, specifying parameters and limits, particularly among classes of individuals. *Pravṛtti* dharma thus achieves an elaborate taxonomy of sex that is deeply concerned with class identity. The categories of gender, *varṇa*, and *āśrama* are crucial reference points in its regulation of sexual life. The overall attempt is to ideologically construct an orthodoxy in which individuals represent their larger genus, and each group conforms faithfully to its specified place and function in society. Thus, for the most part, *pravṛtti dharma* is concerned to locate individuals on interlocking matrices of gender, class, and stage of life, and then to specify a *svadharma* congruent to their specific location.

Universal Ethics?

While the *nivṛtti* stream often speaks to a universal humanity, overriding in its ethical imperatives the specificities of gender and class, there are few places in which *pravṛtti dharma* speaks universally. Indeed, it is apparent that the *pravṛtti* stream does not recognize a universal person; one of its distinguishing features is the classification and hierarchalization of beings, and in such a schema, social privileges and responsibilities vary depending on one's social location. This notwithstanding, however, some cautious generalizations may be admissible.

It should be recognized at the start, for example, that *pravṛtti dharma* is overwhelmingly concerned with procreation, and with maximizing the procreative potential of men and women. Thus, while various types of sexualities may be tolerated, procreation is the fundamental premise on which its sexual ethics are structured. A new life is valuable for a variety of reasons, and should be actively sought. All sexuality should be harnessed toward achieving this primary goal of sexual life.

Given this anchoring premise, a whole host of the text's sexual biases become comprehensible. Thus, homosexuality is disapproved, as is any activity that involves the dissipation or waste of semen. Women are given latitude in choosing sexual partners if their parents have been negligent in getting them married because their procreative periods are passing unproductively. Even women's sexual indiscretions may be forgiven if they either produce children, or are motivated by a desire for children. (More on this in Chapter Six.) In this chapter, we will take account of some of these factors ordering the sexual lives of people in the world. As we move from injunctions covering the petty details of sexual life to the overarching values within which they are inscribed, it becomes apparent that sexuality in *pravṛtti dharma* is a far from happenstance phenomenon, but is finely constructed and rationalized to reflect and support a larger ideology of being in the world.

Wasted Sexuality

The question of a religion's stance on homosexuality is an increasingly recurring one today. In the epic, it is rhetorically disapproved as one variety of wasted sexuality.

Contemporary discourses around homosexuality construe sexuality as an element of identity, whose distinguishing feature is desire. In these definitions, one may be homosexual without ever being sexually active; one is considered homo- or heterosexual by virtue of one's desire. Quizzed from this perspective, one can conclude that the *Mahābhārata* does not speak to the issue of homosexuality at all. Another avenue into the subject, however, is employed by Arvind Sharma, who approaches the problem by looking at the range of sexual activity implied in homosexuality, and then researches the Hindu scriptures for their opinions on these activities. In sum, he interprets homosexuality as implying three types of sexual activity: "(1) copulation between (a) men or (b) women; (2) anal intercourse; and (3) oral-genital contact" (47). Sharma goes on to note the difficulty in reckoning these activities as homosexual: the word *adhorata*, referring to anal intercourse, could imply intercourse among men as well as between a man and a woman, and the word *auparisṭaka*, or oral intercourse, could similarly be applied to both cases (47).

The *Mahābhārata* is witness to several intimate, companionate friendships between members of the same sex and these are unself-consciously rendered in the text. Homosexual "behaviors," however, as defined by Sharma, are summarily denounced. In one instance, oral intercourse is described as one of the hallmarks of the onset of *kaliyuga* (III.186.35). In another, homosexual intercourse between men is more specifically condemned: "Those men of evil conduct who enjoy sexual intercourse with inappropriate wombs, and those preverse-minded who engage in sexual intercourse among men—they will end up as eunuchs"[2] (XIII.133.51). Thus, homosexuality is disapproved in the epic, not from any particular moral ground but as a variety of unproductive, hence wasted sexuality that contributes nothing either to society or to the individual's religious life.

Sexual Etiquette

Sexual ethics in the *pravṛtti* stream in general follow the contours established by earlier works, such as the *Dharmasūtras*. These may be examined in several steps, with the help of the following prompts: (1) Who constitutes a suitable partner for sexual intercourse? (2) To what ends may sexual activity be devoted? What is the rightful purpose of sex? (3) When is sexual activity permissible, and when not? (4) How is sexual activity circumscribed by space?

The ideology of sex in *pravṛtti dharma* is structured around the *homo religiosus* of the twice-born male householder. The most salient requirement about this man is that he must be married. This follows the theology of Vedic tradition; to be formally and sacrally a whole being, a man must have a wife who thus completes him, and this completion then qualifies him for participation in the ritual formality that circumscribes his existence. In Vedic theology, taking a wife and establishing the sacred fires with her was the marker of a *dvija*'s natural progression from adolescence to manhood (XII.234.29). This wife then was not simply an adjunct to his life, but vital to his ritual status, an indispensable ritual agent who was his partner in fulfilling his debts to ancestors, gods, and gurus.[3] For ritual purposes, husband and wife are mystically united to share one *being*; this is reflected even in the broader laws regarding property.[4] Thus, in *Ādiparva*, Jaratkāru's ancestors remonstrate with him for not having married (I.13.15–23); in the Āraṇyaka, Agastya's forebears take him to task for the same reason (III.94.11–15).

There is an even greater concern for women to marry, albeit for different reasons. Women are not born with natural debts needing to be discharged, but as is well known, marriage serves a sacramental function equivalent to that of the *upanayana* that affirms a boy as a ritual agent. Although there is clear evidence of women renouncers in the text, it is expected that women will marry—indeed, so essential is marriage that a woman is advised that if her family has been negligent in finding a mate for her, three years after puberty she should herself seek her mate[5] (XIII.44.15). While these injunctions could be interpreted within the hermeneutics of suspicion, as an attempt to control women's sexuality, it is clear from the context of these passages that the concern is for maximizing a woman's fertility—something that is perceived to be in her best interests. Parents, in failing to arrange a match for her in time for puberty, have deprived her of the possible fruits of her fertility; hence she may take the less desirable step of choosing a partner for herself. (More on this in Chapter Six.)

For a man, a wife is precious not only for her role in confirming a man in his ritual space by conferring wholeness on him; she is also the source of joy and companionship. In a *Śāntiparva* parable, a male pigeon grievously laments the death of his wife: "A householder's home, even full of sons, grandsons, and daughters-in-law is considered empty without a wife. One's house is not one's home; one's wife is one's home. A house without a wife is as forlorn as a wilderness" (XII.142.364*). He continues:

> It is taught that a wife alone is a man's greatest protector. For one without support in the world, there is no greater support than a wife in one's journey in this world. When one is afflicted with illness and is suffering from pain, there is no medicine for a man that is equal to his wife. There is no closer companion than a wife. There is no refuge better than a wife. There is no better ally in the world than one's wife, on the path of *dharma*.[6] (XII.142.8–10)

A wife is held to be a man's best friend. Śakuntalā's celebrated speech on the value of a wife is familiar to all students of Sanskrit:

> The wife is half the man; a wife is his best friend. A wife is the basis of *dharma*, *artha*, and *kāma*; a wife is a friend even in death. They who have wives have rites, they who have wives have homes, they who have wives are happy, they who have wives have fortune. Sweet-spoken wives are friends in solitude, fathers in the work of *dharma*, mothers in calamity.[7] (I:68.40–42)

The relationship of a husband and wife is visualized as one of mutual companionship: "The ordinary relationship of a man and a woman consists only of sexual pleasure. The relationship of husband and wife, however, is special"[8] (XIII.45.10). The interdependence of men and women is noted: "A woman cannot conceive in her season without a man. A man cannot create form without a woman in her season. Because of their union and their dependence on the characteristics of each other, form is created in all wombs"[9] (XII.293.14). Husband and wife are therefore expected to support and cherish each other, and in familial matters, "the conduct of husband and wife should be equal"[10] (XIII.128.43).

Sex Mates and Partners

The question of who is a suitable partner for sexual intercourse is not as simply answered as one might wish. For example, one finds many general statements in the text to the effect that the most appropriate partner for sexual intercourse is one's married spouse. This seems straightforward enough, but it is bedeviled by a host of factors. To begin with, polygyny is a well-established practice in the *Mahābhārata.* This means that in effect, a man may actually have a selection of women with whom he can *dharmically* and legally have sexual intercourse. Furthermore, it is not sufficient simply to speak of "a man." The category of personhood itself is problematized by considerations of *varṇa*, *āśrama*, and relationship.

In the *Śānti* and *Anuśāsana parva*s we find sustained discussion of these issues. These passages prescribe the number of wives that a man may take: a *brāhmaṇa* may take three or four, depending on the passage, a *kṣatriya* two or three, a *vaiśya* one or two of the same class (XIII.44.10). *Varṇa*, therefore, is a major determinant of the number and type of partners with whom a man may be sexually active. The passages also specify the class identity of the proposed wives: a *brāhmaṇa* may take one wife of equal class stature, and one of each of the lower classes. A *kṣatriya* may take one *kṣatriya* wife, and one of each of the lower classes. A *vaiśya* may take one *vaiśya* wife, and the other a *śūdra*, and a *śūdra* may take only one, of the same class. These passages also stipulate the function of the varieties of wives. Wives of the upper three classes are best suited to bearing children, but the *śūdra* wife is to be utilized only for recreational sex; she is designated for when a twice-born man desires pleasure. "The *śūdra* wife exists only for pleasure" (*ratyarthamapi śūdrā syāt* XIII.44.11). The wives are further ranked in relation to each other: the hierarchy of *varṇa* takes precedence over the hierarchy of age. *Brāhmaṇa* wives have a predetermined seniority over wives of other classes (XIII.44.11). By extension, the son of a *brāhmaṇa* wife is to be held naturally senior to the son of a *kṣatriya* wife, regardless of age; the son of a *kṣatriya* wife is senior to that of a *vaiśya*, and so forth. These calculations are of significance in determining not only social relations, but also matters of inheritance. The son of a *brāhmaṇa* wife inherits a greater proportion of his father's wealth than the son of a *kṣatriya* wife, and so on in descending order (XIII.47.11–15).

Only one element is entirely explicit in this network of complex relationships. Several passages in the *Anuśāsanaparva* rhetorically insist that if a man of the upper three class does take a *śūdra* wife, the *śūdra* wife exists for enjoyment only, not for childbearing. Marriage with a *śūdra* woman is a marker of unrighteousness in a man, particularly a *brāhmaṇa*. One passage makes this clear: "A *brāhmaṇa* takes a *śūdra* wife because of lust, or greed, or love . . . The scriptures do not approve of this. A *brāhmaṇa*, by taking a *śūdra* woman to his bed, experiences misery. He should, having done such an act, undergo expiation according to the rites laid down in the scriptures. His penances should be twice more severe if there are children"[11] (XIII.47.8 10). *Dvija* men are not expected to raise children with a *śūdra* wife: "The righteous condemn the practice of fathering children upon *śūdra* women. A *brāhmaṇa* who impregnates a *śūdra* woman must perform expiation"[12] (XIII.44.12). In some discussions, the marriage itself constitutes a crime: in the *Udyogaparva*, a *brāhmaṇa* who marries a *śūdra* woman is listed among various offenders classed as being equivalent to *brāhmaṇa*-murderers (V.37.12). *Śūdra* women, and their children, should be considered no better than defiling carcasses; one passage in the *Anuśāsanaparva* compares them to corpses. "Because they are born of [one whose body is as inauspicious as] the worst corpse, a *brāhmaṇa*'s sons, *śūdra* children, are called *pāraśavaṃ* [meaning one who is born of a corpse]" (XIII.48.5).[13]

While the text is at pains to explicitly discourage such interclass coupling, in the narrative itself one can find plenty to suggest that *dvija* men were in actuality less discriminating about not only marrying *śūdra* women, but also about impregnating them. The case of Satyavatī is one example. The adopted daughter of a fisherman, a *śūdra*, she is herself therefore a *sūdrā*, because according to the rules of inheritance, a child assumes the name and class identity of its parents[14] (Karṇa, for example, notwithstanding his *kṣatriya* and indeed divine parentage, is treated as a *sūta*.) At a young age, however, Satyavatī attracts the attention of the sage Parāśara, who, though of impeccable *brāhmaṇa* pedigree, does not scruple to father a child with her. Later, the same Satyavatī marries the *kṣatriya* king Śaṃtanu, and bears him two male children. These children are moreover specifically designated to be the heirs of the Bhārata kingdom. Furthermore, following Śaṃtanu's death, the *śūdra* queen Satyavatī is active in state politics, and commands an obvious respect in the kingdom. In other examples, the *śūdra dāsī* who serves Vyāsa becomes the mother of "the wisest man in the world" (*loke sarvabuddhimatāṃ varaḥ*), Vidura (I.100.26). The wisdom of Vidura is widely respected, and he functions as the most natural prime minister of the Hastināpura branch of the Bhāratas. In the following generation, this pattern is repeated with Dhṛtarāṣṭra, who fathers a child on a *śūdra* woman (I.107.35–37). The son born of that union, Yuyutsu, is characterized as the wisest and most sympathetic of the Kauravas. He is the only one of Dhṛtarāṣṭra's sons who survives the war, and becomes Dhratarastra's mainstay of support in the postwar years.

Notwithstanding these taxonomical computations of who may legally wed or bed whom, however, there is considerable encouragement to be found for men to content themselves with one *dharmically* married wife. "One should concentrate on one's own wedded wife . . ." (*bhāryāvratam hyātmani dhārayīta* XII.261.23) says one passage. Another submits, "A householder should be content with his own wife," (*svadāranirato* XII.235.12). Householders are advised in various ways to avoid coveting other women: "One should not look at the rising sun, or at somebody else's naked wife"[15] (XII.186.16); older men are warned away from their daughters-in-law: "One may not share a bed with one's daughter-in-law, or eat with her"[16] (XII.186.23). Expiations are devised for taking delight in a woman's company by sitting with her on the same seat (XII.159.56). The householder who follows this course of conduct is promised ambrosial rewards: "residence in the abode of heavenly women, in the lotus-filled region of Prajāpati, which echoes with the sound of music and dance and blazes with rain and fire"[17] (XIII.110.8). Again, the expectation that a man should be satisfied with his legal wife is the norm advocated by the *dharmatrśāstras*; as Wendy Doniger observes, "The bottom line on sex and marriage in the *dharmatrśāstras* . . . is that neither the husband nor the wife should ever have sex with anyone else."[18]

To speak of marriage, however, is to introduce another complication into the equation. The *Mahābhārata*—as Vedic and classical Hinduism—defines marriage broadly as any manner of sexual union between man and woman. Three lists cataloging forms of sexual union are mentioned in the MBh., two in the *Ādiparva*, and one in the *Anuśāsanaparva*. The first two mention eight types of unions, and the last recognizes five.[19] The more comprehensive lists refer to the following eight forms of union: *Brāhma*: the father/guardian of the woman gives her away, "having informed himself about the conduct and learning of the man, his birth and his accomplishments"[20] (XIII.44.3–4); *Prājāpata*: the father/guardian of the woman gives her away to a suitor who asks for her. The guardian may impose a condition for the suitor to fulfill; *Daiva*: the father/guardian of the woman gives her away as a gift on the occasion of a sacrifice; *Ārṣa*: the father/guardian of the woman gives her away in exchange for a modest gift from the suitor (such as a pair of cows, for the use of sacrifice)[21]; *Gāndharva*: a reciprocal exchange of love between man and woman, consummated without *mantra*s, often in secret; *Āsura*: the purchase of a wife after paying a hefty bride-price; *Rākṣasa*: the abduction of the woman after killing her relatives; *Paiśāca*: the abduction of the woman while she is sleeping or drunk (I.67.8–9, I.96.7–12, XIII.44.3–9).

The *brāhma* form, in which the father or male guardian of the woman gives her away to a properly investigated and suitable groom, is the ideal of all forms of sexual union, though the *prājāpatya*, *daiva*, and *gāndharva* are also approved. Some, such as the *āsura* form, are distinguished on the basis of class. The *āsura*, or "demonic" form is said to be uniquely suited to *kṣatriyas*, involving as it does displays of martial skill and valor. As Bhīṣma proclaims at the *svayamvara*, the "bridegroom-choosing" ceremony of the Kāśi princesses: "Those who know *dharma* state that abduction with force is the best. So, kings, I am ready to whisk these girls away by force" (I.96.11–12). The last two forms of union, the "fiendish" and the "ghoulish"[22] while recognized as unions of some variety, are held to be morally perverse. These "should not happen in any way," says one passage of the *Anuśāsanaparva* (*na kartavyau kathaṃcana* XIII.44.8).[23]

To say that a man should content himself with his *dharmapatnī*, therefore, is somewhat misleading. A man may be sexually active with any of various class-ranked wives, acquired through any of several legitimate means, for the purpose either of pleasure or of procreation, depending on the identity of the woman. In addition, a man of means also has sexual access to his female slaves, as well as to courtesans. *Dāsīs* (female slaves) are routinely mentioned among gifts exchanged by wealthy individuals, and it is taken for granted that they are available for sexual service.[24] This is apparent, for example, in the thirteenth year of the Pāṇḍava exile, when Draupadī approaches Queen Sudeṣṇā in the guise of a maid. Sudeṣṇā hesitates to hire Draupadī because Sudeṣṇā's husband, King Virāṭa, would then have sexual access to Draupadī (IV.45.20–26). In another example, one of the key enticements for the Kauravas of the Pāṇḍavas' lost dice game was that Draupadī now became the Kauravas's slave, and would be available to serve them sexually (II.63.1–5). This is one reason for the Kauravas's glee on this occasion. Although on the odd occasion, one finds an injunction that men should avoid sex with their servants (XIII.107.109), in the narrative this directive is followed less than rigorously. Many kings are said to have impregnated their female slaves: Vicitravīrya (by proxy) Vidura's mother, left unnamed in the text (I.100.23–29); Dhṛtarāṣṭra the *dāsī* who became Yuyutsu's mother, also left unnamed (I.107.1); Balin (by proxy) his wife Sudeṣṇā's anonymous slave (I.98.25);[25] and Yayāti his wife Devayānī's slave, Śarmiṣṭhā (I.77.25–78.11).

Men of means also had access to sex workers of various gradations. In particular, courtesans are mentioned in various contexts. They emerge on ritual occasions to impart auspiciousness to festive events. For example, they are summoned by the king of Virāṭa to celebrate the ostensible military victory of his son, Uttara, in the *Virāṭaparva* (IV.63.25). They are utilized by the king in the seduction of the unicorn sage Ṛśyaśṛṅga in the *Āraṇyakaparva*

(III.110.30–113.10)). Yudhiṣṭhira enquires after the courtesans during Saṃjaya's embassy in the *Udyogaparva*: "Well-adorned, well-dressed and sweet-smelling . . . are your visits short and your words few?" (V.30.36).

Thus legally a man of means has considerable choice of sexual partners. In addition to the varieties of *dharmically* acquired wives whom he could be active, he also has recourse to a contingent of other women.

For women, in contrast, the choice is rather limited. Women who were *dāsīs* (slaves) and courtesans clearly could entertain multiple men over their lifetimes, but it is doubtful that these partners were of their own choosing. For the vast majority of other women in the *Mahābhārata*, the only legitimate sexual partners are those to whom they are married. Marriage, again, is construed liberally, as a sexual union of any variety, whether consecrated or not—*brāhma*, *prājāpatya*, *daiva*, and so on. By whatever means a partner may have been acquired, however, women are expected to have only one sexual partner in their lifetimes. This would appear to be the case even in unions in which a woman was abducted or assaulted—as in the case of Ambā. The *Mahābhārata* is on the whole silent on the question of what should happen if a woman is raped, but the *Dharmasūtras* offer some reflection. The Āpastamba DS says:

> If a young man all primped up barges accidentally into the presence of another man's wife or a young woman, he should be verbally reprimanded; but if he does so deliberately and with a malicious intent, he should be punished. If intercourse took place, his penis should be cut off along with the testicles. If it was with a young woman, he should be banished and his property confiscated. Thereafter, the king should support those women and from then onwards guard them from sexual congress. If they agree to perform the expiation, however, he should hand them over to their respective guardians. Once the expiation has been performed, the guardians should treat them as before, for their relationship is based on the Law. (II.26.18–27.1)

Aside from the problematic issue of rape, however, any sexual contact with a second man—even if only in her imagination—is deemed adulterous, held to be not simply a flaw of virtue, but a crime punishable by the husband. The stories of Ahalyā and Renukā, discussed in Chapter Five, attest to this. Once a woman has united with a man, however briefly, she is to conduct herself as a faithful wife. Thus, Ulūpī, who meets Arjuna during his year of voluntary exile in the forest, is sexually attracted to Arjuna and lies with him for one night (I.206.14–33). She sees and hears nothing of him for perhaps fifteen or twenty years later, but she is described as his wife, who has been chaste and faithful to her husband in all the years that she has never had any contact with him. The same may be said of Citrāṅgadā, who lives with Arjuna for three short months (I.207.15–23). After the conclusion of that period, she is forever committed to him so that some fifteen to twenty years after last seeing him, she rejoins him as a wife in Hastināpura, and mourns him as a widow when he embarks on the journey to heaven. Only under very exceptional circumstances is it tolerated (though never formally admitted) that a woman may have more than one sexual partner in one lifetime. These are very special conditions, which explain the sexual histories of prominent characters such as Draupadī, Kuntī, and Satyavatī. These exceptional cases are discussed in greater detail in Chapter Six.

In addition to the varieties of women who are considered suitable partners for twice-born men, there are also specified various types of women who are considered unsuitable. A host of passages in the *Anuśāsanaparva* specify characters who are inappropriate partners: menstruating women, women who haven't bathed after menstruating, virgins, and harlots or barren women (*bandhakī*) (XIII.107.100). For reasons of political safety, one should avoid sexual contact with queens, or friends of a queen (*rājapatnīḥ sakhīstathā* XIII.107.109). One should avoid intimacy with physicians, children, the aged, and servants (*vaidhānāṃ bālavṛddhānāṃ bhṛtyanāṃ ca* XIII.107.109). The *Anuśāsanaparva* adds to this list. One should not marry deformed and crippled women (*vyaṅginīṃ nārīṃ*). One should exercise restraint with the aged, with those who have renounced the world, and with those who are faithful to their husbands (*vṛddhāṃ pravrajitāṃ caiva tathaiva ca pativratāṃ*). One should also avoid women who are too dark or too fair (*atikṛṣṇavarṇāṃ ca varṇotkṛṣṭam*), leprous, epileptic, or generally of low family (*piṅgalāṃ kuṣṭhinīṃ nārīṃ*). The concern with reproduction is reinforced in prohibitions against sex with barren women (*ayoniṃ*), and women with deformed sexual organs (*viyoniṃ*) (XIII.107.122–27).

General Sexual Ethics

The norm for sexual relations in the *Mahābhārata*, then is of conjugal fidelity. Once married, both partners are expected to be faithful (although for women it's a requirement, and for men more a recommendation). Aside from being admonished to be content with their own wives (*svadāraniratāḥ narāḥ*

XIII.132.13), they are advised to treat other men's wives as they would their own mothers, sisters, or daughters (XIII.132.11). They are promised heaven if they avert their gaze from other men's wives and control their senses, and devote themselves to righteous conduct (XIII.132.14). A statement in the *Anuśāsanaparva* advertizes that "Those men who do not seek, even mentally, to associate with the wives of other men, even when they encounter them in deserted places and under the influence of desire, achieve heaven"[26] (XIII.132.32). Where promises do not inspire proper behavior, punitive warnings are uttered: "Those fools who cast wicked eyes upon the wives of other men, by their own evil natures become cursed with congenital blindness. Those men who cast their eyes on naked women with evil intent, those evil-doers become afflicted with disease"[27] (XIII.133.50). Men are warned that promiscuity particularly with women of lower classes results in impotence in the future (XIII.133.51). Adultery is a high crime for both men and women, but where women are occasionally spared responsibility,[28] men are roundly condemned. A statement in the *Anuśāsanaparva* warns about an adulterer: "He will spend as many thousands of years in hell as there are created pores on the limbs of the women [with whom he has fornicated]"[29] (XIII.107.480*).

Function of Sexual Life

For what purpose is sexual activity appropriate? This question is somewhat simpler to answer than the first. As discussed above, some categories of sex are for pleasure only. Thus, sex with *dāsīs*, courtesans, and a *dvija* man's own *śūdra* wives is solely for the purpose of pleasure, and thus pleasure is implicitly recognized as a legitimate end of sexual activity. Sexual gratification, however, while permissible,[30] is not the most appropriate motive for intercourse with one's wives. A fair miscellany of statements found in the text attest that intercourse with one's wives is best suited to one purpose only, and that is procreation. Indeed, in numerous statements, for a man to "approach" his wife when she is not in her productive season is held to be indicative of a lack of virtue, even a sin. Thus, a householder should "never summon his wife to bed, except in her season" (*nānṛtāvāhvayetstriyaṃ* XII.235.6). "A *brāhmaṇa* becomes equivalent to a *brahmacārin* if he goes to his wife only in her season"[31] (XII.214.10). A good householder is one who is content with his own wife, and approaches her "only in her season" (*ṛtukālabhigāminaḥ* XIII.132.13).

In some scenarios, sex for the sake of enjoyment alone is viewed as a variety of unrighteous behavior suited only to the accursed. In the *Anuśāsanaparva*, for example, the seven sages and Arundhatī curse with colorful afflictions the person who has stolen their meal. Alongside curses such as "May that person become a slave" and "May that person become cruel and unrighteous in conduct," one finds curses such as "May that person have sex with women outside of their season" (*anṛtau maithunaṃ yātu* XIII.95.63), and "May that person have sex with his wife when she is not in season"[32] (XIII.96.27). Sex with one's wife for the sake of amusement alone invites condemnation and recrimination. Husband and wife are expected to lie together only when the woman is in her productive phase. While it is expected that they will experience pleasure, and sexual pleasure is implied to be one of the blessings and comforts of married life, it is not to be the motivating purpose of sexual activity in marriage but an accompanying bonus.

The absolute centrality given to procreation in the sexual ethics of *pravṛtti dharma* is clearly a remnant of the theology of debts devised by Vedic religion. This theology is taken seriously in *pravṛtti dharma* also. At various points in the text, individuals are rebuked for not having produced children. Pāṇḍu, for example, when he is cursed to refrain from sexual involvement with his wives, becomes despondent in realizing that his ritual obligations as a householder will not be met.

> People are born on earth bound by four debts (*ṛṇaiścaturbhiḥ saṃyuktā*): to the ancestors, gods, *ṛṣis*, and men, a hundred thousand times over. The man who does not realize them at the due time (*yathākālam*) has no world—so those who know *dharma* have established. With sacrifices he pleases the gods, with study and austerities the *munis*, with sons and *śrāddhas* the ancestors, and with kindness (*ānṛśaṃsya*), men. I am free of my debts to seers, gods, and men, as per *dharma*; but not of my debts to the ancestors and therefore I am in torment. (I.111.12–16)

Time and Space for Sexual Activity

The most appropriate time for sexual activity is similarly circumscribed by the concern for reproduction. Married couples are expected to lie together at the time of the month when a woman is most fertile. Outside of the pleasure-seeking venues outlined above, sexual activity is expected to serve the need for progeny. There are also specific times when it is ritually inappropriate to engage in sex acts. During a *śrāddha*, for example, sexual activity is disapproved (VII.16.32). Other passages in the *Anuśāsanaparva* clarify that sex acts are to take place only in privacy, and never during the day (XIII.107.100).

Summary of General Ethics

A general etiquette of sex, therefore, may read something like this: For a man, it should be contained within polygynous conjugal relationships. For a married woman, it should be confined to a stern and solemn monogamy. Where sex is motivated by desire, a man may indulge himself through concubinage with courtesans and *dāsī*s. (The subject of women's desire is addressed in the next chapter.) The most licit variety of sex is nondesirous; it is a pious and *dharmic* rite, directed to the religiously mandated end of procreation. Sexual activity should occur only in privacy, at night, on the ritually occasioned times. It should be avoided during rituals of sober gravity, such as during sacrifices, or during the obsequial period of a *śrāddha*. These considerations constitute some of the general parameters of sexual activity drawn in the *Mahābhārata*.

Sex-Differentiated Obligations

In addition to the above, men and women also have specific duties suited to each sex. *Strīdharma*, or the *dharma* of women, has been studied in some detail by various scholars, and is examined further in Chapter Five. The subject of what might be dubbed *puruṣadharma*, "the *dharma* of a man," however, has received less attention. One obvious reason for this may be that much of the theorizing on sex (and other matters) in the *Mahābhārata* assumes a closed audience of twice-born males, hence obviates the necessity for a more focused discussion of male duty and privilege. Another reason may be that it is often taken for granted that while men clearly enjoyed a disproportionate amount of privileges, they did not have reciprocal obligations. The evidence of the *Mahābhārata* belies this. There is a theology of male functions that parallels the female, and the two are best read in tandem with each other.

The first point about male duty is that men are expected to provide for and support their wives materially. This goes not only for ordinary householders, but also for *vanaprasthin*s who live modest eremitic lifestyles.

Stories abound about hermits, newly married, pressed to leave familiar habitats to seek fortunes and provide comforts for their wives. This is the case with Agastya. After his marriage to Lopamudrā, Lopamudrā refuses to consummate their marriage until Agastya has provided comforts for their married life. Agastya must therefore embark on a search for wealth. Lopamudrā is not condemned as a superficial materialist for this; rather, she is said to equal Agastya in virtue (III. 97.21).[33] Agastya also does not begrudge her ("feminine") desire; he accedes to her request, recognizing his responsibility as the man to provide for her materially, and later tells her that he is pleased with her conduct (III.97.18). In a similar situation, Uddālaka's disciple Kāhoḍa marries his guru's daughter, Sujātā. To provide for her, and for the family that they anticipate, Kāhoḍa leaves his father-in-law's home and goes to earn wealth (III.132.11–13). To not be able to provide for his family is a source of shame for a man. Nala, for instance, when rendered destitute by Kali, refuses to take refuge in his father-in-law's home out of shame over his penurious condition[34] (III.59.1). When Draupadī faints in the forest in the *Āraṇyaka parva*, Yudhiṣṭhira curses himself for not being able to provide her the luxuries that she had been accustomed to at her father's palace: "How is it that she, this best of women, who was accustomed to well-decked beds in well-guarded houses has now fallen to the ground, even though she was deserving of happiness? How is it that her dainty feet and her face radiant like a lotus, have today through my actions clouded over, when she was deserving of the very best?" (III.144.10–11). In the series of curses pronounced by the sages in the forest, a particularly cursed man is said to be one who lives on the earnings of his wife (XIII.96.22).

In addition to providing for their wives and families, men are expected to be able to defend them physically. Draupadī's most bitter complaint against her husbands is that they did not protect her from the assaults of the Pāṇḍavas. For this, she remonstrates with them in bitter language. "Is it not the eternal way of *dharma*, forever observed by the righteous, that husbands, even those who are weak, protect their wives?" she demands of Kṛṣṇa, and gives mighty vent to her anger[35] (III.13.60). Nobody reprimands her for these vituperations, because it is universally recognized in the text that Draupadī has been wronged. It is a woman's right to expect the protection of her husband, and men who are not able to provide this protection severely castigate themselves for it. Duryodhana, for example, when he is unsuccessful in rescuing his wives from the *gandharvas* without the help of the Pāṇḍavas, resolves out of shame to fast to his death (III.238.10). Similarly, Damayantī complains bitterly at her desertion in the forest by her husband. "A wife is always to be protected by her husband,"[36] she wails (III.67.13); how could he, who understands *dharma*, abandon her so cruelly? In the mongoose story recounted in the *Aśvamedhikaparva*, the *brāhmaṇa* says to his wife: "Even among animals, worms and insects, wives are fed and protected . . . That man who from fear fails to feed and protect his wife earns great infamy and ill repute, and does not achieve heaven"[37] (XIV.93.21–22).

Not only is a man expected to protect his wife, but also other members of his family. Thus, *Aśvatthāman* laments piteously when he is unable to save his father from humiliation: "While I am yet alive, my father's hair was seized. Why should sonless people then wish for sons?"[38] (VII.166.1360*). Arjuna remonstrates the Pāṇḍavas bitterly for not protecting his minor son, Abhimanyu. He disparages their masculinity: "Had I known that the Pāṇḍavas and the Pāñcālas are not capable of protecting my son, I myself would have protected him secretly. Alas, you have no manliness, no prowess, since in the very sight of you all Abhimanyu was killed"[39] (VII.50.76).

In more general terms, repeated injunctions to men include that they should cherish, adorn, provide for, love, and defend their wives. Men should be faithful to their wives. Subhadrā's blessing to Abhimanyu on his death is: "Dear son, may you acquire that end which is attained by those resolute ones who only go to their own wives during their season, and avoid the wives of other men"[40] (VII.155.28). Husbands are also expected to love and cherish their wives. Whatever their other travails, the Pāṇḍavas are always represented as doting on their wife. An example of this may be found in III.144, when Draupadī faints in the forest. Bhīma, in particular, undertakes many dangers to save Draupadī from difficulty. In one instance, he invites serious harm on himself in his determination to pick some flowers that Draupadī had requested (III.146.6 ff.). Draupadī, for her side, had requested the flowers so that they could all show their appreciation and love for Yudhiṣṭhira, their patient elder, who had withstood such abuse on account of his gambling (III.146.10).

One special duty of the husband is to provide his wife with children. Thus, it is a man's absolute duty to lie with his wife when she is in her fertile period. Just as he is not supposed to lie with her at other times, he is not to neglect this sacred duty, by forcing her to remain unfruitful; this position is maintained by the Dharma texts as well.[41] This also explains the crucial participation of the husband in seeking out *niyoga* partners for his wife if he himself proves infertile. On the one hand, it is necessary for him to have children in order to satisfy his debts to his own forbears, but on the other hand, he also has an obligation to his wife to provide her with offspring. It is therefore wrong for a man not to seek the companionship of his wives during their season[42] (see Chapter Six).

In addition to their wives, men are also expected to be chivalrous toward women in general. Bhīma is forbidden from attacking the *rākṣasi* Hiḍimbā because she is a woman (III.143.2). Bhīṣma refuses to fight Śikhaṇḍin because Śikhaṇḍin was formerly a woman (V.169.20–21). This is the narrative device that the text uses in order to accomplish the death of the otherwise invincible Bhīṣma. The Pāṇḍavas similarly exhibit chivalry toward their mother. In his instructions to Arjuna before the latter's departure in search of weapons, Yudhiṣṭhira insists: "Whatever Kuntī wished for you at your birth, Dhanaṃjaya, must all come true" (III.38.20). In the *Mausala-parva*, Arjuna similarly must look after and protect the women of Dvārkā after Kṛṣṇa's and Vasudeva's deaths.

Throughout the text, there are numerous statements from men and women recognizing the comfort and companionship that they provide each other. Thus, where we have statements from women stating their dependence on their husbands, we have many parallel statements from men in apprecia-tion of their wives. "You are always my partner in the practice of *dharma*, you are like a mother to me," says a man to his wife in *Ādiparva*. "You were given to me by the gods as a friend, and you have always been my mainstay. Mother and Father gave you to me to share my life as a householder, chosen from many, and married with the proper *mantras*"[43] (I.145.31–32). Another passage states that "physicians know of no medicine in all sorrows that equals a wife"[44] (III.58.27). The Nāga Padmanābha says to his wife: "I praise my own self greatly since I have you for a wife—you who are ever constant, and possess every virtue"[45] (XII.348.19). The relationship between husband and wife is viewed not as a battleground, but as one of friendship and faith in which the two mutually support, cherish, and love each other. Both parties have crucial obligations that they must fulfill, and when each party acts as he or she ideally should, it is considered that the marital bond is productive of the greatest happiness and comfort *pravṛtti* life can afford. This appears to have been the case with Dhṛtarāṣṭra and Gāndhārī. Their closely supportive and interdependent relationship is attested throughout their text. When preparing to depart for the forest, the blind Dhṛtarāṣṭra publicly acknowl-edges his wife, paying tribute to her wisdom, patience, and self-restraint: "Gāndhārī, even with her sons slain, lives with fortitude, looking to me"[46] (XV.5.15).

Sexual Relations Across Āśramas

In Chapter One, it was suggested that in theory, sexual activity falls within the province only of *gṛhasthin*s, or householders. By definition, none of the other *āśrama*s are expected to engage in sexual activity. It is now time to look at these issues more closely. An overview of renouncers in the text, both male and female, suggests that the above contention generally holds; Śuka and Sulabhā, for example, as two prominent *saṃnyāsin*s, are both clearly beyond becoming befuddled by sexual temptation. Having renounced the world, they cannot be drawn back into it. Śuka's resolve is tested by the many beauteous damsels of Janaka's court (XII.312), and Sulabhā's mastery over herself is tested in a somewhat different way by another Janaka (XII.308). Both prove to have transcended sexual interest. This pattern seems to be consistent for both, those who renounce the world toward the end of life, and those who renounce in youth itself, as in the case of Śuka and Sulabhā.

Formally, celibacy is the defining characteristic of *brahmacārin*s, both among those who practice *brahmacarya* as a phase of life and among those who practice it for a lifetime. In *pravṛtti dharma*, the definition of *brahmacarya āśrama* is the student phase of life, when boys of the upper three classes reside at the homes of their gurus and learn the sacred scriptures. It has no application to women. If we look less formally at the premarital state, however, we may learn something about the conventions governing the sexual behavior of girls. The expectation is that girls will remain innocent until after their marriages; this is articulated in the ideals of *pativratā dharma*, in which a girl saves herself for the man she eventually marries (see Chapter Five). The narrative, however, suggests a more complex picture. Few of the central women characters do not have some sexual prehistory before marriage: Satyavatī and Kuntī, both matriarchs of the Bhārata clan, had both negotiated their virginities and even borne children before marriage. Devayānī, as a young girl, had already desired Kaca before her marriage to Yayāti, and attempted to win his affections. Her marriage to Yayāti also, moreover, was on her own sexual initiative (I.76.29). Similarly, Ambā had apparently already known and avowed herself to Śālva before being abducted by Bhīṣma. Damayantī had had opportunity to meet and fall in love with Nala before her marriage to him. Śakuntalā, the mother of Bhārata, eventual patriarch of the Bhārata dynasty, had already met and consummated her attraction to Duḥṣanta before her father appeared and fortuitously pronounced her married. Of the memorable female characters of the text, in fact, Draupadī and Gāndhārī are exceptional in *not* having some manner of premarital sexual history. No doubt the colorful sexual histories of these characters are important plot devices for the narrative, but they do lead one to speculate about a considerable variance between the ideology governing premarital sexuality, and its apparent practice. It would seem either that the ideology merely represents the ideals of the writers with little connection to factual reality, or—more likely—is a puritanical response to what is perceived as a more libertine sexual environment. Although individuals in the pre-*garhasthya* stage of life were expected to remain celibate in preparation for their fertile roles in the next phase of their lives, many women had already been sexually active before formal marriage.

The situation of *vanaprasthin*s may be discussed in two phases. Where *vanaprasthya* is assumed as an *āśrama*, or phase of life, *vanaprasthin*s are expected to consciously be striving for disentanglement from worldly concerns, including the sexual. Implicit in the narratives of those people who undertake *vanaprasthya* as a stage of life is the reasoning that as persons becoming advanced in age, who had lived full and active lives, their sexual desires have already been satiated. Their weariness with worldly cares is precisely the impetus for their present turning to the forest. There is no suggestion of an active sexual life between Dhṛtarāṣṭra and Gāndhārī, for example, at the point where they retire to the forest. The same may be noted of Sibi, *Bṛhadaśva*, and a host of other kings who seek solitude in the forest after leading colorful worldly lives. Yayāti, for example, bargains for an additional thousand years of youthful play *before* he takes to the forest (I.79). In this way, he satisfies all his worldly desires before undertaking *vanaprasthya.* In these narratives, the forest represents the antithesis of the world, and worldly activities. If it is true, as we speculated in the last chapter, that those who undertook *vanaprasthya* as a stage of life were almost always *kṣatriya*s, then it makes sense to suppose that to them, the forest represented a departure from the decadent and luxurious lives that they had always led, and a yearning for a simpler, less sense-indulgent life.

The perspective of *vanaprasthin*s who have been residing in the forest for generations is rather more complex. Because these *vanaprasthin*s spend their entire lives in the forest, they live their sexually active phases within the forest itself. Various marriages are set in the forest: those of Agastya and Kāhoḍa, for example. These unions yield children who grow up in the forest. The narratives of Śvetaketu, Aṣṭāvakra, and others are indications of this. This class of *vanaprasthin*s therefore lives through its *garhasthya* stage, with its attendant ritualized sexual activity, in the forest setting. It would seem that they remain sexually active even after the arrival of grandchildren. This is suggested in the narratives of Śvetaketu and Aṣṭāvakra, for example. The fatherless Aṣṭāvakra, the grandson of Uddālaka, growing up in his grandfather's *āśrama*, assumes Uddālaka to be his father. He is disabused of this misconception by Uddālaka's son, Śvetaketu, who is said to be of the same age as Aṣṭāvakra (III.132.10). Presumably, at some point the sexual lives of these forest sages comes to an end, but it is unclear from the narratives what the precise time for this may be.

Family and Sexual Ethics

There are clearly demarcated boundaries regulating the sexual encounters of family members. The patriarchal family is most endangered with the arrival of a new bride in its midst. The tension generated by this new arrival is most in evidence in the bride's relationships with her brothers-in-law and her father-in-law. Sexual contact between a father-in-law and daughter-in-law is considered incestuous; according to the *Gautama Dharmasūtra*, it is a crime in penalty of which the perpetrator "should lie on a heated iron bed; embrace a red-hot column or tear out his penis together with the testicles and, holding them in his cupped hands, walk straight toward the southwest until he collapses" (GDh. 23.8–12). Given the severity of the taboo, therefore, there is a self-conscious reserve between the elder male and the young bride. Several statements suggest that the daughter-in-law was never to show her face to her father-in-law, or even to speak to him directly. Fathers-in-law who joke with their daughters-in-law are maligned in one passage of the *Udyogaparva* (V.37.5). Kuntī confesses her premarital parenting of Karṇa to Vyāsa in the *Āśramavāsikāparva* (XV.38.1–18), but outside of that, there are few instances of a daughter-in-law directly addressing her father-in-law. This is in the mongoose story, where she, impelled by duty, hospitality, and generosity, offers her share of food to the guest (XIV.93.42–45). Raibhya encounters his sobbing daughter-in-law after she has been raped by Yavakrīta, and comforts her in a fatherly way before avenging her (III.137.1–21). Vasiṣṭha, after the death of his son and consequent widowhood of his daughter-in-law, in fact leaves his forest dwelling and seeks to annihilate himself. He only returns when he learns that she is with child. The child then neutralizes the potential sexual tensions, casting Vasiṣṭha in the role of a grandfather, and Adṛṣyantī in the role of daughter (I.167). Otherwise, contact between fathers-in-law and daughters-in-law is consciously minimal, and the distance between them self-consciously vast. This is a potent acknowledgment of the sexual natures of both actors. One source of Draupadī's mortification in the assembly of the Kurus is that she is exposed to the gaze of her elder male in-laws, her "father-in-law" Dhṛtarāṣṭra, and her "grandfather-in-law" Bhīṣma (II.60.29). Even more at issue is the fact that she is exposed in her sexualized state: as menstrual, fertile, draped in one length of cloth (II.60.25). She is exposed as a fully sexual being to male elders who should never be permitted to view her in that vein. This is a danger-fraught and humiliating experience for the young bride. This leads to behaviors that are ritualized to be painstakingly discreet and scrupulously modest.

The relationship between a new bride and her brothers-in-law is somewhat different. Yudhiṣṭhira voices an opinion that makes it more complex. One day, the younger Arjuna enters Yudhiṣṭhira's private chambers at a time when Yudhiṣṭhira is occupied inside with Draupadī—an occurrence that all the brothers had specifically agreed to avoid. Interpreting the agreement generously, Yudhiṣṭhira announces that whereas it is a crime for an elder brother to enter the younger's private chambers, which are shared by his wife, the younger brother has more latitude; he may enter his elder brother's chambers without incurring any fault (III.205.27). The logic behind this is transparent. In all social convention, the elder brother is a proxy of the father, and is to be treated as such. For a younger brother to witness his elder brother with his wife is equivalent, therefore, to a son witnessing his parents together. The situation is desexualized by recasting the elder sister-in-law in the nonsexual role of mother. She assumes, in such a scenario, a maternal persona, and interacts with her younger brother-in-law as she would with a son.

By the same rules, however, for an elder brother to enter a younger's chambers would be a gross violation of sexual ethics. In such a scenario, the elder brother again represents the father, and he is expected to relate to his younger sister-in-law with the discretion and courtesy due to a daughter-in-law. For him to enter his younger brother's apartments unannounced, therefore, would be to encroach on his daughter-in-law's intimate sexual space. As we have seen above, such an interaction is considered by the text to be nothing less than incestuous[47] and is to be scrupulously avoided.

Other rules regulating the conduct of elder and younger brothers can similarly be viewed as devices used to avoid potential sexual conflicts within the family. One such rule is that the elder brother must always marry before the younger. This is heard on at least two occasions in the *Mahābhārata*: at the deliberations over Draupadī's marriage (I.182.8), and in the *Śāntiparva* (XII.159.63). It is, however, a common dictum of the *Dharmasūtras*, which hold the marriage of a younger brother before an elder to be an instance of highly unrighteous behavior, necessitating *prāyaścitta* (penance).[48] Such a rule is transparently designed to mitigate sexual tensions between an unmarried elder male and a younger unrelated female. If the elder is safely married, the possibility of the elder's sexual temptation for the younger's wife is resolved, at least in principle. The younger can safely enjoy his wife, without fear of rousing the elder's lust or envy. In another scenario, it is stated that the younger brother who marries first, should present his wife to the elder. Then, with the elder's permission, he can approach her, and she, too is cleansed of all taint (XII.159.65).[49] This again seems to point to the same issue. The elder brother apparently thus only assumes his paternal role on his marriage. Before that, he is viewed as a sexual competitor, even predator; the younger daughter-in-law's sexual safety is constantly at risk as long as an unmarried elder brother-in-law lurks in the background. Through marriage, the elder brother's sexuality is neutralized, and he is rendered safe and fatherly.

Thus, sexual tensions within a family are resolved by being reimagined along familial paradigms. With the arrival of a young bride in the family, all relationships are realigned as being on one side or the other of a kinship model. The new bride symbolically assumes the role of mother to all in the family who are younger to her husband, and the role of daughter to all who are elder. Other relationships in the family are similarly recast in these filial modes. Elder married brothers symbolically become fathers to the new bride; younger brothers become sons. These fictive kin relationships are purposively designed to ameliorate sexual tensions among alien men and women in a family. By each member reimagining him- or herself as parent or child in a familial hierarchy, the potential for sexual chaos is eased. This kind of collective—and protective—reimagining is only provisional, however. If the husband of the new bride dies prematurely, for example, her sexual relationships with her brothers-in-law (elder or younger) may need to be renegotiated along entirely different lines. We will take more account of such cases in Chapter Six, in the discussion on *āpaddharma*.

Draupadī's polyandrous marriage is an instructive case study of how the *Mahābhārata* negotiates these issues of sexual ethics. Draupadī enters the scene when she is won in a tournament by the ace Pāṇḍava archer, Arjuna. By all conventional standards, therefore, she is his prize. The problem arises, however, because Arjuna is only the third of the Pāṇḍava brothers, and neither of his two elder brothers have yet married.[50] For Arjuna to marry Draupadī, therefore, would be a clear violation of the general principle of hierarchical privilege: the brothers are expected to marry in order of seniority. As one statement in the *Śāntiparva* states it, "The younger brother, the elder brother and the woman that is married, all three, because of such a wedding, according to tradition, become fallen" (XII.159.63). The presence of two older, sexually mature but unmarried males creates an imbalance in the family. The stability of the entire family is at risk, since it is likely that the young bride will attract the attention of the elder males. The situation is further complicated in the case of the Pāṇḍavas by the fact that there are also two sexually mature younger brothers who could be attracted to their elder sister-in-law. Indeed, this would appear to be the case; Yudhiṣṭhira observes, for example, that all five brothers are assessing Draupadī with love-smitten eyes: "As all these splendid men gazed at Draupadī, their love became evident, churning their senses" (I.182.10). There is thus a very real danger to the family in allowing only one of the brothers to have a wife, while the others remain unmarried.

Yudhiṣṭhira's reflections in this scene demonstrate that he is cognizant of these dangers. As Yudhiṣṭhira reflects, it would almost certainly cause discord among the brothers. Fearing a breach among the brothers (*tānbhrātṝn-mithobhedabhayān* I.182.15), Yudhiṣṭhira realizes that the situation requires a shrewd solution, and devises the plan of the polyandrous marriage. The need to manage sexual relations within the family is the dominant concern behind this solution.

Even once the solution is achieved, however, much rationalization is required to make it palatable to others. A series of creative explanations are devised to defend this unorthodox resolution. First, we see an exaggerated loyalty to a mother's dictum. Yudhiṣṭhira argues that since Kuntī had pronounced, however innocently, that all five brothers must share their "alms" with each other, the sons were obligated to maintain the truthfulness of their mother's pronouncement. A mother's word, after all, is to be respected above that of the highest guru, for a mother supersedes all in authority (I.199.14). Second, Vyāsa recounts mythic antecedents that foreshadow the polyandrous marriage. One account invokes scenarios from Draupadī's past life, in which she had impetuously requested, five times, that she be blessed with a gifted husband. The god Śiva, interpreting her requests mischievously, assents to five husbands for Draupadī in her next life (I.157.6–15). Another account is that of a complicated myth about five Indras being punished for their pride. These five Indras are reborn as the five Pāṇḍavas, with their common wife, Draupadī, who is the incarnation of Sri-Laksmi (I.189). Whatever the suasive power of these mythic recountings, the polyandrous marriage is arranged and the problem of the younger marrying before the elder is thus resolved in this felicitous way.

The problem of seniority and privilege solved, there still remains the question of the propriety of one woman sexually active with five different men—men who ordinarily would relate to her either as father or son. This problem is addressed in two ways. In the first case, a supernatural device is employed. After consummating each of her marriages, we are told, Draupadī is miraculously restored to virginity (I.191.14). Each of the brothers, therefore, receives an unsoiled virgin bride. The second device is a more pragmatic one. With the help of the *ṛṣi* Nārada, the brothers determine that each brother will take turns with Draupadī. They further agree that when Draupadī is alone with any one of them, none of the others will intrude on the couple's privacy, on pain of exile. In this case, through the management of private time, some semblance of normal sexual relationships is achieved in the Pāṇḍava household. What is interesting about these resolutions is less the devices used, and more what they tell us about the moral ideals of the society. The incest taboo lurks powerfully in the background as solutions are pondered. By making all relationships parallel to natal relationships, a fragile sense of order is achieved.

Sexual Relations Across Classes

The issue of sexual relations across classes is highly complex, because maintaining coherence in class relations is possibly the single greatest preoccupation of *pravṛtti dharma* in the *Mahābhārata*. *Varṇasaṃkara*, the sexual intermingling of classes, is treated as the very worst state of affairs in society, the hallmark of society's descent into chaos before the final dissolution of the world. These apprehensions may be found in the descriptions of *kaliyuga* given in the text. In the age of great turmoil when *adharma* dominates over righteousness in the world, all moral order collapses. The rich prey on the poor, the powerful prey upon the weak; children defy their parents, workers their employers. Righteousness, decency, and learning carry no worth in *kaliyuga*. The world recognizes no values other than those of wealth and power (III:186–89).

One of the key characteristics of *kaliyuga* is the disintegration of boundaries. No distinctions remain between good and evil, high and low, right and wrong. Children rule over their parents, and parents cower before their children. Servants threaten their masters, and masters live in fear of their servants. Men behave like women, and women like men. Finally, *brāhmaṇas* do menial work for their *śūdra* masters, and the *śūdras* are endowed with wealth and power. All descriptions of *kaliyuga* include graphic representations of *varṇasaṃkara*, the sexual corruption of classes. Distinctions between high and low are erased. *Śūdra*s, however untutored, unlearned, take on the functions of *brāhmaṇa*s. They intermarry with women of the higher classs, so that no certainty remains about bloodlines. *Śūdra* blood is mixed with *brāhmaṇa* blood, and all the institutions that defined society crumble. In these grim accounts, the mixture of classes is viewed with more than just distaste. It is imbued with real horror. It is the symbol of a society on the verge of complete moral and spiritual disintegration, a marker of imminent apocalypse in which all the careful refinement of previous ages dissolve into puddles of chaotic nothingness.

The *Mahābhārata* noisily denounces interclass relationships, insisting that people should marry within their own class. Interclass couplings are rhetorically rejected, and considered to be emblematic of vice. As one passage states: "Because of inducements of wealth, greed, lust, or lack of clarity about the *varna* order, or even ignorance of the *varṇa* order, intermixtures of class occur" (XIII.48.1). The most righteous marriages, therefore, are class endogamous, observing the boundaries of one's station.

In narrative, however, the scene is considerably more tolerant, as we have already had occasion to witness.[51] Even a cursory reading of the text reveals that certain kinds of *varṇasaṃkara* are admitted, and are even common. Thus, all the Bhārgava *brāhmaṇa*s have *kṣatriya* wives—Cyavana and Sukanyā, Jamadagni and Renukā, Ṛcīka and Satyavatī, and so on. We have already looked at passages that instruct men on what kinds of wives they may take: a *brāhmaṇa* may take three or four, depending on the passage, a *kṣatriya* two or three, a *vaiśya* one or two, and a *śūdra* only one (XIII.44.10). In these passages, class exogamous marriages are not only admitted, but also regulated.

Clearly, then, the text's rhetorical denunciations of *varṇasaṃkara* are not categorical; certain kinds of union are tolerated. These are *anuloma* marriages, involving the union of a high-class man with a lower-class woman. Men may marry beneath themselves, particularly in polygynous marriages, although their primary wife is still expected to be of equal rank. Women, however, are strongly discouraged from marrying low. Thus, the alliance of a *brāhmaṇa* woman and a *kṣatriya* man is actively disapproved. As king Janaka says to the *bhikṣuṇī* Sulabhā, assuming her to be a *brāhmaṇa*, "You are a *brāhmaṇa*, and I a *kṣatriya*. There is no union permitted for the two of us. Do not cause *varṇasaṃkara*" (XII.308.59). *Pratiloma* marriages, where women marry below their class, are the source of much antipathy in the text. Children born from these marriages take the class neither of their fathers nor of their mothers. Instead, they form a series of subclasses categorized below the class of both their parents.

These fine points are explained to Yudhiṣṭhira in *Anuśāsanaparva* 48.3–37. A *brāhmaṇa* woman with a *kṣatriya* man yields a *sūta*, which is a subclass lower than all of the four traditional *varṇa* groups. A *sūta* earns his living as a minstrel, a bard, or a chariot driver. A *brāhmaṇa* woman married to a *vaiśya* man yields a *vaidehaka*. His occupation is looking after the bars and bolts for protecting the privacy of women in respectable households. The very worst of combinations is that of a *brāhmaṇa* woman and a *śūdra* man. Such a union yields a *caṇḍāla*, a subclass that is the very lowest of the low, even lower than the *śūdra*. All *pratiloma* unions are held in contempt, but the sentiment for *caṇḍāla*s is nothing short of spiteful. The *caṇḍāla*s are worse than the dogs of society; they are the "dog-eaters" (*śvapākāḥ*) the most despised of all. In the *Mahābhārata*, a *caṇḍāla* is described as being "of fierce disposition. He is immersed in slaughter. He lives on the outskirts of cities and towns. Those among *brāhmaṇa*s who father such children are regarded as the disgrace of their lineage" (XIII.48.11). *Caṇḍāla*s are represented as living in self-contained communities outside of towns. This is demonstrated in the story of Viśvāmitra's visit to the *caṇḍāla* colony in the *Śāntiparva* (XII.139.13–94). They are the outcasts of society. They do not mingle with the twice-born classes. Whereas *Śūdra*s work as *dāsa*s and *dāsī*s in *dvija* homes, and *dāsī*s occasionally are even privileged to bear children for *dvija* men, *caṇḍāla*s are objects to be despised or hated. Passages in the *Anuśāsanaparva* presage the attitudes toward outcasts in later Hinduism. A *brāhmaṇa* must not allow the shadow of a *caṇḍāla* to fall on him. If the shadow of a *caṇḍāla* falls on a consecrated space, the space becomes immediately defiled, and so forth. Similar attitudes are also common in the *Dharmasūtras*.

Class considerations are of special significance to the understanding of women's space in the *Mahābhārata*. As we have observed, in most other ways, men and women jointly share responsibility in maintaining the norms. Thus, while women are certainly expected to be faithful and loyal partners to their husbands, so too are men. Men are told various times that women are to be honored and respected. Of a bride, it is said that she "should be honoured by her father, her brothers, her father-in-law, and also her brothers-in-law. She should be treated with every affection by those who wish for good things for themselves"[52] (XIII.46.3). "Manu does not applaud a union without love. It is disreputable, unrighteous, and offensive to *dharma*. Living as wife with a person whom she does not like leads to disgrace and sin"[53] (XIII.44.22). "The sages say that a girl is not to be given to a man who is undesirable"[54] (XIII.44.35). Another passage states, "Women deserve to be honoured. Men should show them respect. Upon them alone depends the righteousness of men. Upon them alone depends the pleasure and enjoyment of men. Men should therefore serve them and worship them. One sees that the birth of children, their upbringing, their care [depends upon women]. Love, and the journey of life itself, is dependent upon women"[55] (XIII.46.8–10). There are various regulations forbidding parents to sell their daughters. "A woman should never be given or married by anybody in this [unrighteous] manner. A wife is never to be purchased or sold. Those who buy women as slaves and those who sell them are considered to be greedy and evil-minded[56] (XIII.44.46). There is compassion expressed for women's sufferings in childbirth: "Undertaking extreme danger and immeasurable suffering, women give birth to children with immense pain, and rear them with great love"[57] (III.196.10); what could be more extraordinary than that? (*kimadbhutataram tataḥ*). There is also recognition of the difficult sacrifices made by mothers in rearing their children (for example, in the reflections of Cirakārin, XII.258).

Similarly, attitudes to women can be generous, and the vulnerability of women to abuse is acknowledged. Thus, when Raibhya's daughter-in-law gets raped, she gets only sympathy (III.137.6–8). Similarly, when Bṛhaspati rapes his brother's wife Mamatā, it is he who is held to be criminal. His actions do not reflect poorly on her (I.98.9–13, XII.328). In an interesting parallel to the *Rāmāyaṇa* central narrative, when Utathya's wife Bhadrā is kidnapped and assaulted by Varuṇa, Utathya mounts a campaign to get her back. The text clearly indicates that the woman was sexually violated. She is not, however, blamed for this. When Utathya finally recovers her, she is accepted back lovingly, and no fire ordeals are expected of her (XIII.138). Indeed, setting aside the major misogynist diatribes found together in the *Anuśāsanaparva*, it is possible to conclude that the text's overall attitude toward women is paternalistic and benevolent. There is a rich sense of chivalry that is extended to women.

It is in the class category that we see a monumental ambivalence regarding women. More specifically, it is in scenarios involving *pratiloma* sex offenses, where women consort with men of lower classes.[58] This would seem to be the biggest single source of anxiety for the writers of the *Mahāb-*

hārata. Women who marry above their class are forgiven, even given commonplace acceptance; thus Satyavatī, Renukā, Sukanyā. Women who marry beneath themselves, however, are virulently condemned.[59] Even the usual injunctions urging chivalry toward women are interrupted before women who commit sex offences with men of lower classes.

The contempt for people who engage in *pratiloma* marriages between high and low classs may be gathered from a litany of statements in the *Śānti* and *Anuśāsana parva*s. These range from mild pronouncements to extreme ones. Thus, "The *śūdra* who has sexual intercourse with a *brāhmaṇa* woman becomes a hog in his next life. He then dies of disease, and is reborn as a rat" (XIII.112.79). Another passage describes the punishment for a *brāhmaṇa* woman who has committed adultery with a *śūdra* man. Unholy glee may be detected in the decree that: "A woman who, abandoning the bed of her high-class husband, desires an evil [low-class] man, should be devoured by dogs in a public place with lots of spectators"[60] (XII.159.59). Further, "The wise bind the man to a bed of heated iron, and burn him severely. There, that sinful man should burn"[61] (XII.159.60).

The connection between class and women's sexuality is unexpectedly drawn for us by Arjuna in the very first chapter of the *Gītā*. In that setting, Arjuna rationalizes why it would be *adharmic* for him to participate in the war at Kurukṣetra. He reasons that if *kuladharma* (the *dharma* of the family), is violated, as it must be when members of the same family fight each other, a major consequence of that will be that the household women will go astray. Women's straying is conceived sexually, because it results in an intermingling of classes: "when women of the family stray," Arjuna worries, "we are left with *varṇasaṃkara*,"[62] (BG.I.40–41). Women are the critical factor between the devolution of *kuladharma* and a descent into chaos. This is the very worst scenario that Arjuna can paint, to persuade Kṛṣṇa that the Kurukṣetra war is *adharmic*. Women will go astray, he says, and create chaos in the class structure.

This is a key passage for the interpretation of sexuality in the *Mahābhārata*, because it makes explicit what is left implicit elsewhere in the text, and that is the critical connection between women and *varṇa*. In this statement, women are recognized as the repositories of class and family identity. It is only they, through faithful sexual conduct, who can preserve the integrity of the *varṇa* system. The relationship between sex with women and *varṇasaṃkara* is drawn in several passages in the text. Those who recognize this relationship are said to be wise and liberated. "Those persons who know that sex is the cause of the intermixture of beings are people of restrained passions, whose faults have been burned away, and they do not again acquire life in a body"[63] (XII.207.24).

At the *pravṛtti* level, it is possible to argue that the preservation of the *varṇa* system is the single biggest preoccupation of the *Mahābhārata* writers. This is because the most salient classificatory scheme of society is *varṇa.*[64] All occupations are divided on the basis of *varṇa*, all privileges and penalties are determined with reference to it. The preservation of the distinctiveness of each class is a matter of singular urgency. We find in the *Mahābhārata*'s presentation of women an intuitive apprehension that women have the potential to jeopardize bloodlines, thereby undermining the entire social edifice.[65] This point may be illustrated through numerous narratives.

The following story is related in the *Anuśāsanaparva* (XIII.28–30). Mataṅga is a young *brāhmaṇa* lad who one day impatiently beats the donkey that is pulling his carriage. The donkey's mother, witnessing the marks of violence on her young son, consoles him with words contemptuously directed at Mataṅga. "Do not grieve, O child," she consoles him. "It is a *caṇḍāla* who is driving you. There is no cruelty in a *brāhmaṇa*. A *brāhmaṇa* is known to be a friend"[66] (XIII.28.10–11). A *caṇḍāla*, as we know, is a member of the very lowest of subclasses, born of the union of a *brāhmaṇa* woman with a *śūdra* man.

Stunned at this unsolicited disclosure, Mataṅga interrogates the donkey's mother further, only to learn that she has spoken the truth. He is indeed a *caṇḍāla*. His mother, a high-class *brāhmaṇa* woman, unbeknownst to his father, had strayed in her sexual conduct, and had fornicated with a barber, a man of the lowest order, a *śūdra*; Mataṅga was the product of that union. This scenario represents the very worst fears of the *varṇa* society. The story has a bravado, suggesting that the sexual and class-injuring perfidy of women will always come to light, through whatever miraculous means. The practical truth, however, is that such adulterous deceptions can easily escape unremarked, and this awareness is the source of a foreboding that is apparent in all discussions of female sexuality. The sexual misadventures of women may likely never be discovered, and high-class men, like Mataṅga's father, could very likely find themselves rearing bastard *śūdra* children as their own. Shalini Shah makes these points in her work, *Gender Relations in the Mahābhārata*. She reads the sexual restrictions on women as being mechanisms of patriarchal control, reflecting male anxiety about the paternity of children. I would add to Shah's analysis that in the *Mahābhārata*, the anxieties of patriarchy are compounded by the anxiety to retain the purity of *varṇa*, and that this has the greatest bearing of all on attitudes to female sexuality.

Mataṅga represents in this story the most loathsome possibility of class relations. The disgust felt by a high-class society for people of his ilk, people born of mixed parentage, where high-class fathers are duped by their wives' nefarious acts of adultery with low-class men, is reflected in the utter malice and hatred with which Mataṅga's story is related. The narrative goes on to describe how Mataṅga, disgusted with his mother and his newly revealed identity, vows to transform himself into an authentic *brāhmaṇa*. In spite of years and years of rigorous ascetic practice, however, in spite of the most fearsome and formidable of austerities, he is unable to change his *varṇa* from that of a *caṇḍāla* to that of a *brāhmaṇa*. After extraordinary persistence, of the kind hardly described anywhere in the text, he is recognized in a small way. He still does not become a *brāhmaṇa*, but he becomes the divinity of a certain measure of verse, and is allowed, with high irony, to receive the worship of *women*.

The contention that a concern for managing class relations is at the heart of the concern to manage female sexuality may be further substantiated by looking at the differential treatment of the sexuality of low-class women. The many regulations governing the sexual conduct of high-class women are reduced to absurdities when applied, for example, to *dāsī*s.[67] While in principle the high idealism of *pativratā dharma* applies to all female behavior, it is clear that these ideals do not apply to low-class women, or at any rate are not respected, or even taken seriously. It is only high-class women who carry the potential to support or subvert the class structure, and therefore it is only their conduct that rouses indignation. Little concern exists for managing the sexuality of lower-class women, and I argue that this is because their sexuality has no serious impact on the social class structure.

Thus, in the Kaurava court, Draupadī's protestations of *pativratā*-hood are treated as pretensions, to be ridiculed and scorned (II.63.11–13). The same attitude is adopted by Kīcaka in the *Virāṭaparva*. Kīcaka meets Draupadī as a servant and desires her. He is warned about her marital status as well as her commitment to *pativratā dharma*, but he laughs both off as the quaint pretensions of a servant girl (IV.13–14). As already noted, *dāsī*s are routinely mentioned as gifts exchanged between people, in references too numerous to belabor. Highly eroticized descriptions of their physical person expose the fact that they are marked for sexual service, among other varieties of labor. While it is formally expected that all women will conform to *pativratā* ideals, this expectation is clearly nominal for low-class women.

Conclusion

In this chapter, I have tried to demonstrate that sexual practice in *pravṛtti dharma* is not random, capricious, or idiosyncratic, but rather is closely tied to the logic of *pravṛtti* religion, reflecting its theological concerns and values. I have tried to make a few points in the above discussion. The first is that *pravṛtti dharma* speaks primarily to the twice-born male householder, and this person is the referent of all *pravṛtti dharma*'s musings on humanity, unless otherwise specified. The second point I made was that there is a general code of sexual ethics that embraces "all human beings" as construed above (i.e., twice-born male householders). This code includes guidelines regulating appropriate partners for sex, and demarcates the proper time, space, and function of sexual activity. The third point was that in addition to these broad conjectures on sexual ethics, there is considerable variation in sexual practice, depending upon the specificities of one's sex, one's class, one's *āśrama*, and so forth. Any discussion of sexuality in the *Mahābhārata* needs to be sensitive to these variations, noting their patterns and their internal logic. Few generalizations may be made about women and sexuality that will hold for all classes and varieties of women discussed in the *Mahābhārata*. The norms for sexual conduct in all interpersonal relationships are based on the larger theological and social goals of *pravṛtti dharma*, so that the management of sexual relations in *pravṛtti* tradition may be seen as something of a science.

Chapter Four

The Unruly Desire of Women

We have now had occasion to discuss the ways in which gender is constructed in the religious discourses of the *Mahābhārata*. We have noted that gender is construed as a quintessentially religious category, critically implicated in the deliberations about life-in-the-world on the one hand, and immortality on the other hand. We have also examined the discourses of *pravṛtti* and *nivṛtti dharma*, and the ways that these metareligious categories demarcate gender boundaries by circumscribing and defining the modes of each sex's participation in religion.

It is now time to look more closely at the tools through which these effects are achieved. Gender is typically constructed in a society in multiple ways—through laws, through religious edicts, through social ideologies and conventions. While all of these are reflected to some extent in the epics, the literary nature of these works means that the primary instrument for the fashioning and shaping of gender is *stories*. Through stories skillfully told, gendered norms are posited as apparently objective realities, given qualities that exist "as if they had always been there, never to be questioned."[1] In this chapter, I entertain some of the narratives that aid, either directly or tangentially, in the development of a mythology about female sexuality. In the first section of the chapter, I recount for the reader's benefit passages that highlight the ideological space occupied by women in epic discourse. In the second section, I evaluate the image of womanhood that emerges from mythic narratives and stereotypes. What becomes quickly clear is that MBh. myths present a profoundly bifurcated image of womanhood, lurching unsteadily between beatific virtue and appalling evil, and this ambivalence remains unresolved in the entirety of the text; indeed, one might argue, it persists in all the subsequent history of Hinduism.

"Myths," says Mieke Bal, "are narrativizations of ideology."[2] They are constructed to support the biases and prejudices of society, and have in common with other stories, as Hayden White puts it, "the latent or manifest purpose the desire to moralize the events" they treat.[3] In this chapter, I propose to apply these insights to a study of myths about women found in the *Mahābhārata*. While several of these narratives have been discussed before by other scholars, my intent here is to read them within the religious context of the epic as sketched so far, remarking the way in which they support and maintain the larger sexual ideology of *pravṛtti dharma*. The epics are powerful didactic works, replete with literally hundreds of stories that involve a continuing negotiation of male and female roles. How is gender and sexuality moralized in these stories? How does narrative serve as a tool to reinforce and perpetuate the larger religio-cultural biases about gender that ground the discourses of the *Mahābhārata*? In this chapter, I will bring these questions to bear on myths and yarns about women in the *Mahābhārata*.

It is easy to close this door even before it's fully ajar to conclude that the gender ideology of the *Mahābhārata* is profoundly misogynist. Some scholars have indeed summarized the *Mahābhārata*'s position in this way.[4] My aim here is not so much to contest this characterization as to nuance it. My interest is less in remarking the prevalence or absence of misogyny as in observing the narrative tools used to construct it, and in theorizing its presence in narrative. An analysis of myths and stereotypes about women reveals that the estimation of women's nature, and hence their virtues and abilities, hinges specifically on assumptions about female sexuality. The chapter will problematize this issue, and query the reasons why sexuality is viewed as a particularly female preserve, generating the anxieties and the disciplining strategies of society.

Myths About Women's Sexuality

Śvetaketu's Law

The *Ādiparva* relates a legend that purports that social attitudes to female sexuality have evolved historically.[5] Pāṇḍu recounts this legend to his wife Kuntī, when attempting to persuade her to bear children for him with the help of another man. His aim in the scene is to impress on her that she does not legally have the right to refuse him what he demands. "In the olden days, we hear," he begins, "women moved freely. Those lovely-eyed ones were independent, and took their pleasure wherever it pleased them. From puberty on, they were promiscuous to their husbands, but this was not unrighteous, for in the old days, such was *dharma*"[6] (I.113.4–5). In Pāṇḍu's evaluation, significantly, "This is the eternal *dharma* that favours women"[7] (I.113.7). In the present world, however, he goes on to say, the rules have changed.

Pāṇḍu goes on to disclose that the great *Upaniṣadic* sage Uddālaka had a son, Śvetaketu.[5] This son was responsible for laying down the current regulations regarding women. "Once," said Pāṇḍu, "in full view of Śvetaketu and his father, a *brāhmaṇa* took Śvetaketu's mother by the hand and said, 'Let's go.' At this, the sage's son [Śvetaketu] became indignant and infuriated, when he saw how his mother, as if by force, was being led away." Śvetaketu's father, however, comforted him. On seeing Śvetaketu angered, Uddālaka said: "Don't be angry, son. This is the eternal *dharma*. Women of all classes are unrestrained (*anāvṛtā*) on earth. As the cows do, so do the creatures, each in its class"[9] (I.113.13–14). Śvetaketu, however, could not abide such a thing. In a fit of fury, he laid down the present rule for human beings. "From this day on," he ruled, "a woman's infidelity to her husband shall be a sin equivalent to that of abortion, an evil auguring misery"[10] (I.113.17). He further pronounced, "Seducing a chaste and constant wife who is avowed to her husband shall also be a sin on earth."[11] Pāṇḍu reinforces his point to Kuntī: "Uddālaka's son, Śvetaketu forcibly laid down this principle of *dharma* in the olden days" (I.113.20).

This little tale is a good starting point for a discussion of myths about female sexuality in the *Mahābhārata*, because it illustrates several issues that converge around the subject. It sums up all the primary concerns that the text has about women, while providing a mythical rationalization for male apprehensions.

First, Pāṇḍu's story purports to relate a historical fact: Women once enjoyed sexual autonomy, he says, but do not anymore. They were deprived of this privilege by a disgruntled child, "a little future patriarch,"[12] who legislated sexual freedom for women as a high social crime. Henceforth, they would consort with only one man, on pain of incurring sin. Second, we find that sexual autonomy for women is treated as uncivilized behavior, equated with lower forms of life. Thus, when women took their pleasure where they chose, they were like all animals, such as cows. Śvetaketu entered the scene and imposed order on this bovine pattern of mating. He civilized women by imposing *dharmic* regulation, and thus culture, on them. Third, the telling is self-reflexive. It betrays a consciousness that women's sexuality is the target of the ordering and disciplining machinations of society, and suggests further that these social programs of control are consciously conceived to serve the interests of men rather than women. Thus, the earlier pattern of mating had been the one that was "favorable to women." The new one, by inference, is less so, and indeed it is one that is favorable to men.

The story that emerges, then, is that in the mythic history of sexual relations in the *Mahābhārata*, women once enjoyed sexual freedom but were deprived of it *against their will*. This supposition is significant, because it provides the rationale for one of the dominant attitudes toward women in the *Mahābhārata*, and in other strands of classical Hindu literature: male apprehension about women's desire. What is suggested here is that a monogamous sexual relationship is "unnatural" for a woman. Women are contained within marital bonds not because of love for their husbands, or any sense of personal virtue; rather, their fidelity is occasioned by the imposition of external bonds. Because they have been harnessed and tamed against their will, therefore, they are resentful and rebellious, always looking for opportunities to escape the constraints placed on them. This is why society needs to be so vigilant about policing women's sexuality.

There is, however, one ambiguity here that seems to escape Pāṇḍu. This is that it is unclear whether Śvetaketu's reaction is directed against the alleged sexual freedom of women, or against the apparent male prerogative to violate other men's wives. It is unclear, in other words, whether Śvetaketu's rule is an act of resentment against the sexual autonomy of women, or an act of chivalrous protectiveness, intended to safeguard them from unsolicited sexual overtures. As we see, although the text states clearly that Śvetaketu's mother was being led away "*as if by force*" (*nīyamānām balādiva*), hence *against her will*, Pāṇḍu assumes that this state of affairs is "the ancient pattern that is favourable to women" (*strīṇāmanugrahakaraḥ sa hi dharmaḥ sanātanaḥ*). Thus, while the first part of the statement suggests a sympathy for women's physical vulnerability before men, the second expresses doubt about them: that women desire sex however they may get it, even if, as in this case, it is forced on them.

As we shall see below, the ambiguity embedded herein is reflected in the ambivalent attitudes toward women in the entire text. The text veers between attitudes of paternalistic benevolence, protecting women from the wolvish and rapacious intentions of men, and virulent denunciations of women's immorality. This ambivalence is never fully resolved, and uncertainties about women's sexual integrity linger on, perpetuating misogynist stereotypes. It is assumed that women would covet any social custom that allows them multiple partners, whether these are of their own choice or not. Karṇa voices this belief in the *Ādiparva*. When Duryodhana tries to devise a way of creating strife among the Pāṇḍava brothers by estranging their common wife Draupadī from them, Karṇa opines that: "It is considered a virtue among women for one to have many husbands. Women think it a desirable virtue to have more than one husband. Kṛṣṇā [Draupadī] has acquired many, so it will not be possible to separate her from them while they are prospering"[13] (I.194.8). The message here is that women love sexual variety. Given the choice, they like nothing better than to have a multiple of lovers and to indulge their desires without any inhibition. A custom that enables them to have intercourse with various men, therefore, of necessity "favors" women. This type of narrative has the effect of rationalizing the management and control of women's sexuality by claiming mythical authority for its necessity.

Indra's Sin of Brāhmaṇicide

Another myth that is fertile ground for examining the associations attached to women's sexuality is the myth of Indra's sin of *brāhmaṇahatyā*, "the killing of a *brāhmaṇa.*" This is an ancient myth, with lengthy Vedic antecedents, and has been discussed by scholars before in different contexts. In the *Mahābhārata*, there are two related versions to be found (V.10–12, XII.283). Both tell of the time when Indra was afflicted with the sin of *brāhmaṇahatyā* after the killing of Vṛtra. The sin of *brāhmaṇahatyā*, the worst sin of all in the classical Hindu lawbooks, is tellingly enough personified as a horrific female figure named Brahmavadhyā, who follows Indra relentlessly so that he is constantly evading her pursuit. One day, identifying a moment of weakness in him, she finally gains her object and attaches herself to him. Indra thereupon loses his powers, and the heavens suffer without their leader. Brahmā is prevailed on for help. He agrees to alleviate Indra's burden of the sin by distributing it among other beings. In one telling, it is dispersed, one quarter each, among fire, the waters, the trees, and the celestial nymphs, the *apsarās* (XII.283). In another, the last quarter is more generally apportioned to women (V.12.17).

The association between women and sin is already apparent in the personification of Brahmavadhyā as a *female* figure, who stalks man persistently, waiting for an opportune moment of male weakness so that she can overpower him—which she unfailingly does. Here, woman is sin itself, and the worst of sins. This linkage is drawn more specifically in further details of the myth. In both tellings, the target of sinfulness is female sexuality.

In the first version, where the sin is distributed among the *apsarās*, the association is quite transparent: *apsarā*s of all creatures in Hindu mythology are the ones defined by their sexuality. Although scholars have argued that *apsarā*s may originally have been mother goddesses and heavenly matriarchs,[14] in the *Mahābhārata*, as in most classical Hindu literature, their roles are attenuated to that of providing sexual service to men; they are often understood as heavenly prostitutes[15] or seductresses, who lure ascetics away from their disciplined focus or meditation into sexual engagements. Alternatively, *apsarās* represent the apex of the heavenly delights promised to heroic men. Warriors are encouraged to envision themselves consorting with *apsarā*s in heaven after valiant deaths in battle. *Apsarā*s are thus crucially identified by the sexual service they provide; hence where Indra's sin is displaced onto *apsarā*s, the association is richly suggestive. *Apsarā*s are the recipients of sinfulness precisely because they, of all female creatures, embody sexuality, its attractions and its dangers. They are thus always a suspicious category, always potentially errant and beyond control.

If the conceptual correlation between female sexuality and sinfulness were not sufficiently apparent in the first telling, the second version of this myth etches deeper lines between the two. In the second telling of the myth, Indra's sin of *brāhmaṇahatyā* is displaced not simply onto *apsarā*s, but onto women in general. When women protest at this unjust pairing, the grandfather Brahmā is reassuring. He states that women will rid themselves of their sinfulness by communicating it to others: "Whoever has sex with menstruating women will assume this sin as a fever of the mind"[16] (XII.283.44). In this way, women may escape from their now primal sinfulness, sloughed onto them by Indra's abdication. The linkage of women, sex, women's unique bodily rhythms, and sin is thus made explicit. Women's sinfulness, hitherto Indra's sinfulness, is transmitted, like a *disease*, through women's sexual and menstrual fluids. Men assume sinfulness only through this kind of *adharmic* sexual contact with women.

In the first telling of the myth, it is female sexuality that is characterized as being sinful because *apsarā*s are the only relatively autonomous females who consort with multiple sexual partners. In the second telling, it is women themselves who are characterized as being sinful. Their sexuality is the *source* of their sinfulness, but the sin does not stop there. In this case, it permeates their whole being so all of womanhood is infected. Men may assume this sinfulness through ritually prohibited, *adharmic* sexual acts, but women are infected with it from their hoary beginnings, and have no recourse to escape from it of their own accord. Their only resort is to invite men to participate in their inherent sinfulness. By transmitting their contagion to others, they release themselves from it. In this telling, Indra's sin targets not only women's sexuality, but generally, crucially, implicates women in *adharma*.

The Curse of Yudhiṣṭhira

A third story is extracted from the central narrative of the *Mahābhārata*, and is cited as an example of the way in which women use duplicity to cover up their sexual escapades. In the *Strīparva*, Kuntī, the mother of the five Pāṇḍavas, finally confesses her girlhood secret to her sons. Seeing Karṇa's body lying dismembered along with the grotesquely mangled bodies of the other warriors on the battlefield, she owns that Karṇa, the late friend of Duryodhana, and the Pāṇḍavas' archenemy, had been her son. Out of shame she had never recognized him publicly, so that the Pāndavas had never been aware of his true identity. In this state of ignorance, they had nursed their mutual hostility, to the point that Karṇa had finally met his death at the hands of Arjuna.

On hearing his mother's words, Yudhiṣṭhira, the conscientious eldest of the Pāṇḍava brothers, is so distraught that he curses all womankind for its deceitfulness. "'I am distressed by your secrecy,' he said to them. Very much saddened, the powerful one cursed all the women of the world, that they shall not bear secrets, or they will suffer misery"[17] (XII.6.10). Aetiologically interpreted, Yudhiṣṭhira's curse is intended to explain perhaps why pregnant women cannot disguise their parturiency in its advanced states. Kuntī had somehow managed to do this while in her father's home, and had borne Karṇa undiscovered by her family. Alternatively, it may be a warning to women that all their sexual indiscretions will ultimately emerge, no matter their attempts to conceal them. Women will henceforth no longer be able to cloak their sexual escapades.

Here again, Yudhiṣṭhira's curse targets women's sexuality, and reflects frustration over women's sexual agency. In spite of all the guards placed on them, women continue to foil social agendas. Their sexual maladventures continue to go undiscovered. Kuntī is one example of this. Mataṅga's mother, cited in the example in Chapter Three, is another, as was the Bhārata matriarch, Satyavatī. Yudhiṣṭhira lashes out in helplessness against this truth. His curse of women represents a wish to alter this reality, to remove from women the means to conceal the deceptions that inevitably occur.

The Creation of Women

A myth from the *Anuśāsanaparva* offers a perspective on the creation of women. The scenario is that all humans were at one time characterized by righteousness, and conducted themselves without hatred, envy, or distrust. This state of affairs became alarming to the gods, who found that it blurred the distinction between human beings and gods. So they appealed to Brahmā to effect some change. "The Grandfather, the Lord, having learned what was in the hearts of deities, to befuddle humanity, created women"[18] (XIII.40.7). Women were created to spread evil and discord in the world.

Women, moreover, were endowed with a particular nature: "The grandfather bestowed upon them the desire of enjoyment, all kinds of carnal pleasure. Tempted by the desire of enjoyment, women began to pursue men"[19] (XIII.40.9). "Beds and seats and ornaments and food and drink and all that is ignoble, indulgence in disagreeable words, and love of sexual companionship: Prajāpati gave all this to women"[20] (XIII.40.12). Men, yielding to the lure of wrath and lust unleashed by the creation of women, sought women's companionship and veered from *dharmic* conduct. Thus Brahmā's objective in creating women was achieved; women became the source of unrighteousness, disorder, and chaos among human beings. Hence, according to this yarn, women are *by their very nature* morally "frail and infirm," "unrighteous" (XIII.40.11). They can hardly help being evil, for they were created with a mandate for perpetrating sin.

Not all women are like this, however. The text hastens to assert that: "In a former creation, women were all virtuous. Those, however, who sprang from *this* creation of Brahmā with the aid of an illusion, became sinful"[21] (XIII.40.8). From this addition proceeds a dichotomization of womanhood that persists throughout the text. There are two types of women. The good are the right-minded, decent, morally mettlesome, who conform to and defend the sexual roles envisaged for women in society, and do not flaunt their sexual power. They are sexually modest and cloaked. They are archetypes drawn from that irrecoverable Golden Age, when "the skies were bluer, the apples sweeter"[22] and women were incorruptible and dignified. These women are acceptable in society, to be honored and esteemed, even worshiped. The evil are the fresh new crop of independent, self-serving, sexually depraved women. They lack all moral earnestness. They exist only to create trouble and to indulge their own appetites. They are ruled by their senses and their desires. Such women deserve to be vilified.

This bifurcated perception of womanhood marches indefatigably throughout classical Hindu literature. We find it in the *Rāmāyaṇa*, in the dichotomous characterizations of Sītā, Kauśalyā, and Anasūyā, on the one hand, and Kaikeyī and Śūrpanakhā, on the other.[23] It prevails in the Dharmaśāstras, where Manu, for example, assumes what appears to be a highly ambivalent stance toward women. We can also find it in abundance in the large variety of the Purāṇic literature that follows the epics. Women who conform to the dominant ideological pattern are reinforced through social approbation; they are praised, adulated, cherished. Those who forge their own paradigms for sexual conduct are brutally dismissed and become the objects of hatred, distrust, and suspicion. This myth about the creation of women justifies the dichotomous conception of women by blessing it with mythic origins. Brahmā himself here is credited with creating these two brands of women.

Stereotypes of Women

The above-cited myths support in different ways attitudes of hostility and fear of women's sexuality. We hear much on the theme that: "There is no creature more sinful than woman. Woman is a blazing fire. She is the glorious illusion created by Maya. She is the sharp edge of a razor. She is poison. She is a snake. She is death. Indeed, she is all of these united together"[24] (XIII.40.4). The mythic framework of the text thus reinforces the prejudices already held by society. In this next section, I will examine some of the prevalent stereotypes and assumptions about women's sexuality.

1. One recurrent proposition to be found in the *Mahābhārata*'s analysis of women is that women are inherently sensually disposed. This preconception comes directly out of the Sāṃkhyan presuppositions on which much of *Mahābhārata* philosophy is based. As noted earlier, in this philosophy, *prakṛti* is the material principle of a dyadic ontology, and *puruṣa* is the self-sufficient, self-effulgent, divinely indifferent spirit. The goal of Sāṃkhya is to work toward achieving a preponderance of the *sattva guṇa* in one's tricolor weave of qualities (*guṇa*s), and eventually to realize one's more basic identity as *puruṣa*, primordially liberated spirit.

Sāṃkhyan philosophy is often viewed as being misogynist, but in its skeletal nakedness it has nothing to do with gender. Its central insight is that of a reality more integral and enduring than the concatenation of material changes one experiences in the phenomenal world. It proposes that one is more than the sum of one's sensual and psychic body of experience; one is more fundamentally an unchanging, blissful, abiding consciousness that remains unaffected by the variety of change one experiences. Sāṃkhyan philosophy urges a hermeneutic shift in the individual, a reassessment of values. While both change and constancy are affirmed as being eternal, Sāṃkhyan philosophy urges a shift that allows one to focus on the constancy, rather than on the dazzling and befuddling varieties of change in which one is enmeshed. The intuitive realization of the constancy of the Self underlying the rapidity of change that registers on one's physical and psychic apparatus, relieves one of the anxiety generated by change, and enables a confident happiness.

Viewed in this way, Sāṃkhyan philosophy is a liberative doctrine that should have only positive bearing on the culture's perception of women. Regrettably, this is not the case, because of its use of gendered language. An abundance of gendered metaphors describe the relation of *puruṣa* and *prakṛti*, in which *prakṛti* is represented as the nefariously intelligent, irresistibly alluring woman who casts out her web of diverse wiles to obscure a seeker's vision. The hapless individual is led into believing that he or she is the endlessly transmogrifying multiplicity of the female, whereas in fact, his or her more primary identity is that of the self-content, radiantly effulgent male (*puruṣa*). Intuiting this integral maleness at the heart of one's femininity is the route to liberation from angst and sorrow.

Logically, all beings are a combination of *prakṛti* and *puruṣa*. The alleged femininity of *prakṛti* is, however, more readily homologized to women than to men. Thus, just as *prakṛti* is material, women are seen as being more attached to the material. Just as *prakṛti* is the domain of the senses, women are perceived as being sense-oriented. Just as *prakṛti* is perceived as being fundamentally ambivalent, possessing as she does the three potentialities of *sattva*, *rajas*, and *tamas*, none of which can be reduced out of existence, so womanhood also is perceived as being fundamentally ambivalent—potentially sage, godly, of lofty ideals, and potentially also deceitful, cunning, evil. This inherent ambiguity is prophetically stated to be the destiny of women, as the daughters of *prakṛti*. The gendered equations embedded in the worldview of Sāṃkhya permit these kinds of transpositions. Thus, the male, homologous to *puruṣa*, is by his nature pure, unmixed, primal calm; the female is by her nature of mercurial heritage, embodying at different times the qualities of *sattva* (truthfulness, idealism), *rajas* (passion, energy), and *tamas* (dullness, stupidity). Each woman is thus a microcosm of the archetypal woman that is the feminine *prakṛti*, embodying the same potentialities and weaknesses.

One of the primary assumptions about women in the *Mahābhārata*, therefore, is that women are naturally more sense-oriented than men. "The *śruti*s declare that women are endowed with the most powerful senses," says one passage[25] (XIII.40.11). Another informs us: women are "sunk in the attribute of passion. They are the embodiment of the senses"[26] (XII.206.9). Like *prakṛti*, women are "restless" (*calasvabhāvāḥ*). Their nature is "unintelligible" (XIII.38.24). While admitted to be intelligent, their intelligence has a sinister and cunning quality, that aids in their many duplicitous acts[27] (XIII.39.9).

It is only a small leap from these anchoring truisms to hypothesize that being naturally more attached to the senses, women possess unreasonable and excessive sensual appetites. They are distinguished by their love of "beds and seats and ornaments and food and drink" (XIII.40.12). These are their less offensive indulgences. Their most voracious appetite, however, is for sex. Women are stated to have an insatiable "love of sexual companionship" (XIII.40.9). The assumption that women suffer from an immoderate and near insatiable lust for sex grounds much of the misogynist theorizing about women that one finds in the text, both in the *nivṛtti* stream and in the *pravṛtti* stream. To indulge it, they will go to extreme lengths. Only the fear of punishment inhibits women in their heedless pursuit of sexual variety. As one passage suggests, "If punishment did not protect the *dharma*, nobody would have studied in the *brahmacarya* phase, no cow would yield milk, and no girl would ever marry"[28] (XII.15.37). Given the choice, in other words, women would rather remain independent of all sexual restraints.

Women's greed for sex is so incontrovertible, that they will in fact bed anybody. Old or young, attractive or ugly, whole or deformed, women do not discriminate. Anybody will do: "From fear of others, women stay with their husbands. But there is none whom they will not admit to their favours: the most worthless of men, whether cultured or not, ugly or handsome, if it is a man, women enjoy them"[29] (XIII.38.15–17). These words are spoken by the sage *apsarā*

Pañcacūḍā, a woman herself, to her interlocutor, Nārada, who is curious to learn The Truth About Women. While coyly declining the question the first time: "Being a woman myself, I am unable to speak ill of women"; Pañcacūḍā is quickly persuaded: "in speaking the truth, there can be no fault"[30] (XIII.38.9). Pañcacūḍā then expatiates on the Truth About Women, warming to her subject as she goes on. She explains: women will bed any man, be he hump-backed, blind, idiot, or dwarf. "There is no man in this world to whom women will not go, O great sage"[31] (XIII.38.21). And she is not simply speaking of lower classes of women, in case this had been one's assumption. *All* women are susceptible to sexual inconstancy. "Even if high-born, beautiful, and already married, women do not remain within the boundaries of propriety. This is a true fault of women, Nārada"[32] (XIII.38.11). If women remain within their bounds, says Pañcacūḍā, it is only because of the lack of availability of male companions. Otherwise, nothing could hold them back: not fear of sin, not compassion, not wealth, nor even affection for family (XIII.38.18).

Not only are women utterly undiscriminating about their sexual partners, but once they have had their pleasure of one, they will go searching for others. They seek constant variety, and thirst for stimulation. "Fire is never satiated with fuel. An ocean is never too full of water. Death is not satisfied even with all beings. Similarly, women can never have enough of men"[33] (XIII.38.25). All they look for is courtship, attention, and flattery. "Women desire most those men who court them, who come near them, and who serve them to even a slight extent"[34] (XIII.38.15).

In one passage in the *Anuśāsanaparva*, the patriarch Manu, nearing death, is heard worrying that women are too easily taken in by the promises of men: "Manu made over women to men, saying they are weak, of little anger, gullible, and disposed to accept the love that is offered to them"[35] (XIII.38.7). In this passage, the mood would seem to be of solicitous paternal concern, fearing for the naïveté of women in sexual relations. Pañcacūḍā's tone, however, is considerably less sympathetic. In her description of women, there is no doubt that women's attraction to men is a fault deserving the severest condemnation and censure.

In the pursuit of sexual variety, women will abandon everything—family, husbands, modesty, shame. They will not care what disgrace they inflict on their families and loved ones. They will abandon perfectly good, virtuous, loving husbands for completely undeserving ones. "Even when they have husbands of fame, wealth, intelligence, and good looks, and who moreover are in their control, women disregard them and await other opportunities"[36] (XIII.38.13).

2. Not only are women said to derive immense pleasure from sex, but their satisfaction is also alleged to be greater than that of men. As always in the epic, a story is cited in support of this belief (13.12.1–49). There was once a king named Bhaṅgāsvana. He performed a sacrifice that required no ritual offering to be made to Indra, the chief of the gods. Even knowing this, Bhaṅgāsvana performed the sacrifice, and through this act, earned the malice of Indra. The god of gods, to punish the insubordinate king, determined to teach him a lesson. The worst punishment he apparently could conceive was to transform the king into a woman. This is what Indra proceeded to do. The king, stopping to drink from a lake while out riding one day, found himself inexplicably transformed into a woman. Bewildered and confused, Bhaṅgāsvana looked about him in terror. How would he explain this uncommon transmogrification to his wife? How would he ride his horse? What would he say to his hundred stout-hearted man-children? These and other questions raced through his distraught mind. Deeply mortified, he pondered for a long time.

With the passage of time, however, he adapted to his new womanly form. Making over the kingdom to his children, he—now she—retired to the forest. She entered into a forest *āśrama*, where she married a *brāhmaṇa* man. With him she produced a hundred more stout-hearted man-children, whom she committed to the care of her erstwhile wife back in the palace.[37] Meanwhile, she herself settled down to living life as a woman.

The god Indra, not a little disconcerted at this unexpected resolution of what he had intended to be a painful practical joke, decided to increase the level of the conflict. Through various contrivances, he orchestrated a war in which the two sets of Bhaṅgāsvana's sons killed each other off in battle. When Bhaṅgāsvana was lamenting in bewildered grief, Indra, finally, out of sheer curiosity approached her. Explaining that he, Indra, had been responsible for the diverse unpleasantnesses, he offered to right the wrongs. In a gesture of extraordinary generosity, he even offfered to reinvest Bhaṅgāsvana with her former masculine form. The king, however, inexplicably declined the offer, saying she'd rather remain a woman. So utterly inconceivable was this desire to the god that he was forced to ask *Why*??! The king responded to this query that there are advantages to being a woman. One gets greater delight out of a maternal attachment to children, and women always derive greater satisfaction from sex than men (*striyāḥ puruṣasaṃyoge prītirabhyadhikā sadā* XIII.12. 47).

We are thus provided the assurance of one who has experienced it both ways, and Indra's locker-room variety of curiosity on this issue is satisfied. Women derive greater enjoyment out of sex than men. Interestingly, strands of Western feminist literature have been making the same assertion for generations, arguing since the 1960s that women's multi-orgasmic capability affords them a richer and "more varied heritage of sexual enjoyment than men."[38] Indeed, feminist theorizing pursues the analysis of female erotic sensibilities into motherhood, childbirth, and nursing, sacred territory where *Mahābhārata* writers do not tread. So in a bizarre paradox, late twentieth-century feminist assessments of female sexuality do not actually differ from the prejudices of the *Mahābhārata*.[39] It is the value assigned to female sexuality that is contested. For feminists, women's allegedly splendid sexuality is a glorious thing, to be liberated, celebrated, and reclaimed. The *Mahābhārata*'s position, as we see, is rather more ambivalent.

A question that may be raised at this time is whether the assertions about female sexuality are borne out by the narratives of women found in the epic. Do women indeed have a special enjoyment of sex? Will they indeed abandon all to assuage their desires? A perspective on this issue is offered by Stephanie Jamison in her work on the sexuality of women in Vedic ritual. Jamison comments that:

> The Indic seductress seems to me a genuinely sexual being, not someone who through innocence or cold calculation enflames sexually susceptible men with purely external charms, without sexual feelings of her own . . . In the Indic pattern, the man is not eager; his drive must be created, and the woman must work hard. She is an *agent*, capable of independent action and resourceful contrivance in the face of resistance. She also wants sex and enjoys it when she finally gets it. (1996, 17)

Jamison's remarks are occasioned by the obvious disjunction between the rhetorical denunciations of women as mentally weak, and the bold, resourceful women whom one encounters in the *Mahābhārata*—women such as Śakuntalā, Damayantī, Sāvitrī, and Draupadī.

She sees this discrepancy as a result of the tension between asceticism and householder religion that defines the Hindu tradition: "The idealization of asceticism so characteristic of later Hinduism is present, in one form or another, from the earliest period, and one of the most powerful forms of ascetic practice is the control of sexuality, the retention of semen. So males are confronted with a conundrum: they do not want sex but they need its products" (16). In Jamison's view, a resolution is achieved by displacing the sexual initiative from men onto women:

> The ideal situation for a man who has both goals is to practice his asceticism (an individual and private pursuit) *actively*, as it were, but to acquire sons from sexual activity in which he is a *passive* and accidental participant. Thus, this ideal male figure is the victim of sex, never seeking it or even welcoming it when it is offered. But, then, for sex to take place at all, we need an aggressor, and who is left? The ideological effort to preserve the image of man as the desire-less ascetic leads to locating *active sexuality* in the female, who chooses her unwitting partner, pursues, badgers, and seduces him, and enjoys sex all by herself (16).

This pattern, moreover, is not new to the epics; it appears "fully formed already in the Rig Veda, our earliest Sanskrit text" (16).

Jamison regards this not as the dastardly displacement of sexual responsibility onto women, but as a sincere portrait of the heroic women found in many of the narratives. "The energy, decision, and intelligence necessary for prodding a reluctant and passive partner into sex cannot be ideologically confined to the sexual arena alone. And so we have the spectacle of a culture that professes to believe women are weak and silly, embracing fictional females whose control of legal niceties or strategic planning far surpasses that of the men who surround them" (17). Sexual aggressiveness in a woman, suggests Jamison, is symptomatic of a personality that is strong and vital in other areas, and vice versa: strong-willed women are likely to take unabashed pleasure in sexual activity.

3. Notwithstanding this reasoned and sympathetic interpretation, the *Mahābhārata* views women's sexuality with considerable suspicion. This is based on the anxiety that women's insatiable erotic desires may not be limited to their legitimate married partners alone. Various statements in the text give voice to the fear that women's sexuality is mutinous and unruly, and cannot be restrained. Women therefore are

frequently characterized as having an innate predilection for wanton and adulterous behavior. They are, says one disgruntled commentator, like the words of the wise: ungraspable and unintelligible for meaning (XII.38.24). Their actions are irrational and erratic, incomprehensible to reasonable people. Because of their monstrous sexual appetites, they cannot be trusted to do the right thing.

These ruminations inevitably beg the question of what should be done about it. How can a woman be persuaded to be faithful to her husband? Yudhiṣṭhira poses precisely this question to Bhīṣma in the *Anuśāsanaparva*. Following an edifying discussion on the true nature of women, their mental frailty and their sense addiction, he asks with the zeal of a newly enlightened man: Is there *nothing* that can be done to alter women's behavior? Has there never been anyone at all anywhere in the world who managed to control a woman's waywardness?

Ever obliging, Bhīṣma recounts the following story (13.40.1–59):

There lived once a famous teacher named Devaśarman Gautama, who had a radiantly beautiful wife named Ruci. So lovely was Ruci, in fact, that she had even attracted the attention of the king of gods, Indra himself. Devaśarman was aware of this, and of Indra's prior history with married women. The subject made him nervous, and when it so happened that he had to be out of town for a time, he knew that he had to take special precautions to ensure the chastity of his wife. So on the eve of his departure, he called his most trustworthy disciple to him and explained the problem. Counseling Vipula, the disciple, on the lustful nature of women and on the unsavory interest of the god, he assigned to Vipula the care of his wife's chastity.

After Devaśarman's departure, Vipula, the hapless disciple, pondered his weighty responsibility. How could he ensure that this woman would remain faithful, given the monumental odds against it? He sat and reflected at length. Finally, realizing that there was no foolproof ordinary way of guarding the chastity of a woman, he designed the perfect solution. He would simply have to force her to be faithful. Briskly, using his *yogic* prowess, he divided himself in two. His body continued to perform its usual functions, but in spirit he entered the woman's body through *yoga*-power, without her knowing. This way he had full access to all her thoughts and desires, could sense when she experienced an attraction toward someone, yet was able to restrain her physical movements. When Indra approached, therefore, to solicit her sexually, as Devaśarman had anticipated that he would, the bewildered woman found that she was unable to move. In what was surely intended to be a comic scene, she tried to invite the god in, but instead ended up reprimanding him in stern language. Confused and astonished, she found herself admonishing Indra in pristine Sanskrit prose about the impropriety of molesting other people's wives. Indra, more than a little perplexed, retreated in consternation, while Ruci witnessed in bafflement the disciple Vipula emerging from her body.

The moral of the story is so transparent, it is hardly even worth belaboring. Women have what is quite literally an irrepressible desire for sex. Only one man was ever able to control it, and that was the brilliantly inspired disciple Vipula. His methods, however, were unorthodox and accessible only to the exceptional few. He had to *yogically* possess the body of his guru's wife, and thus internally arrest her natural responses. Through these acts, he himself entered a gray area of conduct, not entirely vitiated by the purity of his intentions (XIII.42). But his technique was effective: we are told that although Ruci would have liked to receive Indra with gracious hospitality, she was successfully restrained from doing so by Vipula. A hero of sorts, Vipula is the only man in the world who has ever been able to accomplish this magnificent feat. Otherwise, it is not possible to sexually restrain a woman.

This general overview of platitudes entertained by society about women reveal a singular source of anxiety: that women are erotically the more powerful of the sexes. In the fulfillment of their desires, they are aggressive, resourceful, and tenacious. While these markers of concentrated determination are commendable when in the service of *dharmic* bonds, society's anxieties are triggered by the fear that women's desires may lead them afield of familial ties, jeopardizing the stability of families, society, and culture. The text recognizes that a few extraordinary women are able to direct their erotic desire into the appropriate *dharmic* channels. Most of the epic's heroines fall into this category. The majority, however, it is feared, are lax in self-discipline, and need external direction. This assessment results in a characterization of women as inherently untrustworthy and morally frail.

Positive Appraisals of Female Sexuality

We have now spent some time unearthing negative valuations of female sexuality; are there no positive assessments to be found in the *Mahābhārata* that would counterbalance the negative?

Although it may be accurate to say that apprehensive treatments of female sexuality receive more airtime than positive ones, I believe this may be because the positive aspects are taken for granted. It is treated as self-evident, for example, that women's fecundity is mysterious and sacred, and should inspire awe, reverence, even worship. Similarly, it is assumed that the beauty of women's bodies is one of the joys of material existence. As fearsome as it is to one dedicated to *dharma*, *pravṛtti* or *nivṛtti*, passages in the text dwell on its diffuse attractions. It is necessary to take note of these more positive appraisals in order to balance our picture of the *Mahābhārata*'s attitudes toward female sexuality.

Women's Beauty

The beauty of women is an obvious source of poetic inspiration. Even as it is treated with suspicion, it is treasured. The description of Draupadī in *Virāṭa parva* captures the ideal of feminine beauty in the epics.

> Your heels are flat, your thighs are full, you are deep in the three places, high in the six, five in the five red spots, and your voice halts like a wild goose's. Your hair is fine, your nipples are pretty, you are shapely, with full breasts and buttocks, you are endowed with every grace like a filly from Kashmir! Your eyelashes curl nicely, your lips are like *bimba* berries, your waist is slender, your throat lined like a conch shell, your veins are hidden, and your face is like the full moon! (IV. 8.10–12, van Buitenen's translation)

Women are much appreciated for their beauty, even where it becomes the source of anxiety for others.

Women and Fertility

It will come as no surprise to anyone that women's fertility is highly prized. This is reflected in the vast empathy, love, and reverence directed at mothers in the text. Obedience to, and love of a mother will excuse diverse transgressions against *dharma*. The story of Cirakārin sensitizes us to this. Cirakārin ("Slowpoke") is assigned by his father the drastic task of killing his mother Ahalyā after his father learns of her adultery with Indra. True to his name,

Cirakārin procrastinates about his task, weighing the conflicting responsibilities he has to protect his mother, and to obey his father. At length, he determines that his greater duty is to his mother. He reasons: "What rational man is there who would kill his mother, to whose care alone it is due that his own head did not lie on the streetside like a dry gourd?"[40] (XII.258.31). "A person who, though destitute, enters his house, saying 'O Mother!,' need never indulge in grief. Able or disabled, lean or robust, a child is always protected by his mother; there is no one who nourishes like a mother. Only when he is deprived of her does he look old or grief-stricken, and the world looks empty to him. There is no shelter, no refuge, no defence like one's mother. There is no one so dear" (XII.258.225; 27–29). The responsibility of cherishing and protecting one's mother supersedes all responsibilities, including obedience to the injunctions of one's father.

Mothers in the *Mahābhārata* are frequently cast as all-wise, all-capable characters. Numerous instances may be cited of how an individual is inspired, comforted, or advised by a sage mother. Men's dependence on the sagacity of their mothers continues into their adult lives. Gāndhārī is often consulted in *dharmic* matters because of her celebrated wisdom. She is consistently characterized as being a highly intelligent woman (*buddhimatī devī*) who is familiar with the complexities and subtleties of *dharma* (*sarvadharmajñā*) (XV.4.11). The dispirited prince Saṃjaya is revived by the stirring words of his mother, the *kṣatriyā* Vidurā "the wise," who exhorts him in powerful language to persevere after defeat (V.131–34). The story of Vidurā's exchange with her son is moreover used by Kuntī in her message to her own sons (V.130–35). Kuntī seeks to empower her sons to action with her words, advising them that the time for conciliation is over. The Pāṇḍavas's dependence on Kuntī's moral counsel is evident not only in their infancy, but throughout the text. When she insists on entering the forest in the *Āśramavāsikāparva*, the Pāṇḍavas are described thus: "Deserted by Kuntī, deeply afflicted by grief, they were like calves without mothers" (XV.24.15). The mother is similarly cited as an authority by Upamanyu in the *Anuśāsanaparva*. It is she who advises him on devotion to Śiva, and counsels him on the methods of worship (XIII.14.84 ff.). These are but a few samples of the many mothers admired in the text. Pururavas is said to be the son of Ilā, and "indeed, we hear that she was not only his mother but also his father"[41] (I.70.16).

The word of a mother must be honored at all costs. In the *Āraṇyakaparva*, for example, when Bhīma comes perilously close to death in the coils of a snake, his concern is for his mother: "I grieve for my poor mother, yearning for her sons, who has always wished us to be greater than any. When I am dead, and she is left helpless, all her desires for me will be wasted"[42] (III.176.35–36). Her word is sacrosanct, and must be obeyed. This is Yudhiṣṭhira's primary argument to justify the unorthodoxy of Draupadī's polyandrous marriage, an argument that is moreover accepted as compelling: "They say that the word of the guru is *dharma*, and of all gurus, mother is the first"[43] (I.188.14). Adherence to the literal realization of the mother's words is taken to hyperbolic extremes in this situation. Even the omni-capable Bhīṣma is said to do everything "with his mother's [Satyavatī's] consent" (*anumate mātuḥ* I. 96.4).

The word *mother* implies not only one's birth mother, but all women who serve in a motherly capacity to an individual. Identical respect is owed to all of them. As noted above, Bhīṣma's filial regard for his young step-mother is complete. The most famous example of this ethic is furnished by the *Rāmāyaṇa*, where Rāma's insistence on obeying and revering even the much-maligned Kaikeyī becomes exemplary for all later Hinduism.[41] A similar ethic is espoused by Yudhiṣṭhira in the *Āraṇyakaparva*. When given the opportunity to bring one of his dead brothers back to life, he deliberately chooses his step-brother, Nakula. Questioned about his choice, he responds: "As Kuntī was, so was Mādrī. I allow no difference between them. I want the same for both of my mothers"[45] (III.297.73).

The *Mahābhārata* furnishes many examples of powerful mothers: Kuntī, Gāndhārī, Vinatā (who incurred blame by saving the choicest morsels of food for her children), Aurva's mother (who carries Aurva in her thigh, when the *kṣatriya*s are slaughtering the Bhṛgus (I.169.11 ff.). In general, it is held that: "One mother is superior to ten fathers and indeed the whole world in importance. No one carries greater weight than a mother. There is no guru like a mother"[46] (XII.109.16). "The mother has more weight than the earth, the father is higher than heaven"[47] (III.297.41).

The uninhibited, unequivocal appreciation of female sexuality in motherhood may in part be enabled by two considerations. Among younger mothers, it is the thought that female sexuality is being put to the right use—procreation. But it is postmenopausal women who receive the most unambiguous appreciation. This is because their sexuality is no longer a threat to the order of society. We find this candidly stated in one passage: "People praise a wife who is past her youth" (*praśaṃsanti bhāryāṃ gatayauvanāṃ* V.35.59). As much here as elsewhere, the appreciation of women hinges on their sexuality. Sexuality put to productive use for family and society is generously praised.

Even motherhood is not entirely unambiguous, however, for mothers possess powers that are dangerous. Thus, the wrath of a mother is not to be provoked, for a mother's curse has the power to destroy. We hear in the *Ādi-parva* that "One cursed by his mother has no escape"[48] (I.33.5). As an example, there is the story of Saramā, the mother of a dog who is unjustly beaten up by Janamejaya's brothers. She curses Janamejaya with unforeseen danger (I.3.5). This execration then forms part of the frame story of the epic.

The fearsome aspect of motherhood is captured in the characterization of "the mothers" (*mātṛkāḥ* III.215–17). The "mothers of the world" are stated to be both "propitious and unpropitious" (*aśivāśca śivāśca* III.217.8). The mothers are highly ambivalent characters, fiercely protective of their chosen wards, on the one hand, but malevolent, fearsome, and menacing to others, on the other hand.[49] In particular, they embody the perils of ill-health, disease, and death for infant children. In the *Mahābhārata*, the mothers are particularly associated with the Skanda complex of myths. Indra sends the mothers of the world to kill Skanda, but when they are unable to defeat him, they claim him as their son.

The mothers of the world are representations of thwarted motherhood, or motherhood gone askew. They are archetypes of barren women, or of women who have tragically lost children, and are represented as being hungry for children. They are "cruel daughters of the blood sea, who feast on blood"[50] (III.215.22). They live without male companions, suggesting perhaps a pattern of being rejected by their husbands for being unproductive. They represent danger and calamity to infants, unless their more benevolent maternal emotions can be aroused. With motherhood, they become benign, at least to the infant, of whom they are fiercely protective.

Conclusion

A study of myths and stereotypes about women suggests that the primary concern is with women's sexuality. Indeed, there is a collocation of womanhood with sexuality, and these materials reveal a singular source of anxiety: that women are erotically the more powerful of the sexes. In the fulfillment of their desires, they are aggressive, resourceful, and tenacious. While these markers of concentrated determination are commendable when in the service of *dharmic* bonds, it is feared that women's desires may be so immense as to inspire deceit and a reckless pursuit of hedonism. Hence, their desire risks jeopardizing the stability of families, society, and culture. The text recognizes that a few extraordinary women are able to direct their erotic desire into the appropriate *dharmic* channels. Most of the epic's heroines fall into this category. The majority, however, it is feared, is ignorant of the niceties of morals and ideals and is more concerned with self-indulgence. This assessment results in a characterization of women as inherently untrustworthy and morally infirm.

Numerous factors may be responsible for this very conservative sexual ideology. We have already taken some account of the highly vexed political and social clime in which the *Mahābhārata* was most likely composed, a period that betrays the multiple anxieties of an orthodox culture fearing apocalyptic collapse. In the context of apprehensions about *kaliyuga*, women's sexuality is threatening because they are recognized as the repositories of class and family identity. As Sanjukta Gupta remarks, "In the patrifocal brahmanical tradition, . . . *jāti* [caste] is determined by birth . . . A man needs a wife to beget children to perpetuate his *jāti* and lineage (*kula*)." He therefore has to be certain of his own paternity. Women, through chaste sexual conduct, preserve the integrity not only of the individual family, but also of the class structure, which in turn represents the stability of the whole society.[51] "Hence, early lawgivers betrayed their anxiety on this point by setting up an elaborate system of manipulating women's sexuality."[52] Women's sexuality poses a threat to the very foundations on which society is based and is therefore singled out as a frightening and uncontrollable force, potentially beneficial to society, but potentially also destructive.

Literary Considerations

My interest here, however, is in literary considerations for the misogynist presentation of women in the text. It is my view that the negative representation of women in the epic is critically linked to the nature of the text itself, and its larger aims. The epic genre of Hinduism shares the broad didactic purpose of creating a vision of an ideal society, a society that is constrained in all its acts with the preservation of order, *dharma*. The major Hindu epics, the *Mahābhārata*, the *Rāmāyaṇa*, and also the Tamil *Cilappatikāram*, are all preoccupied with offering a vision of society in which it's possible to lead a principled and virtuous existence even in the midst of great adversity. Through stolid adherence to virtue, great personal stoicism and moral resilience, one accrues all the spiritual benefits of renouncing the world. In the epics, this vision of such an ideal society is realized through the creation of paradigmatic characters, who through their actions model the ways that human beings should behave. As Matilal suggests (2002), the *Rāmāyaṇa* provides this vision in a positive fashion, through narratives about stalwart figures who are unflinching in their adherence to *dharma* even in the face of tremendous odds. Rāma, Sītā, and Lakṣmaṇa all represent such ideals of human behavior. The *Mahābhārata* achieves this in a negative way. While it also crafts idealized figures such as Gāndhārī and Vidura, on the whole it posits ideals obliquely, often negatively, by showing in horrific detail the consequences that accrue when people *fail* to act in optimal accordance with *dharma*. *Kṣatriyas* act out of avarice and heedless violence rather than responsibility (Arjuna Kārtavīrya and the series of *kṣatriyas* in the Bhārgava myths); *brāhmaṇas* harbor motives of vengeance and engage in forbidden acts of violence (Droṇa, Aśvatthāman); brothers fight against brothers, women cheat their husbands: these are samples of different kinds of *adharmic* conduct, all transgressions of norm. The result of all of these multitudinous acts of self-indulgence, egoism, and neglect of the larger order is a devastating disorder that leads to cataclysmic destruction.

The concern with shaping and directing women's sexuality, in my view, arises at least partly from this general didactic aim of our text, from its concern with crafting ideals of behavior. Through a highly critical negative style of pedagogy, the writers are paradoxically concerned to sketch out the ideal woman:[53] one who defies all the temptations that are endemic to the human condition and remains chaste, faithful, and exemplary in preserving domestic and social order. The negative images of women are offered as a *foil* to the idealized woman characters of the text. Where the latter are intended to represent the model of *dharmic* conduct in society, the former represents the nadir of moral and social lapse. They are intended to illustrate the destructive potential of moral decline in women, to be negative ideals that will deter women into conforming to their *dharma* and nudge them along the path more salutary to the interests of society. In this way, I believe, the preponderance of misogynist images serve as a negative pedagogical device in the project of inculcating a stern moral and social consciousness among women in society.

These overwhelmingly negative appraisals of female sexuality lead to the evolution of numerous strategies to control and discipline women's unruly desire. In the next chapter, we will examine some of these strategies, legal, social, and psychological, that go into crafting an elaborate and highly efficient schema for the management of female sexuality.

Chapter Five

Disciplining Desire

In Chapters Two and Three of this work, we observed how sexual life, both for men and women, is governed through the imposition of temporal, spatial, and personal constraints. This is true both for the soteriologically oriented stream dubbed *nivṛtti dharma* and for the more worldly stream designated as *pravṛtti dharma*. In this chapter, I would like to explore what might be considered *psychological* strategies aimed at the management of sexual desire. Briefly, *nivṛtti dharma* disciplines desire through a general ascetic deconstruction of social values. *Pravṛtti dharma*, on the other hand, erects the colossal edifice of *pativratā dharma* which, I argue, functions as a most compelling psychological device for disciplining the desire of women. Let us begin with a discussion of the world-renouncing tradition.

Nivṛtti Dharma

The case of *nivṛtti dharma* is complicated by the fact that, on the one hand, women are the objects of sexual desire, and on the other hand they are the experiencing subjects. Much of the ascetic discourse in the *Mahābhārata* assumes an audience of celibate men, hence develops the awareness of women as the objects of male desire. As a result, while there is clear recognition of the challenges *men* face in celibacy, there is little parallel reflection to be found for women. Indeed, though it's apparent that the highest goals were of interest to at least some women, the soteriological aspirations or accomplishments of women are hardly acknowledged. As with much other ancient literature, then, we are forced into a feminist reading of the text, a reading that looks through and between the lines, and extrapolates from other data the detritus of the lives of women.

Given the close link between *nivṛtti* and asceticism, it would seem that the best place to begin such a project would be to examine ascetic discourse.

Ascetic texts cross-culturally are notorious for misogynist attitudes; since the ascetic is generally assumed to be male, texts all too often contain ringing denunciations of women as harlots, temptresses, sybils and scyllas who would distract a man from his lofty goals. Such attitudes were common in early Christian literature, and are encountered in abundance, for example, in early Buddhist literature. The Pali canon is rife with representations of women and women's bodies as hollow facades of beauty, gorgeous on the outside but loathsome and disgusting beneath the surface. Aśvaghoṣa made this attitude famous in his *Buddhacarita*, in which the final element that confirms the young Siddhārtha on his world-negating mission, that which definitively breaks him from the tenacious bonds of attraction, is his view of the women in his father's harem lying in disarray in a state of slumber.

> One woman:
> had her hair loose and disheveled, and with the ornaments and clothes fallen from her hips and her necklaces scattered, she lay like an image of a woman broken by an elephant.
> But others, helplessly lost to shame despite their natural decorum and endowment of excellent beauty, lay in immodest attitudes, snoring, and stretched their limbs, all distorted and tossing their arms about.
> Others looked ugly, lying unconscious like corpses, with their ornaments and garlands cast aside, the fastening knots of their dresses undone, and eyes moveless [*sic*] with the whites showing.
> Another lay as if sprawling in intoxication, with her mouth gaping wide, so that the saliva oozed forth, and with her limbs spread out so as to show what should have been hid. Her beauty was gone, her form distorted.
> Thus these womenfolk, lying in various attitudes according to their natures, family and breeding, presented the appearance of a lotus-pond whose lotuses have been blown down and broken by the wind.
> (V.58–62)

Encountering women thus unguarded, the young Siddhārtha conquers forever his attraction for women and becomes resolute in his conviction about renunciation.

> When the king's son saw the young women lying in these different ways and looking so loathsome with their uncontrolled movements,

> though ordinarily their forms were beautiful, their speech agreeable, he was moved to disgust.
> "Such is the real nature of woman in the world of the living, impure and loathsome; yet man, deceived by dress and ornaments, succumbs to passion for women.
> If man were to consider the natural form of woman and such a transformation produced in her by sleep, most certainly his heedlessness in respect of her would not increase yet, overcome by his impressions of her excellence, he succumbs to passion." (V.63–65)

Siddhārtha penetrates the illusion of female beauty to view the true ugliness inside—the hideousness of flesh and fluid, molded and shaped into the female form. The motif of the sleeping women recurs in early Buddhist literature—it is echoed, for example, in the hagiography of Yaśa (Wilson, 77ff.).[1]

An extreme negative visualization of the female body became a key technique of meditation in early Buddhism. Thus, in the *gāthās*, one finds this technique used with success in the case of several male acolytes.[2] Paradoxically, in the Buddhist *gāthās*, this negative deconstruction of the female body is also used to enable the enlightenment of *women*. Thus, the Buddha's famously beautiful sister Sundarīnandā is taught precisely this by the Buddha:

> Nandā,
> Look at the body, diseased, impure, rotten.
> Focus the mind on all this foulness.
>
> Then the Buddha made an image of a lovely woman, and it aged before Nandā's eyes. He went on:
>
> Your body is like this,
> And this is like your body.
> It stinks of decay.
> Only a fool would love it.

Nandā thus learns to meditate on the innate ugliness of her own body, in order to break her attachment to it.[3]

Later Hindu texts such as the *Saṃnyāsa Upaniṣads* also employ graphic visualization as a technique for breaking a man's sexual attraction to a woman.

> What, pray, is the beauty of a woman, who is a puppet of flesh furnished with tendons, bones, and joints, within a cage of limbs moved by a machine?
>
> Examine her eyes after separating the skin, the flesh, the blood, the tears, and the fluid, and see if there is any charm. Why are you bewitched in vain?
>
> The same breast of a girl, on which we see the brilliant splendour of a pearl necklace comparable to the swift waters of the Ganges rippling down the slopes of mount Meru, is in time eaten with relish by dogs in remote cemeteries as if it were a little morsel of food.[4]

Another passage targets the locus of male sexual interest in women, the vagina, representing it as a hideous wound:

> Even though a woman's private parts are not different from a deep and festering ulcer, men generally deceive themselves by imagining them to be different.
>
> I salute those who take delight in a piece of skin split in two, scented by the breaking of the wind! What could be more rash?[5]

These *saṃnyāsa* texts encourage a visualization of the female body in its raw animal nature, shorn of mystique and beauty. By mentally dismantling what it regards as the façade of female beauty, such ascetic discourse aims to expose its grotesque naked reality.

Examples of such negative valuation are also to be found in some Bhakti literature. Thus, the Sangam-era poet Avvaiyar, deeply attached to the god Śiva, not wanting to marry, transformed herself in youth itself into an old woman, to distance herself from the sexualizing and deluding beauty of a young body (Chakravarti, 1989). The Śaiva *bhaktinī* Punītāvatī took similar steps to efface the beauty of her youthful body. She begged Śiva to transform her into a ghoul, so that she could focus on her *nivṛtti* goals, unfettered by the distractions generated by youth and beauty (Chakravarti, 1989). It would seem, then, that a tradition of cultivating a revulsion for the female body is thus an important psychological device employed by both traditions to break an individual's desire.

It is interesting to note that while men are thus encouraged to cultivate a studied disgust for the female body in order to overcome their attraction to it, women are not given parallel encouragement toward negative contemplation of the *male* body. Indeed, the *Mahābhārata* offers up only one example of a woman expressing a liberating distaste for a man's body. Piṅgalā, the prostitute, following the epiphany that leaves her consciousness transformed, comes to view the bodies of her former male lovers with horror, as "forms of hell" (*narakarūpinaḥ* XII.168.50).[6] This apparent lacunae in the literature is curious, given that, as we have observed, women are alleged to have excessive, indeed insatiable desires for men, uncaring if the male body is old, weak, decrepit or deformed. That being the case, surely one could expect that women would receive ample and detailed instruction on how to overcome their lust? But this is not the case. As Liz Wilson notes in her work on representations of Buddhist women, the meditation experiences of women "do not constitute a female equivalent of what monks do in charnel fields [where they contemplate their own mortality]. These women, like their male mentors and other monks . . . contemplate only female bodies, not the decaying bodies of men . . . Cataloging the deterioration of their own bodies or viewing with horror the dying bodies of female phantasms, these nuns may be said to regard the female body from the perspective of a male subject" (6). Apart from the undercurrent of misogyny that's implicit in such a practice, the inference here seems to be that while men are most challenged in renunciation by their sexual attraction to women, *women's major obstruction is vanity.* Thus Sundarīnandā must visualize her own body in its most degenerate state in order to conquer her attachment to the world; it is thus that she prepares herself for liberation. The *bhakti* saints, no doubt, are more concerned to deface their bodies to forestall the desire of *men*; nevertheless, in the case of both men and women, it is the *female* body that needs devaluing, deconstruction, and discipline.

Another common visualization in Buddhist texts is a meditation of the foulness of the womb. The womb is represented as a fetid and disgusting place in which the fetus experiences only filth, pain, and puerile substances.[7] Through this kind of meditation, birth itself is construed as a profoundly negative experience, with the womb not a sanctuary or refuge, but the portal that signals one's failure to achieve *nirvāṇa*. It symbolizes one's reentry into the world of suffering, angst, and misery.

Similar meditations on the womb may also be found in some of the renunciant tracts of Hinduism. Thus, the Bhagavata Purāṇa represents the womb in this way (Book Three, chapters One and Two).

In the *saṃnyāsa* texts of mediaeval Hinduism, it is not simply the female body that is to be dissected and probed in this captious, hypercritical way, but the very category of the body itself. The body is held to be the site of filth, for which the only appropriate emotion is disgust. It is a bag of skin containing within it a festering putrescence of bile, phlegm, urine, excreta, pus, sweat, and fat. Ascetics are encouraged to inculcate this perspective of the body, and to meditate on its foul loathsomeness:

> Let him abandon this impermanent dwelling place of the elements. It has beams of bones tied with tendons. It is plastered with flesh and blood and thatched with skin. It is foul-smelling, filled with feces and urine, and infested with old-age and grief. Covered with dust and harassed by pain, it is the abode of disease.
>
> If a man finds joy in the body—a heap of flesh, blood, pus, feces, urine, tendons, marrow, and bones—that fool will find joy even in hell.[8]

"These passages," explains Olivelle, "invited the listener to look upon the body not as a whole—an illusory perspective that presents the body as beautiful and pure—but as it truly is when it is dissolved into its constituent parts. When they are found separately, society considers them to be impure. People are polluted when they touch human bones, flesh, blood, pus, and excrement. How, then, can the body be pure or beautiful when it contains and consists of these very substances?" (1995, 191).

The renunciant tradition rejects the physicality of the body, but more, it rejects all the social meaning that is invested in it. In all varieties of Indian asceticism, the body is understood as a fertile symbol of a house (*gṛha*). This "house of nine doors," with its apertures of ears, nostrils, eyes, mouth, genitalia, and anus, is represented as loathsome, with filth and impurity oozing out of every pore. In rejecting the contents and the substance of the body, therefore, in interpreting them as vile impurities from which it is necessary to distance oneself, ascetics reject simultaneously all that the body symbolizes—structure, security, stability, order, domesticity, ritual, sexuality, procreation.

> A house carried a deeply negative value in the Indian ascetic tradition of wandering mendicants. Departure from home to the homeless state was the defining element of this form of asceticism within Brahmanical, Buddhist, and Jain traditions . . . The words *pravrajati* (he goes forth or he departs) and *pravrajyā* (going forth) are used in all these traditions as technical terms for the rite of becoming an ascetic. These terms refer to the ascetic's initial departure from home to the homeless state. (Olivelle 1995, 192–93)

In the act of wandering into homelessness, therefore, ascetics symbolically seek also to leave behind the home, and with it the concerns of the social and political body. But he carries a second home with him, and that is his own body. It is this more intimate "house" toward which the rhetoric of deconstruction is directed so as to elicit in the ascetic a repugnance toward the body, and implicitly toward society of which it is a symbol (193).

Key in the ascetic rejection of home and the body is the rejection of sexuality. The home is the locus of the sexual activity that yields children, one of the central preoccupations of Vedic religion. The body is the instrument that produces children, in particular the ritually all-important sons. *Nivṛtti dharma* repudiates the entire worldview upon which these concerns are predicated. The son and the sexual lust inherent in fathering offspring are regarded instead as two of the main sources of desire and attachment that keep people bound to the rounds of birth and death (Olivelle, 195–96). As we have seen, the *nivṛtti* orientation rejects as hopelessly naive the Vedic view that children, even sons, impart immortality on their ancestors through their ritual exertions. It claims the futility of the ritual and sacrifice that support and maintain order in the world, denying its alleged goodness and denouncing it as a place of sorrow, delusion, and finitude. In rejecting sexuality with its procreative goals, therefore, the *nivṛtti* tradition rejects the entire monument of Vedic theology. It achieves this through a cultivated hatred of the body as a physical, social, and intellectual commodity.

The *Mahābhārata*

To what extent are these patterns characteristic of the *Mahābhārata*?

Passages deconstructing the body can certainly be found in the text; the *Bhārata*, after all, by its own claim, contains everything! Thus, the Śāntiparva speaks of "the unholy wandering of creatures through various wombs, inauspicious wombs where they lie in foul-smelling blood and water, phlegm, urine and faeces; and then in bodies that result from the union of blood and sperm . . . forming an impure structure of nine doors . . ." (XII.290.31–33).[9] It must be noted, however, that on the whole such extreme negative visualizations of the female body are not common in the epic. Owing perhaps to the considerable veneration of the maternal figure in Hindu lore, as well as the womb symbolism that was a foundational element of the Vedic sacrifice, the womb is on the whole represented as a sacred space, the symbol of the goddess in later *Bhakti* tradition and *Tantra*, and a symbol of the wholeness of the universe in Vedic religion. While it is certainly possible to find statements disparaging women in the *nivṛtti*-oriented passages of the text (see Chapter Two), in all, given a text the size of the *Mahābhārata*, these passages are relatively scarce. The *nivṛtti* strand of the text generally relies on more benign techniques for breaking desire's hold on a person, mostly refraining from misogynist diatribes to argue instead that true enlightenment is beyond the prejudice of both class and gender. As we have seen, numerous passages stress the *ethical* content of *nivṛtti* practice; a *nivṛtti* practitioner is one who treats all beings with kindness and compassion, who has an equal love of all.

The primary contemplative technique of *nivṛtti* passages therefore is cultivating a mind-set of hardy stoicism and wisdom through a general deconstruction of the world and of one's relationships. Śuka's rejection of his distraught father on undertaking the *nivṛtti* path is an extreme example, but it is nevertheless a telling one; *nivṛtti* practitioners are encouraged to develop an attitude of detachment from the world and from relationships. Thus, one passage in the Śāntiparva states: "Everyone has had mothers and fathers, sons and wives, by hundreds and thousands in past births—and will have in future births. But whose are they? Whose are we? You don't perform their duties. They don't perform yours. They take birth in accordance with their own actions. You also will leave (this world and take birth depending on your *karma*)[10] (XII.309.84–85).

The same attitude is captured in King Janaka's haunting refrain that occurs several times in the text: "If (my city of) Mithilā is burning, nothing of mine is consumed in the flames."[11] These passages capture the essence of the detachment that the text seeks to encourage in *mokṣadharma*, and they have no reference to men or women. Indeed, some of the best examples of detachment and renunciation are women. The story of the widow Gautamī and the hunter is a case in point. Gautamī's infant son is bitten by a snake and dies. A hunter appears and offers to avenge Gautamī's loss by killing the snake. Gautamī responds that killing the snake will not restore her son to life; rather, the wise remain virtuous, and cannot be provoked into anger by calamity. "Good man," she says, "forgive and release this snake out of compassion"[12] (XIII.1.19–20).

The defining characteristic of *nivṛtti* practice is equanimity. To continue with mental resolve in happiness and sorrow, to retain balance even in the midst of great adversity: this is the ideal of *nivṛtti* practice. The *Mahāabhārata*'s counsel to ascetics tends to move in a liberal direction, deconstructing the notions of class and gender; indeed, the certitudes of gender are consciously relativized in *nivṛtti* dharma, as apparent in the *Janaka-Sulabhāsaṃvāda*. It is through the assiduous cultivation of virtue that one conquers desire and achieves freedom.

It is much more common to find misogynist passages in the *pravṛtti* context of the epic.

Pravṛtti Dharma

The antistructural exercises of *nivṛtti dharma* are conscious antinomies of the structure of *pravṛtti dharma*, which has a more positive appreciation of the body and of sexuality. As in the Vedic tradition, a healthy body is viewed as a blessing, an affirmation of the overall benevolence of the universe. Its functions, particularly those of procreation, are elevated to theological imperatives; to claim wholeness as a human being, a man must produce sons, through whom one assures one's place in the afterworld and achieves a type of immortality. The concern of *pravṛtti dharma*, therefore, is not the negation of the body or sexuality, but rather the superintendence of both. The excesses and effects of both need to be tended and restrained.

The avenues pursued by Vedic tradition in containing the effects of the body are reflected in the intricacies of purity laws devised by the tradition. These provisions seek to distance the body from its polluting effects (blood, urine, feces, mucus, and the like) through ritualized acts of cleansing. Through punctiliously observed routines of purification, the polluting defilements of the body are kept at bay. A similar procedure is at work to check the excesses of sexuality. As already noted, sexual activity is regulated, so that it is limited to ritually specified times, for ritually specified uses, between partners of particular *varṇa* and *āśrama* backgrounds. While sexuality is affirmed as necessary and ultimately beneficial, its anarchical edge is blunted by systems of control.

As remarked in the last chapter, however, women's sexuality comes to be considered particularly problematic in *pravṛtti dharma*. While the fear of sexual chaos is generalized, it is women's sexuality that is targeted. Women's desires, women's personalities, women's intelligence are probed with distrusting suspicion. The supervision of women's prurient natures is a matter of pressing immediacy. In addition to all the techniques implemented for the general government of sex relations in society, therefore, *pravṛtti dharma* also evolves psychological strategies to deal with the menace. Whereas the schemes orchestrating sex relations in society are aimed at the management of sex *acts*, psychological techniques are geared to the disciplining of *desire*. In my view, key among these psychological strategies for the regulation of women's desire is the ideology of *pativratā dharma*.

What Vipula, the student, accomplishes in the individual case of his guru's wife Ruci, is accomplished on the larger scale of *Mahābhārata* womanhood by the ideal of the *pativratā* woman. *Pativratā*: at its simplest, the word literally means a woman who is sworn (*vratā*) to her husband/lord/master (*pati*). In the *Mahābhārata*, for a woman to be sworn to her husband implies many things outside of a marriage vow; it implies being dedicated, committed, staunchly devoted to achieving the interests of her husband. It means placing the interests of her husband before all else in life; valuing his requirements in eating, sleeping, bathing, resting; indeed, in every activity before her own. It means holding her husband's priorities not only above her own, but also above everybody else's in the universe, including her children's, her guests', her family's, and God's. It means, in fact, holding his desires and wishes so dear as to sacrifice all of her own personal desires and wishes to the accomplishment of his.

Draupadī gives us a good description of *pativratā dharma* in the *Āraṇyakaparva*. Describing herself to Kṛṣṇa's wife, Satyabhāmā, as a *pativratā*, she says,

> Be he a god, a man, a *gandharva*, or a well-adorned, wealthy and handsome youth, my mind never goes to another man. Until my husband has eaten, bathed or lain down, I never do so myself, even when there are servants. When my husband returns home from the field, from the forest, or from the village, I get up and greet him with a seat and water . . . Never in any way do I wish my husband ill. When he is away on family business, I do not wear flowers or make-up, and observe vows. What my husband does not drink, what my husband does not chew, what my husband does not eat, I give it all up.[13] (III.222.22–31)

Draupadī goes on to describe how she never "out-sleeps, out-eats, or out-talks" her men (III.222.36). She is always faithful, never complaining, always content. She is sternly vigilant about her conduct, even where it would not seem necessary; as she advises Satyabhāmā: "Though Pradyumna and Sāmba are your sons, you should never sit with them alone"[14] (III.223.10). Nothing should cast doubt on a woman's sexual fidelity to her husband, not even the care of her sons—such care could be misinterpreted. Furthermore, love of children must never exceed that of husband. One statement in the

Anuśāsanaparva laments that women stop caring for their husbands once they have sons. The centrality of the husband in a woman's life must never be displaced. Everybody else in a woman's life must be held to be secondary.

The most crucial tenet of *pativratā dharma* is that a woman should hold her husband to be no less than God. "I believe that taking refuge in my husband is my *dharma*; indeed, it is the eternal *dharma* of women. He is God, he is the path; there are no others. What wrong can he do?"[15] (III.222.35), says Draupadī to Satyabhāmā. In fact, a woman's husband should be held to be higher than God: "Satyā, in all the worlds with their deities, there is none like a husband"[16] (III.223.2). Being an authentic *pativratā* entails nothing short of the mental and physical worship of one's husband as God. This is the one understanding that inspires all others. A woman stands in relation to her husband as devotee to God. All her thoughts, motives, desires, and acts are directed toward achieving the glory of her God. If this necessitates the neglect of all else in her life, that, too should be construed a virtue. This is demonstrated in the story of the *pativratā* woman related in the *Āraṇyakaparva* (III.197). So engrossed does the woman become in providing for the comfort of her husband just returned from work, that she neglects the mendicant waiting impatiently for alms at her door. This negligence is justified in the story by the supposition that the woman was responding to a higher ethic. A woman's first duty is to her husband. In fulfillment of that duty, if she forgets others, it is pardonable. Such a woman is to be recognized as the epitome of feminine virtue.

Pativratā dharma anticipates the radical paradigm of *bhakti* developed in later Hinduism. It insists, for example, on the total surrender of a woman's will to that of her husband-God. Umā says, "That woman who . . . looks upon her husband as god, who waits upon and serves him as if he were god, who surrenders her own will completely to that of her lord . . . is regarded as truly righteous" (XIII.134.630*). As the best kind of devotee is one who is able to subordinate his or her desires entirely to the directives of God, in the same way, the best kind of woman is the one who can wholly yield herself to her husband's authority. Furthermore, the moral propriety of his will is not for a woman to question. "Whether the husband is poor or diseased, fallen into difficulties, harassed by enemies, or afflicted by a *brāhmaṇa*'s curse, a wife should always do his bidding. Even if the task is unrighteous and leads to the destruction of her life, the wife should do it without hesitation, taking recourse in the law of distress"[17] (XIII.134.53–54). A husband's will is verily the commandment of God, and has the same compelling urgency. It must be honored even at the expense, as stressed above, of a woman's life, if need be.

By virtue of being her God, a husband is entitled to the unstinting obedience and worship of his wife. His personal worthiness for such treatment should never be a point of reflection. A woman is advised to care for her husband as she would her child, no matter whether he is "poor or diseased or weak or worn out"[18] (XIII.134.40). Whatever his physical, social, or financial status, he must still be honored. In particular, his appearance should never be considered. Thus, Sukanyā, sprightly young daughter of king Śaryāti, is married off to the aging Bhārgava sage Cyavana, to placate the fury he had directed at her father's troops. However unappealing she may personally have found him, Sukanyā yet serves him with diligence and devotion (III.122.1–26). In a similar story from the *Śāntiparva*, the ubiquitous *brahmārṣi* Nārada is cursed to appear as a monkey before his nubile young wife, Sukumārī. Sukumārī, however, finding herself married to a monkey, remains unperturbed by his appearance. She serves him with equanimity and affection, so much so that on the day that he is transformed back into his usual self, she rushes away in terror, fearing to associate with a man who does not bear the exact semblance of her husband (XII.30.1–42).

The *bhakti* paradigm persists. In descriptions of how a woman should conduct herself toward her husband, for example, we see that *sevā* (service) of the husband is a key ingredient to honoring him, just as in the worship of God. "When you hear the sound of your man at the door, rise up and stand in the middle of the house; when you see he has entered, make haste with a seat and receive him with water to wash his feet. And send your serving woman away, get up and do all the chores yourself"[19] (III.223.6–7). *Sevā* is personal service of God, performed with mind, body, the totality of one's self. A woman should leave all other activities to attend personally to the wants of her husband. Even during his times of rest, she needs to remain heedful of his needs. As Śāṇḍilī explains in the *Anuśāsanaparva*: "When my husband slept in peace, I never woke him, even in sickness or for work. My mind was content by his lying asleep"[20] (XIII.124.18). She remained alert to his cardinal significance in her life, and fawned on him while he slept. Further, as in an earnest commitment to God, where every act one performs may be construed as performed in service of God, in what might be called *patibhakti*, "worship of the husband," all domestic acts performed by a woman may be construed as acts of *sevā* to the husband. The household thus becomes an extension of the husband's body, his person, and deserves the same painstaking attention as his own personage. Umā says in the *Anuśāsanaparva*:

> That woman who always takes pleasure in rising at early dawn, who is devoted to the discharge of all household duties, maintains a clean home, rubs it daily with cowdung, tends the domestic fire . . . who never neglects to make offerings of flowers and other articles to the deities . . . succeeds in acquiring great merit.[21] (XIII.134.44–47)

Similar statements voicing the ideal of dedicated service to the economy of the household are made by both Draupadī and Śāṇḍilī. Draupadī in particular talks of her management of the large and complex household of the Pāṇḍavas when they were the rulers of Khāṇḍavaprastha; her energetic devotion to these matters are viewed consciously as acts of service to her husbands.

The husband's family and friends should also be viewed as being extensions of the husband-body. A woman is discouraged from making her own friends, because they may be sources of distraction for her from her primary duty to her husband. They may also be adverse or corrupting influences. A woman is advised to limit even the small interaction she might have with other women by never staying and chatting too long at the door. Draupadī is particularly zealous in these matters. She goes so far as to say that she never lingers long in the gardens, or even in the toilet (III.222.27). Instead, she hastens back to her duties in the household. These sentiments are echoed by Śāṇḍilī to Sumana in *Anuśāsanaparva* 124. The same woman who in the Udyogaparva was able to humble Gālava with her ascetic power, explains that it is not through her ascetic practice that she earned heaven. Rather, she did it by taking her *pati-sevā* duties seriously. She never stayed and chatted at the door, never laughed aloud. Instead, she committed herself to the service of her husband's family (XIII.124.8–11).

His family being an organic extension of the husband, a *pativratā* woman's relationships with all members are of significance, and defined by the same qualities present in her relationship with her husband: duty, unquestioning devotion, and service. "I always wait on the lady Kuntī, mother of heroes, speaker of truth, myself personally bathing her, dressing her, feeding her, sending the servants away," says Draupadi. "I never outshine her in clothes or jewellery, or out-do her in eating. I never argue with Pṛthā, who equals the earth itself"[22] (III.222.38–39). The person of her mother-in-law is hallowed by its connection with the persons of her husbands. The affinal family therefore deserves the same care and service as does the husband. Śāṇḍilī says in support: "Always vigilant, I waited upon and served my mother-in-law and father-in-law . . . Rising at early dawn, I did and got done whatever was required for the whole family"[23] (XIII.124.14–15). The relatives and kin of the husband are to be conceived as forms of the husband himself. Concern for them dominates the priorities of the wife.

To a somewhat lesser extent, the husband's friends are also understood as annexes of the husband. They therefore deserve some attention, but strictly in *sevā*, or service of the husband. Draupadī advises Satyabhāmā: "Invite for a meal by whatever stratagems those who are dear to your husband, his relatives, and well-wishers, and cut off forever his enemies, opponents, ill-wishers, cheats, and those who are offensive"[24] (III.223.9). A woman should, in other words, foster all relationships that are beneficial to the husband-body, and shun all those that may be malignant. The care of the husband-body in all its forms, as husband, as family, and as household, must be the consuming priority of the *pativratā* wife. In the process, her own self must be negated, and this is what renders *pativratā* a religious exercise. Through the denial of her own self in the service of God and the God body, a woman achieves the highest bliss.

Through negation of herself, and assiduous care of the husband-God, the wife-devotee may obtain the grace of her lord. If the husband-God is pleased, temporal rewards may be forthcoming. Draupadī tells Satyabhāmā: "There is no god like him, Satya, in all the worlds with all their gods. If you fulfill all your husband's desires, you are blessed. If you annoy him, you're dead. From him you get children and colourful delights; a place to sleep and to rest and wondrous sights, and clothes and garlands as well as perfumes and the world of heaven and fame"[25] (III.223.2–3). The grace of the husband-God falls on the wife-devotee, and she becomes blessed with material prosperity, and children. Conversely, if he is displeased, there are attendant consequences. She would be deprived of all the privileges she would otherwise enjoy. One passage sums up: "Limited are the gifts of one's father, mother, and even one's son. Only one's husband's gifts are beyond measure. Who wouldn't worship him?"[26] (XII.144.6); "There is no protector like a husband; there is no joy equal to that of a husband. Setting aside all wealth, the husband alone is a woman's recourse"[27] (XII.144.7).

The directives of *pativratā dharma* are thus simple but formidably comprehensive. A woman's life should entail nothing less than complete mindful attentiveness to the needs of her lord. All her actions should be directed at service to him; all her thoughts should be for his well-being and welfare; all her social world should be constructed around him—his family, his friends; anything that in any way may distract her from complete devoted attention to him should be ruthlessly cut away—her personal friends, her own personal wishes, her very identity; even her children, if need be.

The word *pativratā* is familiar from Vedic scriptures as an adjective denoting a woman sexually faithful to her husband. There is some evidence to suggest, however, that *pativratya* was not the dominant ideology of Vedic tradition. Although marital fidelity was clearly expected of a woman, it was not the most encompassing concern. Vedic literature, particularly in its early phases, was more concerned with delineating the parity of husband and wife in the maintenance of the home and the performance of ritual. As has been abundantly remarked,[28] in Vedic literature, the primary conception of woman is as *sahadharminī*, rather than *pativratā*; hence a woman was understood as the necessary and indispensable ritual partner of her husband. He was as incomplete without her as she without him. Works on Hinduism have remarked this for generations, but recent scholarly work on the Vedic tradition makes this point with emphasis.[29] A woman had a clearly defined ritual role in Vedic sacrifice. Her participation in the ritual was a crucial necessity. She was in this way as implicated in ensuring the solemnity and success of the sacrifice as the man.

Elements of these Vedic origins are preserved in the *Mahābhārata*. Indeed, the text details several royal sacrifices in which Draupadī functions as the *sahadharminī*, the ritual partner, of her eldest husband. During the *rājasūya* that marks the beginnings of the Pāṇḍavas' political ascendancy, she officiates for him and is everywhere conspicuous as Yudhiṣṭhira's chief queen. She describes some of her activities to Satyabhāmā in the *Āraṇyaka-parva* dialogue cited above (III.222–24). In the *aśvamedha yajña* that marks the cleansing aftermath of the Pāṇḍavas' victory, Draupadī is again performing her ritual role to the fullest extent (XIV.91.2).

Notwithstanding this anchoring in Vedic paradigms, the processes of change are everywhere evident. The values characteristic of classical Hinduism—such as the systemization of the *āśrama*s as consecutive stages of life, the expansion of the *puruṣārtha*s to four, including *mokṣa* as a final telos—are in the *Mahābhārata* seen in the process of assimilation. The change in the conceptual place of womanhood reflects these broader intellectual and social currents. Women thus go from being the partners and supporters of their husbands in religious life—which indeed in the Vedic world is *all* of life—to being their uncritical servants and devotees.[30] *Pativratā dharma* is thus an incipient ideology that becomes grafted over the older paradigm of the *sahadharminī* woman, and exercises a powerful ideological appeal.[31] It is seen rapidly emerging as the dominant ethic, subsuming prior ethics into its own rubric. While more ancient practices continue to be recorded in the text, the increasing hegemony of the *pativratā* dogma is evident in the didactic aims of the text.

The depreciation of women's roles in the conjugal relationship coincides with the diminution of women's roles in the ritual sphere. Whereas in Vedic times, women were indispensable participants in the sacrifice, even if in passive rather than active modes, increasingly, we find in the *Mahābhārata* statements that "There are no sacrifices for women, no *śrāddhas*, no observances"[32] (XIII.46.12). These statements parallel statements to be found in the Dharmaśāstras. While they are not accurate descriptions of women in Vedic times, where women clearly did perform various rites, they do reflect the evolving mood that women's religious lives should be located around their husbands. In classical Hinduism, it became common to refer to marriage as the *upanayana* for girls, and to think of the husband as the guru. These formulations reflect the ethos of the *pativratā* creed—that husbands possess both intellectual and religious priority over their wives. In living in humble service of their husbands, women hope not only to propitiate them as they would a deity, but also to learn from them, be intellectually formed by them. This is a very different ethic from that of *sahadharma*, where husband and wife are conceived as complementary partners with different roles, together responsible for the maintenance of order in the universe through their ritual activities.

Methods of *Pativratā Dharma*

The purposes of *pativratā dharma* are underwritten and achieved by a host of congruent cultural practices. In this section, I will point to a few.

Patriliny

The major social institution that both necessitates and reinforces *pativratā dharma* is the tradition of patrilineal marriage, the dominant practice in the *Mahābhārata*. Shalini Shah has commented on this at some length in her 1992 work, *Gender Relations in the Mahābhārata,* and I will not therefore belabor the subject further here. Shah demonstrates that *pativratā dharma* is dependent on patriliny, and is indebted for its success to the profound insecurity experienced by a woman entering an entirely alien environment.

Polygyny

Closely linked to the practice of patriliny, and equally disabling, is the practice of polygyny. The prerogative of the man to take multiple waves serves as a disciplining tool for women and has the effect of disempowering them. Thus, the presence of cowives as rivals is a frequent theme in several narratives and is a continuing source of distress and anxiety for a woman. Thus, Draupadī is pained to learn of Arjuna's marriage to the nubile Subhadrā. Similar tensions are noted in the relationship between Kuntī and Mādrī. While the elder women are represented as having seniority and hence higher status, the younger women are cast as having the husband's amorous attention. These imbalances serve to create situations of continuing insecurity for both women. A particularly fraught relationship between cowives is that of Kauśalyā and Kaikeyī in the *Rāmāyaṇa.* A *pativratā*, however, is expected to handle the situation with stoicism and grace. Draupadī, when faced with the fact of Subhadrā, must concede with dignity; the younger Subhadrā, meanwhile, must conduct herself carefully, so as not to rouse the hatred and jealousy of the elder.

Satī

Satī is the logical end to the *pativratā* practices of a woman. Since all of her life is so much directed at serving her husband, being a *pativratā* also means, possibly, even terminating her own existence when he dies. This decision is typically instigated by two concerns. One is that by following her husband promptly on his death, a wife can better serve him in the next world. This course of reasoning is followed by Mādrī at the death of Pāṇḍu. She is so distraught by his death midcoitus that she decides to kill herself along with him. One of the reasons she cites for this is that he had died before he could achieve sexual fulfillment. She would therefore, she reasoned, follow him to the other world to serve him sexually there. "It is by lying with me out of desire that the best of the Bhāratas was destroyed. So how could I deprive him of his love in death?"[33] (I.116.26). The second sense is that it would be traitorous and disloyal for a wife to continue to enjoy the joys of this world after her husband is gone. Since all of life is structured around service of the husband, what purpose could there be to living once he is gone? The she-pigeon who becomes a *satī* in the *Śāntiparva* says as much in her parting words: "I have no purpose here, O Lord, living without you"[34] (XII.144.8).

She continues: "What decent woman would desire to live when deprived of her husband?"[35] (XII.144.8). The quick answer to this is that no decent woman would; once her husband has died, any *truly* faithful wife's will to live would surely expire. Thus, four of Kṛṣṇa's wives joined the conflagration at his funeral, to unite themselves with him at his death. Four of Vasudeva's wives followed the same course on Vasudeva's death. In this itself, we are told, is a woman's best spiritual interest. In the *Āśramavāsikaparva*, Vyāsa encourages the widows of the Kaurava warriors to plunge into the Gaṅgā and unite themselves with their slain husbands in the *anumaraṇa* pattern (that of following the husband after his death)[36]: "Those among you who want to share the worlds of your husbands, those excellent women should quickly plunge into the Gaṅgā, abandoning lethargy"[37] (XVI.41.18). As the sage grandsire Bhīṣma himself promises: "the woman who immediately follows her lord, as the pigeon did, goes to heaven and shines"[38] (XII.145.15).

It is necessary to point out that *satī* is not the most prevailing practice in the *Mahābhārata*. As one scholar points out, "The *Strīparva* is full of lamentations and funerals, but there is not a single case of *satī*. [It is only] the weapons and chariots of the warriors [that] are burnt with them."[39] Of the thousands of women encountered in narratives in the text, the *satī*s are negligible. Descriptions of *satī*s are distant and impressionistic, and the characters who become *satī*s are on the whole inconsequential.[40] In contrast, many powerful widows are seen in the text who never even entertain the idea of *satī*. Widows such as Satyavatī, Kuntī, Ambikā, and Ambālikā continue to perform their worldly functions much as before, are actively engaged in ritual life, and are influential political figures. The *Rāmāyaṇa* shows a similar pattern: the widows of Daśaratha continue to be active in the social and political sphere, and there is no suggestion of any radical change in comportment or lifestyle to reflect their widowed status. In the epics, therefore, there is little to presage the kind of extreme devaluation of widowhood that becomes commonplace in later Hinduism. Widows such as Satyavatī and Kuntī are some of the strongest, most influential, most politically astute of all characters in the text.

Having said that, however, the ideal of *satī* is clearly gaining ground in the social imagination. Some stories invest it with enough power for it to generate feelings of guilt and anxiety in the surviving wife. The adolescent widow Uttarā, for example, suffers anguished remorse when she delivers her son stillborn. She wails her fear that this is the result of her failure to follow Abhimanyu on his death in the battlefield—"Kṛṣṇa, I had made a vow that if Abhimanyu died on the battlefield, I would follow that hero without any loss of time. I did not, however, keep my vow, wicked that I am and fond of life. If I repair to him now, what will he say?"[41] (XIV.67.23–24) Her sad fear is that she had been an imperfect *pativratā*; she had continued to live even after he had perished. These attitudes reach their logical conclusion in texts such as the *Garuḍapurāṇa*, which declares that a woman does not become free from rebirth as a woman until she becomes a *satī* (II.4.91–100).

Widow Chastity

The same logic shelters the prohibition against widow remarriage, that it would be injurious to the memory of the husband. Again, the same caveat must be entered as above. Widow marriage appears to have been acceptable in at least some strains of the text. To cite one example, in the Nala-Damayantī episode, Damayantī advertises her readiness for a second marriage, assuming the death of her first husband. This advertisement elicits no astonishment or curiosity from the general public. Her suitors respond positively to the invitation, and prepare to assemble for the *svayamvara*.[42] Widow remarriage, therefore, even for a member of a high-profile family, may at one time have been acceptable. This apparent tolerance, however, is seen rapidly being superseded by the ideal of a single husband.

That widow remarriage had begun to be prohibited, or at least actively discouraged, is attested by the Dharma texts as well as by many statements in the text. In an episode in *Ādiparva*, for example, where members of a family argue about who should be sacrificed to the *rākṣasa* Baka, the wife insists that it should be she. Her reasoning is that if she died, at least her husband could marry again and raise their children. If he died, on the other hand, she would have to continue alone.[43] "After you have given me up, lord, you will find another woman, and then your *dharma* will once again be established. It is not against *dharma* for a man to have many wives . . . but for a woman it is a serious transgression of *dharma* to pass over her first husband"[44] (I.146.34–35). It would be a violation of *dharma* for a woman to marry again. Thus the she-pigeon in *Śāntiparva* would sooner die than live widowed: "All widowed women, even with many children, are miserable. O high-minded one, without their husbands, they become the object of pity for their relatives"[45] (XII.144.2).

Numerous statements in the text express disgust with women who remarry. In the *Anuśāsanaparva*, a *brāhmaṇa* who marries a widow is classified among those who lose their caste. The *brāhmaṇa* Gautama is held to be fallen because of his marriage to a widow, and is despised by his peers. "A heavy curse was pronounced upon him by the gods to the effect that having fathered, within a few years, numerous children in the womb of his remarried wife, that awful sinner should sink into hell"[46] (XII.167.17). Becoming a widow therefore ideally means conducting herself in a state of intense bereavement for the rest of her life. If a woman does not follow her husband immediately to the other world, she should continue to be loyal to him, to worship if not him personally, then at least his memory. It would be a "terrible breach of *dharma*" for her to attempt to start another life. She should live with the expectation of being rejoined with him when she herself dies. Thus Kuntī, in the *Āśramavāsikaparva*, will not allow herself to enjoy the sovereignty earned by her sons. Insisting that she had had her share of wealth and glamour when her husband was alive, she tells Yudhiṣṭhira that she had only stayed alive to see her sons achieve success. She will now live in austerity in the forest, in anticipation of her reunion with Paṇḍu (XV.23.17–21).

Virginity

The obsession with lifelong sexual partnership with but one single man, naturally leads into the exaggerated concern with female virginity to be found in the text. In principle, the *Mahābhārata* approves sexual involvement for a high-caste woman with only one man in her life. As noted above, it is expected that a woman will never "step over" her first husband. In exceptional cases, however, it can accept that she is sexually active with several different men, but the ideal of female virginity is never compromised. Each new male partner receives a virgin bride. Thus, the unorthodox nature of Draupadī's polyandrous marriage is resolved with the promise of serial virginity. She is stated to be restored to purity after each of her five marriages (I.191.14). Kuntī shows herself to be worldly-wise and savvy about these matters: she agrees to sexual intercourse with Sūrya only after he promises to restore her virginity (I.104.12). Satyavatī is enticed into negotiating her sexuality with the same tools; after *ṛṣi* Parāśara promises to reinstate her virginity, she yields to his desires (I.57.64). The fear that Uttarā's virginity had been jeopardized motivates the king of Virāṭa to offer her in marriage to her erstwhile dance instructor, Arjuna (IV.66.27). The desire to *allay* that fear motivates Arjuna to accept Uttarā as wife for his son (IV.67.2–9). In the most notorious instance, Mādhavī, after four virgin marriages and four children borne to four different men, is restored to virginity yet a fifth time, in preparation for her *svayamvara* (V.114.10)! There is thus a strong attachment to the ideal of virginity, at least for high-caste women.

Seclusion

The seclusion of women is not practiced in the *Mahābhārata*. We see it in specific instances, such as when a woman is menstruating. In the most notorious case, we know that Draupadī was dragged into the assembly hall by Duḥśāsana while she was in her monthly seclusion in the women's quarters, and this fueled the sense of outrage felt by her supporters in the *Sabhāparva*. Apart from that, there seems to be little evidence for the seclusion of women as a practice. All the primary female characters of the text are seen in public arenas at one time or another. Gāndhārī is present for numerous events in the assembly hall. Kuntī and Satyavatī are both visible in the public sphere, without any inhibitions. Draupadī, outside of that one instance, may be witnessed on the battlefield, in active discussion with her husbands and the sages of the forest, as well as in conversation with strangers in the forest (as in the case of Jayadratha III.251). Uttarā is spied speaking freely to her brother in the assembly hall of Virāṭa (IV.35). In the *Udyogaparva*, we are told that women came out onto the streets, to witness Kṛṣṇa's arrival in Hastināpura (V.82.14). Similarly, at the close of the *Sabhāparva*, we are informed that women appeared on the streets, grief-stricken at the departure of the Pāṇḍavas (II.72.20).

At the same time, however, we see the ideal of female seclusion creeping into the text. In the *Strīparva*, we are told that women who had never been seen by the sun or moon now appeared in public disarray, uncaring of decorum in their grief (XI.9.15). We see thus the ideas of gentility being connected with privacy and seclusion. Women thus assume their commitment to their husbands long before they ever meet them, and possibly, long after their husbands have departed the world. Increasingly, we see their lives circumscribed by this one relationship. They grow up sheltered from the public gaze, away from the eyes of prospective admirers. They protect their virginity for the man they marry. They exercise stern mental and physical loyalty to their husbands while they are married. They prefer to die before their husbands, but if they do not, they remain committed to their memory, in moderate or extreme ways.

Reinforcement of Pativratā *Ideals*

Not only do cultural practices underwrite the aims of *pativratā dharma*, but these aims are consistently and continuously boosted in both positive and negative ways. A *pativratā* woman is supplied with a selection of eminent role models to help her mold her own behaviors. She is also promised a generous package of benefits and rewards, to be reaped both here and in the afterlife. On the negative scale, women who dissent in their behavior are either virulently condemned, or else effaced altogether from their religious symbology.

ROLE MODELS. On the positive scale, *pativratā* values are endorsed by a bevy of highly exalted role models. There are many, many examples in the *Mahābhārata* of women practicing one or other element of *pativratā dharma*. We have witnessed Draupadī above, but in *Śāntiparva*, we hear Śāṇḍilī espousing the same faith. When asked by Sumana by what means she had earned residence in heaven, she responded that it was through *pativratā dharma*. She says, "I did not wear red robes, nor barks of trees. I did not shave my head, or wear matted locks. It is not because of these that I am so blessed. I never spoke harsh or hurtful words to my husband. Never did I speak to him carelessly"[47] (XIII.124.8–9).

In the *Āraṇyakaparva*, the entire *Rāmāyaṇa* is pressed to the service of the *pativratā* creed. It is retold as an illustration of the sufferings of virtuous and devoted wives (III.258–75). Draupadī is clearly shaped and encouraged in her efforts by reflecting on the lives of famous *pativratā* wives. The story of Sītā is told to her, so that she may draw inspiration from it for her own conduct. Close behind Sītā follows the love story of Sāvitrī, the most formidable of *pativratā*s, who wrested her husband Satyavat away from the grip of death itself (III.277–83). The story concludes with the statement that "Thus Sāvitrī by her toils saved them all—herself, her father and mother, her mother-in-law and father-in-law, and her husband's entire dynasty. So will the auspicious Draupadī, esteemed for her character, rescue all of you"[48] (III.183.14–15). This is preceded by the evocative narrative of Damayantī,[49] who, through misfortune and sorrow, clung tenaciously to her husband, until by dint of sheer perseverance, she finally got him back (III.50–78). These women are shown to be of heroic temperament and strenuous resolve. They are resourceful and intelligent in pursuit of the goals to which they are committed. Draupadī and the Pāṇḍavas pass their years in the forest listening to such edifying discourses. That Draupadī was clearly moved by them, and had deeply internalized ideals of *pativratā* behavior herself, is evident in her conversation with Satyabhāmā, cited earlier. Here, it is Draupadī who expatiates on proper womanly conduct. She has self-consciously modeled herself on the *pativratā*s of old, and by this time, has joined that distinguished species to achieve the same heights of glory.

If one were concerned that God might be disgruntled at His/Her displacement in the lives of women by mere mortals, one need not fear. Draupadī's attestations and demeanors are approved by God Himself. The *Aśvamedhikaparva* relates an instance where Kṛṣṇa mildly suggests that Arjuna's cheekbones are too high (XIV.89.7). Peeved at this ascription of any fault whatsoever to one of her husbands, Draupadī bristles with indignation. Kṛṣṇa notices it, and approves her show of loyalty to her husband (XIV.89.10). Similarly, in the *Śāntiparva*, Umā, the Mahādevī, herself endorses the *pativratā* campaign. The same Umā who in other traditions is represented iconically as standing triumphant on the prone body of her husband, the mother of the universe, a match for her husband in every respect, is here heard espousing *pativratā* ideology. She says: "The husband alone is the god of women. The husband is their only relation. The husband is their destiny. There is no refuge like that of the husband, there is no god like him"[50] (XIII.134.51). She goes on to say that if the husband, however lacking in personal virtues himself, should command the wife to accomplish anything at all, even what is improper or unrighteous or leads to her very death, the wife should unhesitatingly accomplish it, taking recourse in the law of Distress (XIII.134.54). The invocation of the doctrine of *āpaddharma* elaborates that, just as hunger, thirst, privation, and severe emergency can extenuate an individual from observing the usual ethical precepts, in the same way, the command of the husband extenuates a wife from usual ethical conduct. At the command of her lord Sudarśana, therefore, Oghāvatī prostituted herself with a stranger—with no reprisals, because she did it in deference to her husband's wishes (XIII.2.33–95). For the sake of her husband, the "devoted wife" in *Āraṇyakaparva* neglected the usual imperatives of hospitality toward *brāhmaṇa*s, because she was engaged in the service of her husband (III.197). The Great Goddess not only approves these violations of *dharma*, but herself decrees them, since they are committed in the service of the husband. Similarly, Mahādeva, the great god Śiva, also shows no resentment at being ousted in women's worship by the husband. Umā's homilies on women are fully applauded by him[51] (XIII.134.56).

REWARDS OF *PATIVRATĀ DHARMA*. The *pativratā* woman is also promised many rewards. In the stories cited above, Sukanyā, married to the cranky, aged, but nevertheless libidinous Cyavana, is rewarded for her service by her husband being transformed into a handsome youth (III.122–24). In the parallel story of Sukumārī, Sukumārī is rewarded for her punctilious service of her monkey-husband Nārada, with Nārada eventually being transformed into his usual, presumably appealing, self (XII.30.37). We have in the *Āraṇyakaparva* an entire chapter (*pativratopākhyānam* III.197) that illustrates some of the powers of "the devoted wife." In this episode, the wife, through her devoted ministrations to her husband, is able to divine the inner turmoil of the *brāhmaṇa* mendicant Kauśika, as well as to clairvoyantly see into his recent past. Her mastery of *pativratā dharma* had given her such insight. In this scenario she, although a simple housewife, is elevated above the *brāhmaṇa* in her knowledge of esoteric truths. Understanding his quest, she directs him in his search, and points him in the direction of the hunter from whom he acquires wisdom (III.197.41–42).

Such rewards come naturally to a woman who is earnestly devoted to *pativratā dharma*. The rewards that ascetics gain after many years of rigorous austerities, a *pativratā* can accomplish simply by controlling her sexuality and remaining a chaste and faithful conjugal partner. As Umā says, "That auspicious woman who holds her husband to be the highest lord, and is avowed to her husband achieves merit, austerities, and eternal heaven"[52] (XIII.134.50). In other words, a *pativratā* woman need not stand on one toe for a hundred years, or sit amid blazing fires in the merciless heat of summer. She need not live eating one leaf every fourth day, or stand perfectly still on one leg, with arms raised above her head, in a pool of icy water. If she takes her husband to be her very God, and serves him as one in every way, completely forgetful of herself, this will suffice to achieve the same effects. We have a legion of examples illustrating this in the text: some of the most famous women of the *Mahābhārata* achieve their fame through commitment to their partners, and discipline over their sexual urges. Gāndhārī, Draupadī, Damayantī, Sāvitrī, and others, for example, all have the power, acquired through sexual chastity alone, to curse people and to vaporize or incinerate them. Damayantī, when assaulted by a would-be rapist, has only to solemnly intone: "If even in my heart I have never thought of any man but Nala, so let this brute who lives off animals fall dead!"[53] (III.60.37). She has only to pronounce this once to have it come true: the man immediately keels over dead. Sāvitrī similarly is able to revive her dead husband by the same means; she uses her devotion to her husband as a bargaining tool for the release of her husband from death. She gains sway over the hitherto implacable god of death himself; Yama grants her wish, and Satyavat shortly returns to life (III.277–83). Gāndhārī is famed for her generous empathy for her blind husband. Her singular refusal to see anything that he himself could not see is one of the most spectacular examples of *pativratā dharma*, and the source of her astonishing paranormal powers. Thus, she is able to curse Kṛṣṇa himself, along with his clan, to extinction, and have it come true (XI.25.36–42). Similarly, at the end of the war, Yudhiṣṭhira seeks to avoid Gāndhārī, because he knows that if enraged over the death of her hundred sons, she could burn each of the Pāṇḍavas to ashes. Gāndhārī, however, maintains her self-control for all but one moment. In that one instant, her fiery gaze scorches Yudhiṣṭhira's toe (XI.15.6). Draupadī is said to be able to demolish her assailants by her own inner power, but restrains herself for the greater glory of her husbands. And Sītā's example in the *Rāmāyaṇa* cannot be outdone: in the *Yuddhakāṇḍa*, she is able to forestall fire itself from burning her. Not a hair on her head is singed, or even a flower on her garland withered (*Rām.* VI.120). In the *Uttarakāṇḍa*, she is able to command the earth to open up beneath her (*Rām.* VII.97). Such is the power of her extraordinary chastity. Another famous *pativratā* from the *Rāmāyaṇa*, Anasūyā, is able to revive the dead, while others elsewhere are able to keep the sun from rising.[54] In the southern epic, the Cilappatikāram, the *pativratā* Kannaki is able to destroy the entire Pandya kingdom with her curse.[55]

Pativratā dharma yields the rewards of asceticism because it is conceived as a discipline equivalent to asceticism itself. This is because the level of self-negation required to practice it truly, to hold somebody else as the center of oneself, and to devote every ounce of one's attention and energy to anticipating and fulfilling that person's needs, cannot be any less difficult than the physical negation of the desires of the body, or the effacement of the self in surrender to God. It requires exceptional conviction, discipline, and will. This is why the *tapas* accumulated through *pativratā dharma* is deemed no less than that generated by asceticism or *bhakti*.

Pativratā dharma is also interposed into society in negative ways.

MARGINALIZATION OF DISSENTERS. No space is envisioned for women outside of the *pativratā* ideology. At all stages of life, women's lives are seen to be absorbed in their husbands, present, future, or past. As young unmarried girls, women are seen fretting about guarding themselves for marriage. Kuntī voices this concern when solicited by Sūrya: "Father, mother, gurus and others rise to give away this body. I do not want to violate *dharma*. Women's protection of their bodies is honoured in this world. I called you only to learn the power of my *mantra*, O resplendent one. Considering it the childish act of a child, you must forgive me, Sir."[56] (III.290.22–23). Similar reservations are voiced by Tāpatī to Saṃvaraṇa: She refers her suitor to her father because, "I am not mistress of this body, for I am a girl with a father. I cannot come near you, for women are never independent"[57] (I.161.16). Satyavatī expresses similar concerns to Parāśara, but they are quickly foiled by the powerful sage[58] (I.57.61–62). Because of the high premium placed on virginity, a young woman seeks to protect herself from any who would encroach on it, because she is saving herself for the one man she will marry.

Once women marry, however, one might think that the fears of jeopardizing chastity could be put to rest, but this is not the case. As married women, women's vigilance over their sexual conduct only increases. In the first case, if they spend any time at all apart from their husbands, they have to guard against the despoiling of their reputations. Śakuntalā's father recognizes this when he advises her to go to her husband, saying that a woman's reputation is jeopardized by living too long at her father's home: "It is not good for women to live too long with their family; it imperils their reputation, good conduct, and virtue"[59] (I.68.12). Sītā's story from the *Rāmāyaṇa* is well-known already. Even after her heroic resistance to Rāvana, she is not able to escape the suspicions of her husband (*Rām.* VI.117). So, the women's concern about reputation are not entirely misplaced. In the case of the *saptārṣis*' wives, for example, when it is alleged that six of them had slept with Agni, they are rejected by their husbands. Even when their innocence is attested by the culprit herself, Svāhā, who had impersonated them, the sages refuse to accept their wives back (III.215.13).

Second, women must be wary of sexual temptation of any sort. Hardly any example of female adultery can be found in the *Mahābhārata*, and yet the fear of women committing adultery looms as the biggest source of anxiety. When adulterous acts happen unwittingly, as for example, in the case of Ahalyā, who was beguiled by Indra's disguise as her husband into having intercourse with him, the reaction is quite severe. As we have seen previously, Ahalyā is ordered by her husband to be killed (XII.258). (In the *Rāmāyaṇa* story, she is turned into a stone *Rām.* I.48–49.) We have also encountered Renukā, the hapless wife of Bhārgava Jamadagni. She is punished by her husband with death, after he divines her momentary attraction to king Citraratha. Her head is struck off with an ax by her own son, Rāma Jāmadagni (III.116). In the *Umāmaheśvarasaṃvāda*, Umā specifies the standard for the behavior of married women. She says: "She who will not even look upon the Moon or Sun or a tree that has a masculine name, she who is committed to her husband, that lovely-waisted one is truly righteous"[60] (XIII.134.39). A truly faithful woman, therefore, one who is *truly* righteous, will allow nothing male whatsoever into her consciousness. She will not even allow her gaze to fall on objects that possess grammatically male gender.

If their married lives are cut short by widowhood, women's lives still continue to be dominated by concern for their husbands. As we have already noted, widows are not expected to remarry, out of respect for their husband's memory. In some cases, as cited above, they summarily *satī* themselves, like Mādrī and others. In other cases, like that of Bhadrā Kākṣīvatī, she mourns with such intensity at her husband's death that she compels her husband to return to earth to father children with her (I.112.15-ff.). In most cases, therefore, widowed women are expected to live lives of genteel austerity and forbearance. Though nowhere do we see any hint of a suggestion that they are inauspicious, or that they do not participate in daily life—Satyavatī, Ambikā/Ambālikā, Kuntī, and Uttarā certainly do—they live the remainder of their lives in anticipation of their heavenly reunion with their husbands. The question of remarriage is never entertained. The society is so constructed around the *pativratā* ideal of lifelong—and even beyond that, posthumous—devotion to one single man, that this is the only normative role envisioned for women. No space can be imagined outside of it. Thus, we have statements like, "The father protects her in childhood, the husband protects her in youth, and the son protects her in old age. A woman should never be independent"[61] (XIII.21.19). There is no space recognized for a *kulaṅganā*, a woman of a respectable household to live in the world, outside of the *pativratā* paradigm. Ambā discovers this when she is rejected by her lover, Śālva. She is left with no recourse but to either marry Bhīṣma, or to renounce the world altogether and take the ascetic path. Eventually, she takes to austerities with a bitter purpose.

Pativratā Dharma as a Strategy of Sexual Control

It is possible to read the ideal of *pativratā dharma* as a sophisticated mechanism for the psychological control of women's sexuality. With simplicity, it achieves what Vipula could accomplish only crudely with Ruci: it internally binds and gags a woman so as to severely inhibit her sexually. It tames a woman's desire, shapes and molds it into one direction so the woman herself embraces it. It is a self-imposed restraint, but the more effective for being self-imposed, because it is a standard that a woman unconsciously adopts and internalizes; she herself aspires to emulate it in her life. She herself exercises vigilance over her conduct, monitoring her thoughts and movements so as to conform to it. As a strategy of sexual control, therefore, *pativratā dharma* is prodigiously effective. It is self-perpetuating, self-monitoring, and self-disciplining. And it is reinforced at every step. Where a truly fearless woman does penetrate its ideology, she learns that in the social sphere, there is no space envisioned for her. All the supports, myths, and even divinities of the society valorize the *pativratā dharma*. She is not represented anywhere in the symbolism of her world. Every representation of decency in womanhood is of *pativratā*-hood. To break the mould under these circumstances, therefore, is to risk not only social ignominy, but psychological dysfunction.[62]

Pativratā Dharma as *Karma Yoga*

We have so far interpreted *pativratā dharma* through the hermeneutics of suspicion, as an immensely potent strategy for the control of women's sexuality. Through an emic hermeneutics, it may also be interpreted as a technique of *karma yoga*. The *karma yoga* doctrine taught by Kṛṣṇa in the *Gītā yoga* aims for the relocation of one's religious focus from one's own limited ego onto something else—one's socially prescribed duty, or *dharma*. In the case of Arjuna, the duty most pertinent to his situation at the commencement of the *Gītā* was his class duty—his responsibility as a *kṣatriya*, a warrior, to fight the *dharmic* fight forsaking all other considerations. Kṛṣṇa advises Arjuna to simply do his duty, setting aside thoughts of both, personal gain and personal aversion. The practice of *pativratā dharma* may also be viewed as a variety of *karma yoga*. Here, a woman is enjoined to do her socially prescribed duty as a woman, setting aside all thoughts of her own person. By disentangling herself from her own ego-desires, the gratification of her own likes and dislikes, and by directing her attentions outward, she aspires to the kind of egolessness that premises all religious striving in the Indian traditions. She disengages her actions from the emotional vicissitudes of her will, and places herself on a course that is predetermined by society, that is held to be true and constant: the path of *dharma*. The dedication to *dharma* is then both empowering and liberating. The loss of self-esteem one might anticipate in a woman's effacement of herself before her husband is mitigated by the empowerment she experiences in her stolid commitment to *dharma*. This is why the most engaging *pativratā*s to be found in the text—Sāvitrī, Draupadī, Damayantī—are women of towering self-esteem. They are strong, confident, self-assured and resolute. Their epic fortitude is derived from the knowledge that they live in principled devotion to *dharma*. While on the superficial level, these women live in subjection to the wills of their husbands, devoted to their husbands before all else, in actual fact their prior commitment is to what they perceive as being their authentic duty as women, their truest *dharma*. Draupadī says as much in her spirited defence of herself in the Kaurava court: "The king, son of *Dharma*, abides by *dharma*, and *dharma* is subtle, even for the skilled to find out. But even at the behest of my husband, I would not act wrongly and abandon my virtue"[63] (II.60.31). Her attachment to what she perceives as her *dharma* is absolute. Sāvitrī demonstrates the same resolve in her commitment to Satyavat. When her father attempts to dissuade her from marrying him, she flatly refuses to reconsider her choice. "Long-lived or short-lived, virtuous or virtueless, I have become avowed to my husband, and will not choose another. Having made the decision with my mind, I am stating it in words, and shall accomplish it with my actions later. My mind is my authority"[64] (III.278.26–27). Women's agency is everywhere apparent in these narratives.

Pativratā women are by far the best and most common examples of *karma yogins* that we have in either of the epics. They fulfill all the ideals of the doctrine. They act without desire for themselves, in a mood of *niṣkāma karma*; they care not what trials and challenges they face on their path—exiles and abductions, unremitting physical hardship and various types of personal indignities: all these they take in stride, undeterred from their larger purpose. Uncowed by threats (as in the *pativratopkhyāna* narrative), unimpressed by offers of better lives (Sāvitrī, Draupadī), they fulfill perfectly the ideals of *yogic* equanimity.[65] These women view themselves as being on the path of *karma yoga*, scrupulously avoiding the direction of their own petty wants and desires, and functioning instead studiously on the path of higher duty. They adopt the course charted by society of their own will and volition, and take tremendous pride in epitomizing the ideals they embody. Viewed in this light, *pativratā dharma* is not anything alien ascribed onto society. It is entirely consistent with the logic of the overall society, a society that encourages a virtuous adherence to principle, and a stoic tenacity to it in the face of all unpleasantness. Thus, paradoxically, while on the one level, *pativratā dharma* is clearly an ideology that limits and effaces the talents and potentials of women, on another level, as *karma yoga*, it is potentially also liberating in that it involves the quintessentially *yogic* technique of decentering oneself as the focal point of one's exertions, and committing oneself to a higher ideal (*dharma*).

The difficulty that a contemporary reader may have with the *pativratā* ideal, therefore, cannot be either with the women who embody it, or with the religious techniques that it employs. Both are heroic conceptions. As we have seen, the *pativratā* women of the *Mahābhārata* are some of the most powerful, intelligent, and resourceful characters of the text—certainly among the most memorable of epic heroes. In their stories, they embrace the dogma of *pativratā* consciously and with determination. They exercise their own agency, and claim the ethic as their own method of practising *dharma*. By interpreting it as *dharma*, moreover, and by pouring their allegiance into *dharma*, they in a sense even subvert the centrality of the husband. While the husband functions as the titular recipient of their devotions, therefore, the devotions are actually offered to *dharma*—something that is construed by the culture as universally true and eternal.

In the same way, the difficulty cannot be located in the religious methods mobilized by *pativratā dharma*. The *karma yoga* techniques exploited by *pativratā dharma* form the basis of all religious striving in Hinduism. Any way that one approaches it, liberation (*mokṣa*) can only be achieved by distancing one's exertions from the gratification of personal motives. Some people achieve this kind of distance by redirecting their lives to God (*bhakti yoga*). The service of God then motivates and grounds their actions. Others aspire to the same kind of distance by positing a spirit, or Self, anterior and more ancient than the limited ego (*jñāna yoga*). The concern for the actualization of the Self then motivates them. In every case, the insights of *karma yoga* are presupposed. All traditions hold that one cannot take the pendulous oscillations of one's mind as the guide to right action. One must commit oneself to a higher *dharma*.

The difficulty then, may be located in the *content* of the *dharma*. One may, in other words, quarrel with the social biases that frame *dharma* as inegalitarian and hierarchical. One might argue, for example, with a *dharma* that privileges male above the female in such a way that the female is represented as secondary and subservient, while the male is represented as primary and worthy of devotion. This would be the right perspective from which to quarrel with the doctrine of *pativratā dharma*, a doctrine that is, to my mind, a transparent, highly potent and ultimately most pernicious device for the psychological control of women's sexuality.

Chapter Six

Āpaddharma

So far in this study, we have looked closely at ideologies of sex as they are embedded within the renunciant orientation referred to as *nivṛtti*, and the more world-affirming orientation called *pravṛtti*. In this chapter, I would like to highlight a third category of *dharma*, called *āpaddharma*. *Āpaddharma* is one of the three broad categories of *dharma* explicated at length to Yudhiṣṭhira in the *Śāntiparva* of the *Mahābhārata* (the others being *rājadharma* 'the *dharma* of kingship' and *mokṣadharma*, 'the *dharma* of freedom'). *Āpaddharma* refers to the "*dharma* of difficult times"—times when the limits of ordinary life are stretched to the point where individuals are forced into unorthodox actions to help themselves. The section on *āpaddharma* in the *Śāntiparva* is an exploration of how the laws and regulations applicable during ordinary times may be abrogated in circumstances of unusual stress.

The discussion of *āpaddharma* begins with Yudhiṣṭhira's question to Bhīṣma:

> When true righteousness declines, when everybody violates *dharma*; when the wrong is deemed right, and the right becomes wrong; when tradition has been decimated; when the resolve to do right has been shaken; when, Lord, the world is oppressed by kings or thieves; when all the paths of life are confused; when rites are obstructed; when everyone is imperilled by lust, attachment, and greed, Bhārata; when no one feels trust and is always fearful, Prince; when people are killed through nefarious means and people deceive each other; when countries burn and Brahmanism is oppressed; when the God of rain has not rained; when ruptures occur; when every earthly occupation has been usurped by *dasyus*—when that darkest of times has come, how is a *brāhmaṇa* to live?
>
> Tell me, grandfather, how can one go on in times of distress? (XII.139.1–8)[1]

In response, Bhīṣma expatiates on the complexity of *dharma*. There are, he says, circumstances in which "speaking a falsehood is better than speaking the truth";[2] when the wise rely upon the "power of discriminating knowledge" (*vijñānabalam*) to discover the right course of action (XII.130.3); when one must follow the course of true wisdom instead of one's received learning (XII.140.9); when the book learning of people is revealed to be the way of simple-minded fools (XII.140.13 *apakkamatayo mandā*) who don't understand that there are two paths, two ways, two levels of knowledge and wisdom[3] (XII.140.8). He then speaks of *āpaddharma*: under extraordinary strains, people must sometimes do extraordinary things; if they atone for these lapses later, they suffer no net loss in merit.

Descriptions of the conditions necessitating recourse to *āpaddharma* might lead one to suppose a connection between the theory of *āpaddharma* and the doctrine of the four successively degenerate ages, particularly the *kaliyuga*, in which much that should not happen, does. Indeed, this would be suggested by an explicit reference to the *yuga* context; Yudhiṣṭhira asks Bhīṣma: "How, Grandfather, does one remain steadfast, when the ages are in decline, *dharma* wanes away, and the world is oppressed by the uncivilized?"[4] (XII.138.1). In such a time, diseases, droughts, famines, and other natural disasters occur with greater frequency. Wars are endemic. People's moral sense is thick and dull, and their ability to discriminate between right and wrong is weak. In the four *yuga* conception, *āpatti*, or distress of all varieties is more likely to occur in *kaliyuga* than at any other time, but because *kaliyuga* also bespeaks diminished intellectual and moral capacity, people are less able to cope with distress. Such a connection, however, while suggested in some passages, is avoided in others; indeed, some of the examples of *āpatti* are cited as being at the cusp of the *tretā* and *dvāpara yugas* (XII.139.14). Conditions of *āpatti* reveal humanity at its most frail, most vulnerable to physical, social, and moral lapse; severe afflictions test people's moral resolve, hence a greater flexibility is required.

There are several kinds of exceptions sanctioned by *āpaddharma*. One refers to actions that are necessary to cope with natural disasters. An evocative story illustrating this use of *āpaddharma* is that of the sage Viśvāmitra, told in the *Śāntiparva* (XII.139). Starving because of the severe drought conditions prevailing, Viśvāmitra stumbles across a *caṇḍāla* settlement. *Caṇḍālas*, as we have had occasion to observe, are the lowest of the low subcastes, despised as impure and unclean, worse even than dirty dogs;[5] they are "dog-eaters" (*śvapaca*). The scenario is intended to illustrate the extreme measures that are justified in times of most uncommon distress. In the midst of a famine, Viśvāmitra is so starved for food that he attempts to steal the food of a *caṇḍāla*—the backside of a dog (*śvajāghanī* XII.139.47). This represents the worst possible state of affairs in terms of Viśvāmitra's class purity. The derriere of a dog is obviously the most unclean part of what is considered a most unclean animal. Further, it belongs to a *caṇḍāla*, who performs dirty work in the community, and therefore represents ritual uncleanliness. Taking the food without asking furthermore constitutes stealing, which represents moral uncleanliness. The levels of uncleanliness are compounded in the story to yield the idea that what Viśvāmitra goes to do here would under ordinary conditions be considered highly reprehensible for somebody of his status, physically repulsive but also so defiling as to entirely compromise his *varṇa* status. Viśvāmitra, however, appeals to *āpaddharma*. When caught red-handed stealing from the *caṇḍāla*, he argues that in times of extreme crisis, his first duty is to ensure his survival: "A long time has elapsed without my having eaten any food. I see no means for preserving my life. One should, when one is dying, preserve one's life by any means, practising *dharma* if possible"[6] (XII.139.58–59). He goes on to argue that the body is one's closest friend, and it is one's duty to ensure its continuance before worrying about the moral propriety of one's actions (XII.139.73). "By whatever means life may be preserved, it should be done without scruple. Life is better than death; living, one may practise virtue"[7] (XII.139.61). This explanation is accepted as reasonable, and Viśvāmitra's moral purity is not besmirched through these actions.

A parallel story is told of the seven sages (XIII.94). They are shown wandering through the wilderness in a state of desperate starvation, unable to procure food at a time of drought and famine. With them, they have the body of king Śaibya's son, who had been given to them as a *dakṣiṇā*, but had died. Realizing that they would all die of starvation if they did not eat, they resolved to cook the dead body, and to eat it. This again represents the nadir of human experience—where, because of sheer desperation, seven eminent *brāhmaṇa*s are forced to cannibalism. Taking recourse in *āpaddharma*, they resolve to eat the body, to enable sheer survival.[8]

The above are the kinds of situations to which the theory of *āpaddharma* generally speaks: situations in which people are so distraught or stricken by circumstance that they are led to performing acts ordinarily considered grossly reprehensible. *Āpaddharma* thus may apply to the conduct of either an individual, or society at large. Less moral endurance can be expected of the entire society in difficult times, and less strength can be expected of individuals when in crisis.

Since *āpaddharma* represents deviations from prevailing norm, its primary application is to *pravṛtti dharma*. As suggested earlier, the *nivṛtta* path itself necessitates the abrogation of social conventions and meaning complexes. Considerations of high and low, of pure and impure, clean and unclean, are of minimal significance in the *nivṛtti* worldview, which aims to extricate itself from these categorizations of experience altogether. Thus in the *nivṛtti* view, *āpatti* represents only the extremes of the sorrow, anxiety, and deprivation that characterize ordinary existence. *Āpatti* therefore should inspire not wonder or dismay, but wisdom; it serves a soteriological purpose, in that it may radically induce in an individual the realization of the futility of life. *Āpaddharma* thus is of relevance to the boundaries of *pravṛtti dharma*—those that direct people's interactions with each other, and with their environment.

The questions pertinent to our discussion of gender, then, are the following: Aside from the natural catastrophes that afflict equally all human beings, are there any conditions that are thought to constitute distress specifically for a woman? And if so, what deviations from norm are permissible to women in distress?

Women in *Āpatti*, "Distress"

While there are numerous contexts in which women are represented as the *source* of distress to society, the distress *of* women is comparatively little theorized. Thus, women figure as key ingredients in the breakdown of society in descriptions of the *kaliyuga*. In that time of painful chaos, women are of weak moral fiber. They are corrupt and deceitful, and lasciviously fornicate with slaves and cattle.[9] They are aggressive and rude of tongue (*krūravādinyaḥ*), easily unsettled emotionally, and are disobedient to their husbands.[10] They even kill their husbands, cherishing their sons instead.[11] In general, they are intolerant of their husbands and bear many girls. Their moral failings are reflected in their physical unattractiveness; they are ungainly and hirsute.[12] These descriptions of women are typical of others that characterize *kaliyuga*, and are consistent with the state of chaos that prevails in *kaliyuga*: juniors question and exert authority over their natural seniors, servants treat their masters as slaves, and *śūdra*s employ *brāhmaṇa*s to do menial work in their homes. Women contribute to the general collapse of civilization through neglect of social and familial duty. They lose reverence for the codes of behavior encouraged by *pativratādharma*, and act in ego-indulgent, idiosyncratic ways. Hence they are critical agents in *creating* the distress signaled by the age and are the source of disquiet and difficulty.

Women are also, however, thought to *suffer* distress of a variety that excuses errant behavior. Thus, there is a general recognition in the text that women are often sexually victimized by powerful men. Consequently, some latitude is extended to women who suffer in such ways (more on this below). More formally, however, women figure in the allowances of *āpaddharma* in primarily two contexts: (1) Explicitly, women may take refuge in *āpaddharma* when the situation of distress involves procreation; (2) implicitly, women may act in undesirable ways when *pativratā dharma* is at stake. In several instances, *pativratā dharma* itself is construed as a variety of *āpaddharma* admitting deviation from recognized orthodox conduct.

Women Desiring Children

One compelling factor mitigating women's departure from sexual norm centers on the desire for children. As is well known, ancient India placed a high value on progeny. In the epic, this is the object of many a character's prayers, austerities, and other efforts: Satyavatī contrives various stratagems to acquire descendants for her son Vicitravīrya; Pāṇḍu performs austerities for children; Gāndhārī similarly appeals to Vyāsa; Drupada undertakes sacrifices for the birth of Draupadī and Dṛṣṭadyumna. In the Anuśāsanaparva, even Kṛṣṇa is seen engaged in austerities for the sake of a son. The value of children is further attested by the number of significant characters adopted and reared by nonbiological parents. Śakuntalā is adopted by the *ṛṣi* Kaṇva (I.66.13), and Pramadvarā by the *ṛṣi* Sthūlakeśa (I.8.7). Satyavatī is adopted by the fisherchief who later exerts himself to protect her interests. Kuntī is adopted and raised by Kuntībhoja (I.104.3). Karṇa is adopted by the *sūta* couple Adhiratha and Rādhā (I.104.14). Though boys are inarguably deemed more desirable than girls, children in general are treated as a profound blessing, the most treasured of gifts. Apart from obvious emotional, genealogical, and economic benefits they could bring, offspring number among the three debts to be repaid to one's forbears in Vedic society. Thus, *ṛṣi* Mandapāla is barred from heaven because he does not have offspring (I.220). *ṛṣi* Agastya chances upon his forebears suspended upside-down because they have not been propitiated through offspring from him (III.94). Procreation is thus both a need and a duty, and its purposes are supported in the text through ritual, devotional, and social apparatus.

Āpatti results when a couple is deprived of progeny. Whatever the causes of the childless state, it occasions genuine and acute distress. Thus, Satyavatī is deeply worried about the political and religious ramifications of her widowed daughters-in-law being childless; Pāṇḍu is equally anguished about his own inability to engage in procreative sex. Such distress, as Satyavatī argues to Bhīṣma, warrants drastic measures; through appeal to *āpad-dharma*, one may circumvent the norm of sexual relations for the express purpose of gaining children[13] (I.97.22). The practice of *niyoga* is proposed as one such unorthodox measure.

Niyoga is the custom of levirate marriage, a special provision in the sexual ethics of ancient and classical India. It is a response to the *āpatti* occasioned by childlessness; its express allowance is for a woman to obtain children through the instrument of another man, if her husband has been unsuccessful in giving her any. *Niyoga* is quite a common occurrence in the text; indeed, it is critical to the plot of the epic, which hinges on *niyoga* for the birth of two generations of its major characters—Dhṛtarāṣṭra, Pāṇḍu, Vidura, as well as the five Pāṇḍavas are all born of *niyoga* unions. The practice also has distinguished mythic referents. We are told that just as a woman, in the absence of her husband, accepts the husband's brother in his place, so Earth, in consequence of the refusal of the *brāhmaṇa*s, accepts his next-born, the *kṣatriya*, for her lord (XII.73.12). In the Bhārgava Rāma complex of myths, every time the *kṣatriya*s are obliterated from the earth, the *kṣatriya* women are said to revive their lineages through *niyoga* with the *brāhmaṇa*s (I.98.4–6). *Niyoga* is thus a well-established custom in the *Mahābhārata*, given the sanction of both myth and tradition.

Niyoga is employed under two circumstances. If a woman's husband proves unable to father children,[14] she could, with the permission of the family, resort to another man. Alternatively, if he died before impregnating his wife, she could take the same recourse. In both cases, the children ensuing would be the legal heirs of the husband. Brothers are favored above other choices of men,[15] but virtuous *brāhmaṇa*s are also lauded for their mental and spiritual *tejas*, "splendour"; indeed, in the *Mahābhārata*, all the cases of *niyoga* involve either gods or *brāhmaṇa*s.

The agency implied in statements saying that women should resort to other men (statements also found in the *Dharma* texts), is illusory, however, because in almost no instance does the woman initiate the process. Sometimes, the person most painfully in distress is the heirless husband. This is the case with Pāṇḍu, the father of the Pāṇḍavas. Desperate for children but unable to father any himself, Pāṇḍu pleads with his wife Kuntī to resort to *niyoga* and bear children for him with somebody else. In other examples, the *ṛṣi* Vasiṣṭha is invited by Queen Madayantī's husband Kalmāṣapāda Saudāsa to father children on Madayantī (I.113.21). The blind sage Dīrghatamas is invited by king Balin to father children on Balin's wife, Sudeṣṇā (I.98.17–32).

In other cases, children are solicited by concerned grandparents to continue an endangered family line. The most famous instance of this in the *Mahābhārata* is Satyavatī, the matriarch of the Bhāratas, who persuades her two widowed daughters-in-law to rescue the Bhārata clan from extinction by assenting to *niyoga* with Vyāsa.

Thus, while it may be tempting to interpret *niyoga* as an allowance that shows compassionate consideration for a woman's maternal sentiments, the urge is best restrained. As most of the narratives demonstrate, the *āpatti* at issue is that of the husband or the patrilineal unit, not of the woman; it is to redress the *man's* ritual incompleteness that *niyoga* is permitted. The woman is merely the *kṣetra*, the field of the husband, which he invites another man to implant.[16] It is for this reason that the husband (or his proxy) is the decisive agent. In the case of Kuntī, Pāṇḍu takes the decision for his wife to pursue *niyoga*. He determines the criteria for suitable *niyoga* partners, and is vitally involved at every step of the process. To prepare himself for his most formidable request, the request for Arjuna, it is *he* who fasts for a full year and undertakes austerities. In the case of Ambikā and Ambālikā, it is their mother-in-law Satyavatī who makes the decisions, determining the solution of *niyoga*, soliciting partners for her daughters-in-law, making all the attendant arrangements. The women themselves apparently have very little say in the process and are hapless and passive instruments for the will of their husbands and their affinal kin. Their own maternal ambitions receive no consideration.

It is the perceived desire of women that renders the practice problematic, on the hazy margins of sexual ethics. There is a clear recognition that through *niyoga* society may be flirting with disaster. Thus in the *Dharma* texts, the practice is outright forbidden by some thinkers (Āpastambha II.27.2–7). Others permit it, but cautiously (Gautama 18.4–8; Vasiṣṭha 17.55–66). Yet others very carefully specify that *niyoga* is explicitly for the purpose of reproduction; it is not sex for enjoyment, and must not to be approached with desire.[17] Indeed, it is a rite that needs to be engaged with the appropriate solemnity and seriousness of purpose.[18] Kuntī underscores this point to Pāṇḍu when he requests her for a fourth child through *niyoga*. Three, she tells him sternly, are enough. More than that would take her into murky moral territory since by that time, clearly, the need for children has been satisfied (I.114.65–66). Pāṇḍu accepts this explanation, and Kuntī's sacred *mantra* is then lent to her cowife Mādrī, so that Mādrī also may have children (I.115.15). *Niyoga* is thus a deeroticized variety of sexual activity; were it otherwise, it would constitute adultery. Thus, while *niyoga* represents a departure from the ideal of absolute monogamy prescribed for a woman, through such caveats against desire, it actually underwrites the objectives of female chastity. The woman's sexual agency is expressly for the sake of her husband; her procreative function is enlisted specifically for the perpetuation of the male ritual sphere. Personal maternal fulfillment may be a bonus, but it is not a motivating factor. Even where she acts on her own initiative,[19] the concern is to enable the man to thrive in the afterlife, to ensure the longevity of his lineage.

In many narratives, however, it is not only married women who acquire children by soliciting men. Unmarried woman also seek out men out of desire for children. We see this in the case of Sarmiṣṭhā, recounted in *Ādiparva*. When Sarmiṣṭhā is given to Devayānī as her slave, and has no prospects of marriage herself, she finally approaches Devayānī's husband, Yayāti. She tells him that although he has vowed to avoid intercourse with his slaves, he must not refuse her. A woman in her season must not be turned away. This argument carries weight; it is reinforced by pronouncements in the text as well as in the *Dharma* literature, all of which is unanimous on the point that if parents are remiss in marrying a woman off shortly after puberty, she may choose a man for herself. Yayāti is therefore persuaded. Having considered the issue, he allows: "If a man chosen by a woman who begs for her season refuses her, the wise call him an aborter"[20] (I.78.32). A woman who desires to bear children should be supported in her efforts to do so, even if she is not formally married to the man.

Prima facie, this attitude appears exceptionally liberal in a text that overall advocates conservative sexual conduct. A feminist might be tempted to view this as an instance of the text's regard for the maternal aspirations of women. Once again, however, caution is advised; as Patton, Schmidt, and Jamison have demonstrated, the latitude allowed the woman is more out of concern for the maximization of her fertile life. An unproductive menstrual period was viewed as akin to abortion, a most heinous crime; furthermore, if Patton is right, it was viewed as the abortion of a potentially learned Brahmin. It is to preserve the life of this *veda*-knowing *brāhmaṇa* that the departure from norm is sanctioned. This is the proper context for understanding the apparently coercive regulation that: "Those who know *dharma* have said this about it, that at the time of her season, a woman who is committed to her husband may not avoid her husband"[21] (I.113.25). This is matched by numerous parallel statements that it is a man's obligation to approach his wife during her fruitful season. The *āpatti* here is the potential murder of a potential (male) fetus, and the latitude extended is precisely to preclude that happening.

There are other instances of women importuning men sexually, expressly or implicitly out of the desire for children. The *rākṣasī* Hiḍimbā is one example. She falls in love with Bhīma after seeing him one night, sitting awake and guarding his family while it sleeps. When Bhīma's mother, Kuntī awakes, Hiḍimbā pleads with her to let her marry Bhīma (I.143). Kuntī agrees, but unlike a conventional marriage, when Hiḍimbā gives birth to a child, Hiḍimbā's marriage to Bhīma dissolves, and Bhīma returns to the care of his family. Thus, when Ghaṭotkaca is born, Hiḍimbā takes her child and departs, and is never heard from again. A similar situation occurs with Ulūpī and Arjuna. Ulūpī seduces the unresisting Arjuna, and lies with him for one night (I.206.14–33). Arjuna departs the next morning, and Ulūpī later gives birth to her son, Iravat, whom she raises on her own. Arjuna has no contact with either of them until much later, when Iravat participates in the war on the Pāṇḍava side. In yet another scenario, Arjuna falls in love with Citrāṅgadā, princess of Manalurā (I.207.15–23). They marry and Arjuna lives with her at her father's home for three months. By that time, she is pregnant and able to provide an heir for her sonless father. Arjuna, therefore, leaves them and continues on his adventures.

The latitude given to women desiring children may be seen even more pointedly in the case of Atri's wife (Anasūyā? She is left unnamed in the text), who is mentioned only briefly, in *Anuśāsanaparva* (XIII.14.65–67, 91*). We are told that the sage Atri's wife leaves her husband because she is tired of his domineering nature.[22] Leaving him, she takes to devotion of the god Śiva. Śiva grants her asylum, and sanctions her abandonment of her husband by promising that she can still bear children. Through Śiva's grace, she gives birth to a boy, and the text expressly states that she does not return to her husband; the child grows up with his mother's name.[23] This is a remarkable story from various perspectives. First, it is possibly the only example that we have in the entire text of a woman leaving her husband. It is also extraordinary that Anasūyā's abandonment of her husband is condoned, and supported, by a personage no less than Śiva himself, who in another context lauds *pativratādharma*. Her desire for a child is honored without her having to return to her husband.

All of the above women's behavior is unconventional in that it represents a departure from the ideal of gender relations, in which a woman is given by her parents to one man, and subsequently never even considers sexual involvement with another. While no doubt some of these departures serve the functions of an interesting narrative, these women's unorthodox behavior may also be construed as an appeal to *āpaddharma*—that a woman's duty to produce children is of such paramount importance that it functions as an extenuating condition overriding the usual conventions of society.

Pativratā Dharma

Another extenuating circumstance, it would seem, is *pativrata* itself. Women acting in accordance with the higher ideal of *pativrata* are in several cases excused from the usual expectations of womanly conduct. The *pativratā* in Āraṇyakaparva is one example. So absorbed is she in ensuring the comfort of her husband that she neglects the imperative to hospitality, leaving the mendicant *brāhmaṇa* standing at the door, to his great irritation. She is excused for this departure from norm because she was acting in service of her husband, forgetful of all else. This forgetfulness of self and the world, absorption of her self in the person of her husband, is precisely the condition that the ideology of *pativrata* seeks to achieve; hence the woman is lauded for her conduct and held to possess esoteric knowledge.

Another example of this forgetfulness may be located in the descriptions of bereaved women at the end of the *Mahābhārata* war. So distraught are they over the loss of their loved ones that they quite forgot themselves. The text says: "Those women who had never before been seen by the very gods, now, with their husbands slain, were seen by common people. Those who used to be embarrassed even before their own women friends now felt no shame, though clad in one cloth, before their fathers-in-law" (XI.9.15). While this is a departure from their usual discretion before strangers, their actions attract no *dośa*, or fault. Their neglect of decorum here is entirely appropriate to their widowed state; it is meant to underscore their status as loyal *pativratās*. Here *pativratā dharma* operates as a variety of *āpaddharma* that allows for deviations from the ideal.

Similarly, women appointed to *niyoga* are also deemed as acting in accordance with *pativratā* doctrine. As one passage states, "The virgin wife or widow may either pursue asceticism, or may go to the brother-in-law. Through such a marriage, she becomes known as a devoted and virtuous wife"[24] (XIII.44.50).

An extreme instance of such a situation may be seen in the case of Oghāvatī (XIII.2). Oghāvatī lies with a *brāhmaṇa*, a stranger, even though she is married to Sudarśana. She does this because her husband has made a vow of extending unstinted hospitality to whoever should visit his home. No matter what the visitor may solicit, the husband will unhesitatingly give it. When the *brāhmaṇa* impudently solicits Oghāvatī herself in her husband's absence, Oghāvatī is afraid to refuse for fear of jeopardizing her husband's vow. As a result, she engages in adulterous sex, in order to honor her husband's vow. Her act is excused precisely because she is viewed as acting not out of her own desire, but to protect her husband from the curse-wielding *brāhmaṇa*. Her concern is for the welfare of her husband hence she suffers no ill consequence.

In these scenarios, *pativratā dharma* permits deviations from proper conduct, but only for the overall valorization of the larger institution. The effect is therefore, arguably, more insidious. Women transgress the ideology of womanly behavior only to reinforce it at a deeper, more integral level.

Gray Areas

Having said all this, it must be noted that the *Mahābhārata* exhibits an overall generosity toward its major women characters; its attitude is generally charitable. As Sutton notes, "Whatever distaste the modern mind may feel for the discrimination against women embodied in the text, one cannot deny that it is the work of civilized men of largely compassionate intent" (2000, 430). The "genteel tone" of the epic is evident particularly in narratives where women are smitten by love, or where they are seen to be under the duress of powerful men. In these cases, there is a recognition that women are often victimized by oppressive patriarchal norms, and are treated with an empathic liberality, as laboring under exceptionally trying conditions.

Women in Love

Perhaps naturally for a creative literary work, in several narratives, love earns the indulgence of the writers, breaking the confining hold of dogma and ideology. Let us look, for example, at the story of Ambā (V.170–93). The eldest of three sisters abducted during their *svayamvara* by Bhīṣma, Ambā had already privately chosen her mate, the king Śālva, and was to make her choice public in the *svayamvara*. Before this could happen, however, she and her sisters were abducted. On arriving at the Kuru palace, Ambā bravely declares her involvement with Śālva and is given leave to return to him. But the story takes an epic turn when Śālva rejects her, citing fear of reprisal from Bhīṣma. When Ambā returns to Bhīṣma and demands that *he* marry her instead, and Bhīṣma, true to his vow of celibacy, refuses, Ambā, now twice rejected, departs into the wilderness, vowing revenge against Bhīṣma. Through extreme austerities, she is reborn into Drupada's family, and in adulthood transformed into the man Śikhaṇḍin, who eventually becomes the instrument of Bhīṣma's death in the war.

This story is handled with some sensitivity to the justice of Ambā's sentiments. She is cast as a woman genuinely wronged, and deserving redress. Of all the people who are blamed for her misfortunes—her father, Śālva, Bhīṣma—Ambā herself is never targeted for blame. At no point is it ever suggested that she had departed from womanly virtue for having known and loved Śālva before marriage, and for pledging herself to him. The sages of the forest accept her grievance as authentic, and support her desire for revenge. "Your words about *dharma* are correct, O beautiful and auspicious one," affirms one sage. "Listen also to my words: the revenge that you have fixed upon for Bhīṣma is proper" (V.176.9, 12).

The story of Svāhā is another example. Svāhā is one of the sixty daughters of the mythic king Dakṣa, with powers out of the ordinary. Later tellings of the same myth identify her with the goddess Umā. The first telling is found in the *Āraṇyakaparva* (III.213.42–215.23). She is a young woman deeply infatuated with the god Agni. Agni, however, has an adulterous infatuation of his own: he is smitten with the wives of the seven sages. The text describes him as suffering intensely in his love, his heart so aflame with desire (*kāmasaṃtaptahṛdayaḥ*) that he sets his mind to renouncing life (III.213.49). "Svāhā, seeing this, undertakes a bold deception. When she sees Agni depart for the forest, she decides, 'I will assume the forms of the seven seers' wives, and when he has been deluded by their shapes, I will make love to Agni who is tormented with desire. This done, he will be happy, and my own desire will be satisfied' "[25] (III.213.50–52). She transforms herself into a likeness of six of the seven wives, one at a time, and in that likeness, lies with Agni. After each encounter, she deposits the sperm in the wilderness. Eventually, this collection yields a six-headed child, who becomes known as Skanda.

What is remarkable about this account, given the overlay of *pativratā* ideology in the text, is that there is complete lack of moral judgment about the propriety of Svāhā's conduct. Throughout the narrative, Svāhā is depicted with sympathetic concern, characterized as "blameless" (*aninditā*), "radiant" (*bhāminī*), and so on. Even at the conclusion, when Svāhā, without any remorse, owns Skanda as her own child, Svāhā's sexual conduct is not disparaged in any way.

It could be argued that this story is a myth in the style of early Vedic myths, and carries with it the same kind of amoral consciousness that is prevalent in many of the myths of Vedic literature. The same kind of compassionate attitude, however, also pervades the narratives of other women suffering from love. Even dubious heroines such as Devayānī are treated with compassion. The willful and spoiled daughter of the renowned sage Śukra falls in love first with one man (Kaca I.72), and then with another (Yayāti I.73), in direct contravention of the ideal of *pativratā dharma*. Yet, she rouses nobody's moral ire. Similarly, even Renukā, who is so brutally punished by her husband for lusting after another man, is not disparaged by the writers of the text. The text reveals her husband to be a harsh tyrant, overbearing and authoritarian, and sympathetically contrasts his domineering presence with her own frightened timidity[26] (XIII.97.6–16, III.116.1–19).

It should be noted that the text has a natural admiration for the kind of obsessive single-mindedness shown by characters such as Svāhā, Ambā, Damayantī, and others. This is because, while departing from the ideals of *pativratā dharma*, they reinforce them at a more subversive level. *Pativratā dharma* is premised on the same kind of single-minded dedication to one man, the same purposeful determination to honor commitment to one man. Amba's fixation on Bhisma is inspired by hatred and revenge, but it is nevertheless an all-consuming devotion, worthy of admiration. Much unorthodox behavior may be forgiven in the service of that ideal.

Women Under Duress

Another area where the *Mahābhārata* makes allowances for unconventional sexual conduct is where women act under pressure from men. The parallel stories of Kuntī and Satyavatī are two examples. Satyavatī consorts with the puissant *ṛṣi* Parāśara after she finds herself alone with him on a ferry. Kuntī is helpless before the exalted Sūrya, and yields to him after he threatens the destruction of her family. Both women even bear children before marriage. These acts, which may be viewed from the dogmas of *pativratā dharma* to be unforgivable transgressions, worthy of stoning and other indignities, are defended by the text, and justified within the narrative. When Satyavatī confesses her story to Bhīṣma (I.99.5–17), he is respectful of her discretion, and does not question her moral fitness. Similarly, when Kuntī confesses her story to her father-in-law, Vyāsa exonerates Kuntī: "No fault can be ascribed to you. You were restored to virginity. The deities are powerful and are able to penetrate human bodies" (XV.38.20). He excuses her completely (XV.38.20). No moral judgment is passed on these women. Even where it is clear that both women negotiated their sex acts, and materially gained from them—Satyavatī an irresistibly fragrant body, and Kuntī an exceptional son—they still are not condemned for their actions. I believe that this is because of an attitude in the text that recognizes that when women are pursued by powerful men, the women are at a decided disadvantage. Their complicity is forgiven, or ignored, because it is acknowledged that they have little control in the situation.

The story of Mādhavī is perhaps the most colorful departure from the usual sexual code prescribed for women.[27] The story is recounted in *Udyogaparva*. The king Yayāti is solicited for eight hundred of a special breed of horses by a *brāhmaṇa* student, Gālava, who must pay his guru *dakṣiṇā*, his guru's "fee." Yayāti, however, does not possess any of these horses. Since it would be against his *kṣatriya dharma* to let the seeker go without being satisfied, however, Yayāti arrives at a novel solution. He offers his beautiful young daughter, Mādhavī, to the *brāhmaṇa*, to trade for the 800 horses wherever the *brāhmaṇa* is able to find them. Mādhavī thus becomes "the gate to the horses" a kind of currency with which the *brāhmaṇa* may purchase the horses when he locates them (V.113–18). Mādhavī goes voluntarily, impelled by a sense of duty to her father. In order to honor his promise, she rents herself out to four different men for two hundred horses each. With each man, she bears a male child. After the child is born, the *brāhmaṇa* Gālava reappears to claim her, and the two of them leave, proceeding to the next king who possesses the same breed of horses. In this manner, Mādhavī is married four different times to four different men, and bears four different children. With the birth of each child, her marriage is presumably dissolved, and she enters into a new one. In any other context such conduct would be considered wanton and disreputable. Mādhavī, however, is honored in the text, encountered later giving counsel to her four sons, and depicted as something of a sage. Her unorthodox behavior is excused because it is at the behest of powerful men. Mādhavī acts for the sake of her father's promise, and hence she incurs no moral calumny.

The episode featuring Atri's wife may be read the same way. Anasūyā's unorthodox behavior is excused because her husband is recognized as being overbearing, and she herself is recognized as being of unflawed virtue. Anasūyā is a character who is familiar from other sources. In the *Rāmāyaṇa*, she is depicted as a chaste wife who gives counsel to Sītā on the proper observance of *pativratā dharma* (*Ram.* II.117–19).

Beyond these outstanding cases, the text has a considerable compassion for women whose husbands take second wives, women who are abandoned, and women who are otherwise victimized by men. This may be gathered from the passages that include among lists of people with the most legitimate serious grievances, a wife deserted by her husband, and a bigamist's wife (II.61.75). Women who have been raped are never blamed for their plights, but are treated with great sympathy.[28] This may be seen in the story of Mamatā, the highly esteemed wife of the seer Utathya. She is raped by her brother-in-law Bṛhaspati while she is pregnant, and the sympathy of the text lies with Mamatā (I.98.7–16). The same may be noted of Raibhya's daughter-in-law, who agrees to lie with Yavakrī because she is afraid of him (III.137.1–21). When her father-in-law finds her crying and in pain, she confesses the events, and he curses Yavakrī in fury. She herself is treated with gentleness, and is not condemned for her suffering. Similarly, Utathya's wife Bhadrā is kidnapped by Varuṇa. Utathya mounts a campaign to get her back. Varuṇa is finally prevailed upon to return the woman, who is joyfully reclaimed by her husband. No fire ordeals are demanded here, and the text clearly indicates that the woman was sexually violated. Bhadrā is never held responsible for the events that were beyond her power to prevent (XIII.138). Rapists are unequivocally said to be "evil doers" (*pāpasya kartāraḥ*), who will suffer from colourful afflictions in the future (XIII.45.23).

Unlawful Sexual Offenses

All of the above represent violations of *pativratā* ideology, and they are violations excused for one reason or another. In contrast, let us look at attitudes to women who violate the sexual codes of married life through adultery. How are their violations viewed? Given the dominant *pativratā* ideology of the text, one would expect that its position on adultery would be clear-cut, since adultery represents a volitional transgression of sexual mores. The reality, however, is more complex. Variations are produced by several factors. First, there is a considerable disjunction between the pronouncements made in the explicitly didactic portions of the text, and the actual narratives involving adulterous women. Several of the didactic passages, located in the *Śānti* and

*Anuśāsana parva*s of the text, are very harsh, advocating brutal penalties for adulterous women and their lovers (see Chapter Three). Even here, however, the text's stance is not uniform. Other passages in the didactic portions suggest that a woman's adultery may be forgiven through pilgrimage or fasting. "Those who know *dharma* state that women are cleansed by observing the vow of *caturmāsya*, by piety, and by their menstrual periods"[29] (XII.36.24). In other places, we are advised that women's private sins do not cling to them, and that these are erased through menstruation. "Whatever they do, no fault can be ascribed to them, nor does it stick to them. Without a doubt, the sins women commit do not attach to them. Women are automatically cleansed by their menstrual course, like a utensil scoured with ashes"[30] (XII.36.25,27).

This pattern of seeming ambivalence is apparent in narratives as well. When a woman's adultery is first discovered, the immediate reaction is harsh. Ahalyā, for example, is condemned to death by her husband, and her son Cirakārin "Slowpoke" is ordered to kill her (XII.258). Cirakārin, however, true to his wont, reflects long before doing anything so drastic. Considering seriously the sin of injuring a mother, who is held to be sacred in every context, and the sin of injuring a woman, he concludes with the extraordinary statement that: "A woman is never guilty; only the man is guilty. In great sins and adultery, only the man is guilty"[31] (XII.258.36). Women may not be blamed. The point is underscored by the fact that the narrative is framed within a discussion of the virtues of patience and reflection. Cirakārin, the son, represents ideal wisdom in his refusal to act with haste. Through haste, one can perform evil and regrettable acts. Through reflection, however, one can achieve the higher goal of understanding and forgiveness. The story, therefore, is told with the implicit reasoning that the adultery of women should be forgiven. To condemn an adulterous wife in outraged haste would be unwise and wrong. This point is reinforced by the conclusion of the story. Gautama, after ordering Cirakārin to kill his mother, shortly after regrets his command, and is relieved to find that his son has been characteristically slow in obeying him.

The same pattern of hasty judgment and forgiveness may be observed in the episode involving Renukā. Renukā is condemned to death by her husband, for harboring an adulterous thought. In a repeat of the above story, Jamadagni orders his son, Rāma, to kill his offending mother. Rāma, faithful to his father's word, decapitates her immediately. Later, however, he intercedes on her behalf. When his father offers him a boon for his obedience, he requests that his mother be forgiven and revived. Renukā is thus revived, with no memory of the events that have elapsed (III.116).

These considerations suggest that in both didactic and narrative sequences, adultery is a variety of sexual transgression that is wrong. This is because, being a volitional act, there is no authentic situation of distress existing, which would mitigate it. Adulterous women are not, however, beyond redemption. Forgiveness is offered to them, though sometimes premised on an assessment of women's moral weakness. As Cirakārin reflects, "It is said that in principle, women are susceptible to sexual solicitation . . . their predilection for *adharma* is known and evident; there is no doubt about this"[32] (XII.258.38). Women's putative moral inferiority qualifies them for forgiveness.

Conclusion

The concept of *āpaddharma* represents the ultimately pragmatic and nondogmatic turn of the *Mahābhārata*, which, while it expatiates energetically on right and wrong, *dharma* and *adharma*, in the end always reserves the last word for something that interrupts all the careful calibrations, to hold that the essence of *dharma* is elusive and mysterious. When Yudhiṣṭhira notes the inconsistencies in what is the stated norm and what Bhīṣma holds permissible in times of *āpatti*, Bhīṣma displaces the priority of tradition:

> These *dharma* lessons that I am giving you are not derived simply from pure tradition. It is the highest wisdom, it is honey collected from diverse sources by visionaries. A king must draw upon many kinds of wisdom from various sources. The world's progress forward is not based on a linear interpretation of *dharma* ['*dharma* with just one branch'].[33] (XII.140.3–5)

A contemporary feminist might interpret women's distress in the classical period of Hinduism as being of so many varieties that they're hard to enumerate: intellectual deprivation; economic dependence; lack of independent social recognition, opportunity, or value; lack of independent religious expression; a general lack of physical and intellectual freedom in society—not to mention the powerlessness bred by sexual vulnerability and abuse. It is telling of the patriarchal preoccupations of the *Mahābhārata* that in all the detailed discussion about the varieties of *āpatti* and the measures that are permissible in coping with them, there is no reference to women whatsoever. The subject of women's *āpatti* is simply not treated. The primary area in which women figure in the theorizing of *āpaddharma* is in the context of childlessness; here also, however, as noted, it is clear that male ritual priorities dominate the concern. One is therefore forced into the feminist practice of looking for women in the lacunae and pauses of the text. Through such reading, one can find some recognition of women's distress, particularly their vulnerability to sexual abuse. There is an overall paternalist regard for women that advocates affection and care. On the whole, however, there is little specific appreciation of the difficulties experienced by women, and this bespeaks the broader upper-class male discourse of the work, in which women figure only to the extent that they impact on men's lives.

The theory of *āpaddharma* rounds out the *Mahābhārata*'s conception of *dharma*. It applies to times of extreme distress or emergency, and does not explicitly address issues of women's sexuality, except in a tangential, negative way. Its spirit suggests, however, that there are situations that may extenuate an individual from the proper performance of his or her socially sanctioned duties of sex, caste, stage of life, and ordinal position. I have applied this spirit to understanding the sexual allowances extended to women. Although these exceptions are not recognized by the text as having any official status, in practice, the *Mahābhārata* makes numerous compassionate allowances for women, acknowledging the potential for their victimization in a patriarchal world. I have suggested that there are several circumstances in which women may be excused from proper observance of their *strīdharma*. The sanction given these acts, however, should not be abused, and should be seen as contingent and provisional. The text makes clear that where authentic violations of *dharma* have occurred, forgiveness should be sought for them later on (XII.128.8).

Conclusion

In embarking on this inquiry, I initially feared that sexuality in modern times is an overtaxed hermeneutic, often reduced in its illuminating power to the status of a cliché. So why undertake a discussion of sexuality in the *Mahābhārata*? What is gained from a look at the minutae of sexual relations, sexual practices, and injunctions; the discrete ideals, norms, affirmations, and violations that we find in the Great Epic?

For me, one key motivating factor was the consideration that the gendered ideologies of the epics still have tremendous currency and continue to be powerful forces in molding the way that Hindu society constructs gender. Any woman growing up in even a moderately observing Hindu household will recognize the sway that this ideology exercises on her. From every angle of society—public media, ritual, social convention, even law, she is beamed images of the *pativratā* woman, that towering ideal of virtuous womanhood in whose image she must shape herself. Even in an age where urbanization, globalization, and increasing sexual parity in the public sphere all augur change, the *pativratā* woman is a deeply internalized ideal for Hindu women, reinforced through the modern avenues of television and Internet. This is apparent in the contemporary television reworkings of the epics, but it is also startlingly cognizable in the numerous soap operas airing on Indian TV today. Though cloaked in stylish Western garb, the *pativratā* woman prevails as the stock motif of this genre of television, and through her disarming fashion sense, she amplifies, magnifies, and reinforces *pativratā* ideals for a new generation. Thus even today, Hindu women dissenting from this paradigm risk suffering a psychic dissonance that they may never entirely lose in their lifetimes.

Locating, contextualizing, and in multiple ways accounting for ideologies is one of the functions of scholarship, and given the enormous affective power of the Hindu epics, a critical study of the source of their gendered ideology was long overdue. Narrative is an unthreatening and gentle vehicle for ideology, but prodigiously powerful for all its charming traits; through stories skillfully told, the audience receives a moral education that informs and forms its own moral sense, and teaches it to discriminate between contrary values. To my mind, it was important to identity the source of ideologies billed in the tradition as eternal and transcendent. It was important to deconstruct the monument and analyze its roots in particular historical, political, and social impulses, and to enable the scholarly apparatus to subvert their claim to ontological truth. In this work, we saw that the Hindu tradition's gendered biases emerge from deep concerns for the preservation of orthodoxy and the stability of the social order. Women's potential to jeopardize the hierarchical classification of society constituted the major rationale for the control of their sexuality, even as fears of women's erotic power led to a devastating characterization of womanhood as morally feeble and sexually depraved. I have argued here that the behemoth of *pativratā dharma* emerges directly out of these discourses based on fear of female sexuality, and the first step to drawing it down from the transcendent into the historical is to appreciate its intellectual moorings in a particular moment of Hindu history.

Scholars have noted that "the Sanskrit *Mahābhārata* came to be the continuing repository of crisis in the public discourse of classical India."[1] It is a text situated at the cusp of what we may loosely call the Vedic and the Classical periods, when Hinduism was reinventing itself in response to the numerous challenges it encountered. It represents the concerns and reflections of a particular group of people reacting to these rapid changes: the ascendancy of the heterodox traditions, their scathing critique of Vedic religion, the numerous social and economic upheavals of society, the repeated foreign invasions; all these factors were the source of pause for orthodox Brahmanism, and the cogitations of the *Mahābhārata* are a creative response to these circumstances. In the words of one scholar, "The *Great Bhārata* was a dramatic new beginning for the Brahmin tradition."[2] In the idiom of literature, the Brahmanical community tries to take account of its tradition, and to come to terms with the developments of several centuries. The text grapples with these issues, trying to understand, analyze, and systematize them, trying to impose some kind of theoretical cohesion on the varieties of ideals and practices that have infiltrated Brahmanical culture. It makes broad synthesizing movements, trying to assimilate desirable elements and to eliminate undesirable ones, to weave new values within the larger broadcloth of the old, so as to make the new appear to be ancient, and to exercise the same authority. The *Mahābhārata* self-consciously undertakes such activity; hence its presentation of itself as "the fifth Veda."[3]

The *Mahābhārata*'s presentation of sex and gender is part and parcel of this larger project of synthesizing tradition, while at the same time anticipating the future's need for social stability along the hierarchical model of Brahmanism.

These processes are most clearly evident in the *Śānti* and *Anuśāsana parvas*. Fully one-quarter of the entire text, these sections tackle both the big and the small questions of existence, trying to identify the most crucial human goals, and then on the basis of that, to map out human life in painstaking detail. In doing so, it tries to synthesize the compelling ideals and ethics of the *śramaṇa* traditions, with its own strongly affirmed Vedic roots. While one driving goal of the exercise is clearly to preserve tradition, another is to incorporate worthy innovations that have arisen in the culture since Vedic times. The first section of the *Śāntiparva*, the *rājadharma*, ponders extensively the place of beings in society. What are the duties and privileges of a king, the executive bearer of authority in society? What are the duties and privileges of all other beings in relation to him? How should people conduct themselves in relation to each other? What are the rules for all varieties of interpersonal relationships, and what are the exceptions to these rules? How should violations of rules be handled? What constitutes appropriate punishment? Who has the power to punish? All of these matters are discussed at length in the *rājadharma*, providing an extensive code of social ethics for the functioning of society.

In the second section of the *Śāntiparva*, *āpaddharma*, exceptions are formulated to the rules evolved in the first section. Under what circumstances may rules be violated? Which rules are pliable, and which are not? What compassionate allowances may be made for times of extreme distress? How should people compensate for rules violated? In presenting this law of emergencies, the *āpaddharma* section tries to formulate answers to these questions, anticipating numerous varieties of uncommonly stressful situations.

In the third section of the *Śāntiparva*, the writers focus on the larger questions of existence. Who is the person? What is the individual's relationship to the larger world? Where do we come from? Where are we going? How do we get to where we are going? What mental attitudes are appropriate to the path we pursue? What conduct is fitting? What material supports are necessary? For whom is this path appropriate? These are properly the most basic questions of religion, and it is in the answers given to these questions that we must begin our understanding of the worldview articulated by the *Mahābhārata*.

In the *mokṣadharma* section of the *Śāntiparva*, we learn that most fundamentally, the individual is a Person (*puruṣa*), a Self or a soul (*ātman*) that is trapped in the world, ignorant of its true identity. Mired in a perplexing and changing world, it identifies itself with those changes and hence suffers pain and misery. The answer to this problem is to realize one's true identity as the stable, unchanging, calm and blissful Self. The acquisition of this knowledge liberates one from delusion, and so liberates one from anxiety and unhappiness, setting one free of the world.

A crucial feature of this understanding of the individual is that *the Self is unsexed*. Notwithstanding the gendered language that is sometimes applied to *puruṣa*, the Self has no sex: "*Brahman* has no sex—it is not male, female, or neuter."[4] Sex is a consequence of one's *karma*. The fine details of what *karma* yields which sex are not elaborated in the *Mahābhārata*, but the basic point is that the Self has no sex; it is simply spirit lost in a confusing world, and in search of itself.

This understanding of the world most fundamentally grounds the *Mahābhārata*'s interpretation of individuals, and how they should conduct themselves in the world. Some individuals are intensely interested in Self-realization. These are the people the *mokṣadharma* says are on the *nivṛtti* path. They are entitled to pursue it through whatever means they discover are conducive to Self-realization, but the text makes some basic observations of people on the *nivṛtti* path. Thus, the search for Self-realization is inconsistent with a wish to harm other beings. It is inconsistent with hatred, anger, and attachment. It is inconsistent with a desire for possessions and comforts. It is inconsistent with a dependence on companionship and society. It is inconsistent with any type of ill-will, greed, wrongful conduct. Most importantly for our purposes, *it is inconsistent with social prejudice of any sort*. Sex, caste, age: all manner of social markers are of no consequence to the search for Self-realization. Numerous passages in the text insist that people who nourish such prejudices are spiritually naive and ignorant, and have not yet acquired the wisdom and the detachment to see the truth clearly.

People on the *nivṛtti* path, however, are few; the majority of people cherish no burning desire for Self-realization. They are content to live in the world, but want to do so in a way that is consistent with righteousness. This is the *pravṛtti* path. The *mokṣadharma* section has little patience with people of this hue, characterizing it as the way of the unenlightened and the inferior, but other sections of the *Śāntiparva*, and most of the *Anuśāsanaparva*, volubly describe the ideals and the methods of the *pravṛtti* path.

This constitutes the *Mahābhārata*'s primary analysis of existence, and sets up the principal categorizations that emerge from that analysis. Individuals are of two basic types. Both are lost, but one is interested in Self-realization, while the other is a long way from seeking it. Depending on the category that applies, the expectations differ. If an individual seeks Self-realization, and desires renunciation, the codes of society hold little value, but the spiritual and ethical discipline are demanding. If one seeks involvement with the world, the spiritual and ethical demands are less rigorous, but social roles are more confining. *These categories hinge on a person's own personal religious aspirations.* The *Mahābhārata* speaks to both types of people, but its viewpoint varies noticeably depending on which category of religious practice it seeks to evoke. If it is addressing the *nivṛtti* practitioner, its pronouncements are significantly different from if it is addressing a *pravṛtti* one. These two basic categories of *pravṛtti* and *nivṛtti* are thus key hermeneutics for understanding the *Mahābhārata*. Indeed, they are the only way for making sense of the numerous statements the text makes about women and sex—statements that, if one weren't sensitive to the larger worldview of the text, would appear whimsical and contradictory. The text's understanding of sex is as contingent on these two categories as is its understanding of all other phenomena.

If nothing else, a study of the gendered ideology of the *Mahābhārata* reveals that sexuality in the text is a far from haphazard, arbitrary, idiosyncratic affair; rather, it is a deeply religious concern, a conscious and refined construction closely premised on the religious aspirations of the individual. Devoted to soteriological pursuits, one is responsible for one set of sexual ethics—an ethics that are simultaneously more rigorous in their practice of abstinence, and liberal in their deconstruction of gendered boundaries. Immersed in the world, one is responsible for an entirely different set of sexual ethics: that of preserving order, tradition, social harmony, and through them, Brahmanical values and hierarchies. Sexuality, then, is contingent on an individual's personal religious goals. To that extent, it is always fluid, and open to reformulation at any time.

In conclusion, one note that may be entered is that it is fundamentally unmeaningful to make generalizations about "women in Hinduism," or even "women in the *Mahābhārata*." As we have seen, the concept of personhood itself is problematized by a host of factors, not least of which is the epistemological sophistication of the individual. Once that has been identified, numerous other variables come into play—for example, questions of *varṇa*, *āśrama*, and so forth. The gender ideology of the text has several complexities such that no one generalization is accurately descriptive of all *Mahābharata* womanhood. The urge to essentializing generalizations is therefore best resisted.

Notes

Introduction

1. The term *ideology* is wide-ranging and has been used to signify many discrete phenomena. This work employs the conventional definition as summarized by Terry Eagleton, as referring to a body of beliefs propagated by society and reinforced through a variety of sociocultural mechanisms (1994, 5–6).

2. For example, Jung, Hunt, and Balakrishnan, eds. (2001); Lancaster and di Leonardo, eds., (1997); Laqueur, (1990).

3. Or at least, they lean toward an "irreversible cultural determinism." See Donovan (107 ff.).

4. See, for example, essays in Holt, Rinehart, and Winston, eds. (1987).

5. Even this very rudimentary definition, however, has its problems. As Thomas Laqueur reflects in his introduction (1990): "It seems perfectly obvious that biology defines the sexes—what else could sex mean? Hence historians can have nothing much to say on the matter. To have a penis or not says it all in most circumstances, and one might for good measure add as many other differences as one chooses: women menstruate and lactate, men do not; women have a womb that bears children, and men lack both this organ and this capacity . . . [These are facts] although if pushed very hard they are not quite so conclusive as one might think. (A man is presumably still a man without a penis, and scientific efforts to fix sex definitively, as in the Olympic Committee's testing of the chromosomal configuration of buccal cavity cells, leads to ludicrous results)" (viii). The relationship between sex and biology has been increasingly questioned by feminist scholars. See, for example, Luce Irigaray (1989), Ruth Hubbard (1989), and Ruth Bleir (1988).

6. Jung, Hunt, Balakrishnan, xi.

7. See 1980, 1985, and 1999.

8. See Parrinder (1980); see also Narayanan (1990).

9. See Leslie (1991); Patton (1994); Jamison (1996).

10. Sharma (1993); Kripal (1995).

11. See Gold and Raheja (1994); Feldhaus, 1995; Wadley and Jacobson, 1970, among other works.

12. Nandy (1992, 1995); Kakar (1982, 1990, 2002).

13. For example, Wulff and Hawley, eds. (1993, 1996).

14. White (1996), Urban (2001).

15. The many works of Doniger, for example.

16. Orr (2000); Marglin (1985).

17. Coburn (1985, 1991); Brown (1990); Caldwell (1995); Erndl (1993).

18. Faure (1998); Wilson (1996).

19. Other scholars would seem to have the same criticisms. Jamison notes that in these works, "legal maxims or narrative skeletons are abstracted out of context and strung together like so many beads on an ideological necklace. The richness of each individual text, the effect on the text of its genre and intent, the ambivalence and internal contradictions, both deliberate and unconscious, that complicate the text—all of these are often ignored" (1996, 10).

20. These works offer, says Patton, "a kind of sweeping time line that moves from the Vedic golden age to the age of Brahmanical repression to the more hopeful era of Hindu reform . . . [or] an inventory of references to and about women." There has been a tendency to merge human, semidivine, and divine figures into a "potpourri" of characters united only by an essentialized femaleness (2002, 4).

21. Patton makes a similar observation with reference to works on women in the Veda: that they have a "tendency to create a separate category of 'female' which distinguishes only sketchily between various kinds of 'female'" (1996, 22).

22. He supported his position with reference to the fact that while the ancient Vedic literature is familiar with the Kurus and the victorious Bhāratas of the *Daśarajña* war recorded in the *Ṛgveda*, it is wholly unfamiliar with a clan called the Pāṇḍavas.

23. These arguments are detailed in *The Destiny of a King* (1973).

24. "Whatever the advances of archaeological research in India, one will never find sufficient traces of the epic events of their cultural context, simply because these are mythical events without even the most elementary historical basis" (1995, 9). The only appropriate approach is an ahistorical one, that shows acute cognizance of "the Indian collective consciousness" (9).

25. "In short, the ideals sponsored by the Veda have long since ceased to operate as the exclusive motive forces so far as the Indian way of life and thought is concerned" (11).

26. Other "structural" approaches are attempted by Fitzgerald, 1983; and Minkowski, 1989. Fitzgerald looks at the commonalities of structure between the *Mahābhārata* and the architecture of the Hindu temple: "The *Great Bhārata* and the Hindu temple converged on that common ground which was and is the major locus of the religious activities and expression of Hindu people, the materially and socially constituted world of everyday life" (612). Minkowski points to the frame stories of the epic, and the ways that secondary narratives are embedded into primary ones, forming

concentric rings, or frames. Minkowski proposes that this narrative structure may be the most consistent source of unity in the epic (402).

27. Hiltebeitel's three-volume work on *The Cult of Draupadī* (1988–97); Nancy Falk (1977), Sally Sutherland (1989).

28. Vidyut Aklujkar, 1991; Aurobindo's epic poem of the same title.

29. For example, one of Jayal's explanations for the relative rarity of *niyoga* in the Vedic period is that "the need for such a custom may not have been then felt . . . because the Aryans were a virile race." By the time of the epic, however, "the aristocratic society as traced in the *Mahābhārata* had become lascivious and lost its virility" (1966, 156).

30. Or "growth rings," as Fitzgerald terms them (2003c, 2).

31. These points are developed in detail in Dhand (2005).

Chapter One. Religion in the *Mahābhārata*

1. One might well question what is meant by this expression. In recent years, scholars have proposed that while the *Mahabharata* does show signs of textual accretion, that its final composition was achieved by a group, or even a school of authors who, judging from the concerns of the text, were almost undoubtedly Brahmins.

2. Several of R. S. Sharma's works also detail these socioeconomic changes. See in particular, *Śūdras in Ancient India* (1958).

3. For the politically motivated contemporary reworkings of this period, see Chakravarti (1998).

4. This period is succinctly summarized by Shastri (1911).

5. On these points, he meets broad agreement with other scholars, such as Biardeau, Hiltebeitel, and Fitzgerald.

6. Fitzgerald speaks of two stages of composition and redaction, with the final composition being a product of the Gupta empire (2003).

7. The conference on "Between the Empires" at University of Texas at Austin (April 2003) narrowed the margins for the composition of the epics to the period between the Mauryan and the Gupta empires, respectively.

8. See, for example, Thapar (1979, 173–88).

9. Fitzgerald, for example, sets the historical context for the MBh as "post-Nandan, post-Mauryan, particularly post-Aśokan, north India after 240 B.C.E." (2003, 7).

10. This point is made, for example, in Fitzgerald, 2003.

11. One recent volume on the *Mahābhārata* as a whole is by Nicholas Sutton (2000).

12. See, for example, the work of Biardeau 1994, Hiltebeitel (forthcoming), Sutton (2000).

13. An observation made famous by Hopkins, 1895 (1967).

14. The word *dharma* is, of course, most notoriously difficult to translate into English. It has a broad semantic range, as reflected in its various translations as "norm," "duty," "command," "religion," "faith," "justice," "custom," "law," "piety," "moral fitness," "virtue," "good work," "religious merit". "Law" is favored by van Buitenen in his translations, "Law" or "Lawful Meritorious Deed" by Fitzgerald (2003a, 11). "Taken in its fullest post-Vedic sense, the concept of *dharma* places every individual under a duty to behave appropriately in every circumstance. For each individual, action is seen to be implied by, and to have its effect on, the cosmic whole" (Menski, 52). Others point to the slippery quirkiness of the concept of *dharma*: "To put it rather cynically, it is symptomatic of its [the MBh's] approach that Yudhiṣṭhira, who is so often referred to as *Dharmarāja*, is the least decisive of the five brothers" (Brockington, 242). One of the best overviews of its history and usage is Halbfass (1988, 310–48).

15. The categories of *nivṛtti* and *pravṛtti* have been discussed by others, most notably Strauss (1911) and Bailey (1985). I expand on them here to lay the groundwork for the discussion that follows. Fitzgerald refers to the same divergent metaphysical and ethical systems as the "older" and the "newer" *dharma* respectively (2003, 2004). To the extent that *pravṛtti* represents a reformulation of older Vedic material, this is a helpful way of understanding them. On the whole, however, it is clear that they are *both* "new" forms of *dharma*, derived from older traditions of different sorts. *Pravṛtti* theology, while it borrows substantially from the old Vedic one and is concerned to preserve and extend it, is nevertheless as new a theology and ethics as is *nivṛtti*.

16. *dvāvimāvatha panthānau yatra vedāḥ pratiṣṭhitāḥ*
pravṛttilakṣaṇo dharmo nivṛttau ca subhāṣitaḥ

Bailey argues for *three* categories: *pravṛtti*, *nivṛtti*, and *bhakti* (1983, 235). His categorizations are followed by Sutton (2000, 9–16). I have chosen to go with the categories literally provided by the text itself, which doesn't recognize a privileged category for *bhakti* in its *mokṣadharma* section.

17. Jaiminīya Brāhmaṇa I.18.45 ff.; Bṛhadāraṇyaka VI.2 (Śatapatha Brāhmaṇa XIV.9.1); Chāndogya Upaniṣads (V.3–10). "The 'way of the gods' is the way of those who, because of their knowledge and faith, reach the 'world of brahman' beyond the sun, and liberation from earthly existence. The 'way of the fathers,' on the other hand, is the way of those who have relied on rituals and similar works and have enjoyed the reward resulting from these deeds, ie. the sacrificial merit, in heaven, but have ultimately been unable to avoid returning to an earthly existence" (Halbfass 1991, 92).

18. Apte (1965, 669–70).

19. Olivelle (1993, 8); see also Jash (1991, 21–25).

20. *Akrodhaḥ satyavacanam saṃvibhāgaḥ kṣamā tathā*
prajanaḥ sveṣu dāreṣu śaucamadroha eva ca
ārjavam bhṛtyabharaṇam navaite sārvavarṇikāḥ (XII.60.7–8).

21. *Strībhogānām viśeṣajñaḥ śāstradharmārthatattvavit*
nārhastvam surasaṃkāśa kartumasvargyamīdṛśam (I.109.21).

22. In fact, it is more specifically the duty of *kṣatriya*s to *dispose* of wealth than to acquire it, for it is assumed that they always have wealth. Thapar points this out (1982), observing that *kṣatriya*s were expected to expend their wealth in sponsoring sacrifices, and in making gifts (*dāna*) to the *brāhmaṇa*s who were dependent on them. See also Jamison (1999).

23. *Pravṛtti lakṣaṇo dharmo gṛhastheṣu vidhīyate* (XIII.129.16)

24. This may also be because *saṃnyāsa* functions in later history as the definitive springboard into the "religion of *nivṛtti*." It is one of the points of connection between the two "religions."

25. The process of rebirth is described, for example, in XII.212, as the cyclical union and disunion of the elements of water, space, wind, heat, and earth.

26. Apte (1965, 562).

27. To illustrate this to the grieving Dhṛtarāṣṭra, Vidura uses an extended parable about existence (XI.5): This is that of a man, lost in a dark and terrible forest, teeming with beasts of prey. There are lions and elephants, roaring and stomping about. There are deadly poisonous snakes and lizards, wolves and wild beasts of different varieties. His hair stands on end, and he is filled with terror. He begins to run around, mindlessly fleeing, casting his eyes frantically about, looking for a place of shelter. But he can't get away from the predators. Then he sees that the entire forest is surrounded with a net, and that a frightful monster stands there, with its arms outstretched. Fleeing from the monster, the man falls into a hidden pit that is full of thick clusters of thorny, abrasive vines. He becomes entangled in these vines and creepers, and hangs there, feet up, head down. While in this posture, other calamities overtake him. He sees that the pit is full of writhing, hissing, poisonous snakes that are straining upward toward him. He also sees a gigantic wild elephant at the mouth of the pit. It is, however, of a peculiar character—dark in complexion, with six faces and twelve feet. And it is heading toward him! Meanwhile, there are rats gnawing on the vine on which he hangs, some black rats, some white ones. In the midst of all this, from a tree above, some sticky substance starts to drip onto his face. Curious about what it is, he tastes it, and finds that it is honey. In the tree just above his pit are a series of honeycombs. Honey is dripping from them, and falling right into his mouth. Drunk with the taste of its sweetness, the man strains toward it even more. He can't get enough of it. He waits from one drop to the next drop, forgetting the terrible danger of the situation in which he lies.

This is a parable about our existential condition. The harsh wilderness of the forest is the world in which we live. The beasts that haunt the man are the various diseases to which we are so vulnerable. The monster of gigantic proportions is Age, which destroys our health, youth, and beauty. The pit is the physical frame of our bodies. The cluster of vines is the sum of the desires that keep us clinging to life. The six-faced elephant heading for the pit is time, the six seasons, and the twelve months.

The rats gnawing at the vine are the days and nights continually reducing our life. The snakes at the bottom of the pit are the perils to which our lives are always subject. But amid all these difficulties, the man is addicted to the honey that intermittently drips into his mouth! The drops of honey represent the pleasure that we derive from the gratification of our desires, the pleasures to which we are so strongly addicted. The wise know that this is in fact the existential state of beings. Surrounded on every side with suffering, injury, death, and decay, we remain drunk on our desires, intoxicated with petty pleasures and wishes. The real issues of existence remain ignored, unattended, looming larger and more urgent every day, but we remain wrapped in our desires, forever oblivious. (The folkloric roots of this parable are discussed by Vassilkov, 1995.)

28. *durgam janma nidhanaṃ cāpi rajanna bhūtikam jñānavido vadanti* (XII.306.106).

29. These questions are entertained in Dhand, 2005, using Śuka and Sulabhā as two illustrative examples.

30. *bījānyagnyupadagdhāni na rohanti yathā punaḥ*
jñānadagdhaistathā kleśairnātmā sambadhyate punaḥ
"Just as seeds that have been scorched by fire do not sprout again, the same way, the Self is no longer bound by miseries that have been scorched by knowledge" (XII.204.16).

31. *sarvabhūteṣu cātmānam sarvabhūtāni cātmani*
yadā paśyati bhūtātmā brahma saṃpadyate tadā (XII.231.21)

32. *sarvabhūtātmabhūtasya sarvabhūtahitasya ca*
devāpi mārge muhyanti apadasya padaiṣiṇaḥ (XII.321.23)

33. *Yena bhūtāny aśeṣeṇa drākṣyasy ātmany atho mayi* (BG.IV:35).

34. *ekaḥ śatrurna dvitīyo 'sti śatrurajñānatulyaḥ puruṣasya rājan*
yenavṛtaḥ kurute saṃprayukto ghorāṇi karmāṇi sudāruṇāni (XII.286.28).

35. *Prabhāvārthaya bhūtānām dharmavacanam kṛtam*
yatsyādahiṃsāsaṃyuktam sa dharma iti niścayaḥ (XII.110.10)

36. *dharmam . . . sanātanam . . . sarvabhūtahitam maitram purāṇam yam janā viduḥ* (XII.254.5).

37. *dhāraṇāddharma ityāhurdharmeṇa vidhṛtāḥ prajāḥ*
yatsyāddhāraṇasaṃyuktam sa dharma iti niscayaḥ (XII.110.11).
Hiltebeitel, following Halbfass, argues that in this passage "support" implies support of the *varṇāśramadharma* (2001). Thus, *dharma* here is taken to be upholding the social values of *varṇa*. I have, however, argued to the contrary that given the context of the passage, it is very clear that the intent is to universalize the concept of *dharma*, undermining its relation to *varṇa*. See Dhand (2002).

38. *vāsyaikam takṣato bāhum candanenaikamukṣataḥ*
nākalyāṇam na kalyāṇam pradhyāyannubhayostayoḥ
na jijivīṣuvatkiṃcinna mumūrṣuvadācaran
maranam jīvitam caiva nābhinandanna ca dviṣan (I.110.14–15).

39. *Yena pūrṇamivākāśam bhavatyekena sarvadā*
śūnyam yena janākīrṇam taṃ devā brāhmaṇam viduḥ (XII.237.11)

40. *na krudhyenna prahṛṣyecca mānito amānitaśca yaḥ*
sarvabhūteṣvabhayadastam deva brāhmaṇam viduḥ (XII.237.14).

41. The ideal of not causing harm to others is retained as one of the cardinal vows of the renouncer in the Saṃnyāsa Upaniṣads, which inscribe it into ritual. The ritual of renunciation also involves the ceremonial promise of imparting fearlessness to others. See Olivelle (1978b).

42. *yadyatra kiṃcitpratyakṣamahiṃsāyāḥ param matam*
ṛte tvāgamaśāstrebhyo brūhi tadyadi paśyasi (XII.260.19).

43. *śūdre caitadbhavellakṣyam dvije caitanna vidyate*
na vai śūdro bhavecchūdro brāhmaṇo na ca brāhmaṇaḥ (XII.182.8).

44. *tulā me sarvabhūteṣu samā tiṣṭhati jājale* (XII.254.12).

45. *vidyābhijanasaṃpanne brāhmaṇe gavi hastini*
śuni caiva śvapāke ca paṇḍitaḥ samadarśinaḥ (XII.231.19).

46. *rājan naitadbhavetgrahyamapakṛṣṭena janmanā*
mahātmanām samutpattistapasā bhāvitātmanām (XII.285.12).
vaidehakam śūdramudāharanti dvija mahārāja śrutopapannaḥ
aham hi paśyāmi narendra devam viśvasya viṣṇum jagataḥ pradhānam
(XII.285.28).

47. *api varṇāvakṛṣṭastu nārī vā dharmakāṅkṣiṇī*
tāvapyetena mārgeṇa gacchetām paramām gatim (XII.232.32).

48. *prāpya jñānam brāhmaṇātkṣatriyādvā vaiśyācchūdrādapi nīcādabhīkṣṇam*
śraddhātvam śraddadhānena nityam na śraddhinam janmamṛtyu viśetam
sarve varṇā brāhmaṇā brahmajāśca sarve nityam vyāharante ca brahma
tattvam śāstram brahmabuddhayā bravīmi sarvam viśvam brahma caitat-samastam (XII.306.85–86).

49. Sutton states about *nivṛtti* that "In terms of causality, *nivṛtti* emphasizes the absolute control of destiny over human existence, thereby indicating that action in this world has no real meaning for it cannot change the preordained outcome of events" (2000, 11). I hesitate to settle the question of fate and human initiative quite so categorically; indeed, in portions of the text such arguments are presented as being sophistical (XII.137.45–49; XII.137.79: *daivam puruṣakāraśca sthitāvanyonyasaṃśrayāt / udattānām karma taṃśra daivam klībā upāsate* "Fate and human effort are both ever-present because they are interdependent; Actions are the preserve of the elite, while the cowardly take recourse in fate."

50. This line of interpretation was made famous by the writings of Louis Dumont, and subsequently pursued by others such as T. N. Madan, J. C. Heesterman, and M. Biardeau in various works.

51. See Doniger (1973), Jamison (1996), Olivelle (1995).

52. *Atraivavasthitam sarvam trailokyam sacarācaram*
nivṛttilakṣaṇam dharmamavyaktam brahma śāśvatam

pravṛttilakṣaṇam dharmam prajāpatirathābravīt
pravṛttiḥ punarāvṛttirnivṛttiḥ paramā gatiḥ (XII.210.3–4).

53. *tam gatim paramāmeti nivṛtti paramo muniḥ*
jñānatattvaparo nityam śubhāśubhanidarśakaḥ (XII:210.5).

54. *iyam sā buddhiranyeyam yayā yāti param gatim* (XII.205.3).

55. *yuge yuge bhaviṣyadhvam pravṛttiphalabhoginaḥ* (XII.327.53).

56. *paśuyajñaiḥ katham hiṃsrairmādṛśo yaṣṭumarhati* (XII.169.31).
ātmanyevātmanā jāta ātmaniṣṭho 'prajo 'pi vā
ātmanyeva bhaviṣyāmi na mām tārayati prajā (XII.169.34).

57. *karmaṇā badhyate janturvidyayā tu pramucyate*
tasmātkarma na kurvanti yatayaḥ pāradarśiniḥ (XII.233.7).

58. Dhṛtarāṣṭra, for example, deeply distressed on the eve of the war, receives a visit from Sanatasujāta (V.42–45).

59. *śarīrapaktiḥ karmāṇi jñānam tu paramā gatiḥ* (XII.262.36).

60. *so 'yam prapadyate 'dhvānam cirāya dhruvaṃdhruvaḥ* (XII.307.7).

61. The other is the admission of *mokṣa* as a fourth *puruṣārtha*, or aim of human striving. Both *saṃnyāsa āśrama* and the *puruṣārtha* of *mokṣa*, however, are consigned to the end of life. In this way, their sharp antinomian revolutionary edges are rendered blunt and innocuous.

62. As Olivelle notes, in the longer history of Hinduism, the attempt to cast the two *dharmas*, *pravṛtta* and *nivṛtta*, as stages of a lifetime, or as levels of practice did not ultimately work as harmoniously as it was designed to do. It simply gave rise to rival theories, articulated in the literature of orthodox renouncers, that again asserted the unambiguous superiority of *mokṣadharma* and world renunciation, undertaken at any point in one's life, entirely shunning the *pravṛtta* elements if one were inclined to do so. "The possibility of choosing between these two opposing life-styles had come to stay" (1978a, 32).

63. I have retained here traditional views of ancient Indian history, of an Indo-European migration into India, but recognize that this is an ongoing subject of scholarly contention. Edwin Bryant (2001) outlines the numerous factors pertinent to the debate.

64. For more on the *śramaṇic* roots of *nivṛtti* ethics, see Chapple, 3–20. See also Thapar, 1979. Fitzgerald remarks that the existence of the *mokṣadharma* section itself, in fact seems "at least in part to be an innovation reacting to the socio-political position, rhetoric, and success of the *nāstikas*" (2003, 8).

65. This last is not a highly developed concern in the *Mahābhārata*, although it is addressed at points. One finds, for example, many statements that assert that a *brāhmaṇa* who does not behave like a *brāhmaṇa*, should not receive the privileges due to one.

66. *kāmātmanaḥ svargaparā janmakarmaphalapradām*
kriyāviśeṣabahulām bhogaiśvaryagatim prati
bhogaiśvaryaprasaktānām tayāpahṛtacetasām

67. *bhogaiśvaryaprasaktānām tayāphṛtacetasām* (BG.II.44).

68. This possibility has been explored by Knut A. Jacobsen

69. *yadyatra kiṃcitpratyaksamahiṃsāyāḥ param matam*
ṛte tvāgamaśāstrebhyo brūhi tadyadi paśyasi (XII.260.17)

70. *prāṇairviyoge chāgasya yadi śreyaḥ prapaśyasi*
chāgarthe vartate yajño bhavataḥ kiṃ prayojanam
anu tvā manyatam mātā pitā bhrātā sakhāpi ca
mantrayasvainamunnīya paravantam viśeṣataḥ (XIV.28.11–12)

71. *darśam ca paurṇamāsam ca agnihotram ca dhīmatām*
caturmāsyāni caivasaṃsteṣu yajñaḥ sanātanaḥ (XII.261.19).

Tamar Reich has pointed out that Kapila here plays the role of the reviler, who was a part of the traditional sacrifice, and concludes that to construe Kapila's discourse as a higher moral path would be a mistake. His structural position within the sacrifice is meant to underscore the idea that he is a malicious reviler and that his views are mistaken. Reich makes a valuable contribution in pointing out the ritual structure at the basis of the dialogue, but I find it difficult to agree that this is the conclusion intended by the text. Kapila's words are very much valorized. Syūmaraṣmi is the supplicant looking for knowledge and his words reflect no irony. Kapila is given the last word in the passage: "I bow to that *brahman* who is identical with he that knows it." The dialogue, moreover, is introduced by Yudhiṣṭhira's query as to which set of duties is superior, those of domesticity, or those of Yoga" (XII.260.2). While the episode makes some room for domesticity, it concludes unequivocally in favor of *mokṣadharma*. This would seem, therefore, to be another instance in which an orthodox form has been appropriated and reinterpreted to assert a reformed and novel ethic.

72. *Tretāyuge vidhistveṣām yajñanām na kṛte yuge*
dvāpare viplavam yānti yajñāḥ kaliyuge tathā (XII.224.62)

73. In Biardeau's evocative image, the values of *saṃnyāsa* "englobe" the values of sacrifice (1976, 1981).

74. See, for example, J. C. Heesterman, 1978. Looking at the evolution of sacrifice from its *śrauta* variety to its domestic *agnihotra* variety, Heesterman notes the elimination of the bloody aspects of the sacrifice. In his interpretation, however, the change from sacrifices of blood to sacrifice that did not involve death but a "dry and perfectionist ritualism" (90) eased the dangerous positioning of the Brahmin priest. "The brahmin priest, instead of having to carry the burden of death and destruction, simply repairs the mistake by technical ritual means . . . without any dire consequences" (91).

75. The many works of Biardeau interpret the development of this process. See especially, *Le Sacrifice dans l'Inde Ancienne* (1976).

76. Although this impression may be deceptive. As Thapar argues, "the householder is perhaps given even greater importance [in Buddhist texts] than in the Brahmanical tradition" (1982, 283). This is because the "the householder is the source of *dāna*," and "the institution of the *saṃgha* makes the pendant relationship much sharper than in the Brahminical tradition" (284).

77. As has been recognized by scholars, the *Mahābhārata* narrative is intended to be a Brahmanical response to the famous legend of King Aśoka as developed in Buddhist sources. Aśoka, after the particularly bloody battle of Kaliṅga and conquered the territory, is said to have visited the battleground. So repulsed is he by the carnage that he witnesses, that he determines on the course of *ahiṃsā*, and embraces *Buddhadharma*. Yudhiṣṭhira's actions parallel those of Aśoka. He visits the battleground of Kurukṣetra after the *mahā bhārata* war, witnesses the thousands of bloodied and mangled bodies, with the mothers, wives, and sisters of the warriors weeping over them. So moved is he by the sight that he resolves to renounce the world forever. In the Brahmanical ending, however, he is restrained from doing so. He is repeatedly urged to recall himself, to remember his duties to the world, his diverse responsibilities, and his proper function as a king. Eventually he is persuaded, but only with great reluctance. Where Aśoka banned animal sacrifices and criticized brahmanical festivals, Yudhiṣṭhira sponsors both a *rājasuya* and an *aśvamedha*. He is established as the *brahmanya* king after the purging of the evil *kṣatra* represented by the Mauryan and Nanda kings. See James Fitzgerald, 2001, 2003, 2004; Hiltebeitel 1976, 2001; Sutton, 1997.

78. *Na hi paśyāmi jīvantam loke kaṃcidahiṃsayā*
sattvaiḥ sattvāni jāvanti durbalairbalavattarāḥ (XII.15.20)

79. *udake bahavaḥ prāṇāḥ pṛthivyāṃ ca phaleṣu ca* (XII.15.25)

80. *sūkṣmayonīni bhūtāni tarkagamyāni kānicit*
pakṣmaṇo 'pi nipātena yeśām syātskandhaparyayaḥ (XII.15.26)

81. "Everything in this world functions by punishment. A person naturally pure is difficult to find. It is from the fear of punishment alone that one strives for good" (XII. 15.34).

82. "If punishment did not hold sway, then there would be chaos in the universe. All barriers would be swept away, and the idea of property would disappear" (XII.15.38).

83. As Fitzgerald has argued, "the acceptance and employment of violence as Meritorious, Lawful Action (*dharma*)" is one of the primary agendas of the *Mahābhārata*, as encapsulated in the figure of Yudhiṣṭhira, the ideal king who "stands firm in battle" and does not turn his face away from it in *śoka* (grief, a deliberate foil to Aśoka, the legendary king trumpeted by the Buddhists (2001, 65).

84. See, for example, Kaelber, 17–18.

85. Olivelle (1990, 130).

86. *bhāryām gacchanbrahmacārī ṛtau bhavati brāhmaṇaḥ*
ṛtavādī sadā ca syājjñānanityaśca yo naraḥ (XII.213.10).

87. As is the case in most cultures, violence within the home may represent a special category of violence that is countenanced for the alleged purpose of discipline. The question of the extent to which violence is permissible in the home is unclear from the text. Although there are many passages in the text that express chivalrous attitudes toward women, and the violence against Draupadī is strongly condemned (to

say nothing of the fact that it becomes a major justification for the war), other passages leave one wondering. One passage excised from the Critical Edition states "The *devas* and *pitṛs* destroy that disgraceful house in which a woman is beaten at festival times" (XIII.App.I.14.87–89). At festival times? This begs the question of whether beating women was to be tolerated at other times.

88. The exception to this is in times of dire distress. For example, the *brāhmaṇa* Rama Jāmadagni earns some notoriety by bearing weapons in the defense of the *brāhmaṇa*s.

89. David Gitomer draws attention to the conflictual relationship between Duryodhana and Kṛṣṇa, developed in the *Mahābhārata* and subsequent Sanskrit drama. Duryodhana's stubborn resistance to Kṛṣṇa's counsel represents the *atikṣatriya*'s ("super-*kṣatriya*" 's) refusal to capitulate to the Lord Kṛṣṇa's plan "to Pāṇḍavize, i.e., theocratize Āryavarta" (1992, 223).

90. I have presented here Krsna's own justifications for the war, but recognize that there are scholars who have interrogated Krsna's motives in urging Arjuna to fight. See, for example, Matilal.

91. This pattern of role-reversal, of *śūdra* instructing *brāhmaṇa*, is discussed by Laine (1991).

92. This would seem, at face value, to contradict Wendy Doniger's assertion that "Hinduism has no 'golden mean'; . . . It was perhaps as a reaction against this extremism that the Buddha called his teaching 'the Middle Path,' " but we are in apparent agreement in her larger assertion that "Compromise is never the Hindu way of resolution, which proceeds by a series of oppositions rather than by one entity which combines the two by sacrificing the essence of each" (1973, 82).

93. Fitzgerald (1983, 622).

Chapter Two. *Nivṛtti Dharma*: The Search for the Highest

1. "There are traces of this discourse in various later Vedic texts, it is flowering in the oldest *Upaniṣads*, is thoroughly evident in some of the Brahmin *sūtra* literature and in the *Mahābhārata*, and has become the most prestigious kind of Brahmanism in Manu's Teachings of the Laws by the beginning of the Christian era" (Fitzgerald, 2001, 72).

2. This perspective is reflected in the famous parable of the man lost in the forest, recounted in the last chapter (XI.5).

3. Fitzgerald (2001, 72).

4. This is the interpretation of *yoga* favored by Biardeau (see, for example, 1995, 91 ff.).

5. In a striking passage from the Śāntiparva, Bhīṣma entertains the question of whether theism is necessary. Yudhiṣthira asks about the differences between Sāṃkhya and *Yoga*, and receives the response that both are equal in their purity and their

compassion toward beings, and both are equal in their adherence to vows. Ultimately, Bhīṣma concludes, it is up to one's personal preferences. There is no crucial difference between the two (XII.289.1–9).

6. Nick Sutton seems to make the same points (2000, 98, 103).

7. *Na cāpyavahasankaṃcinna kurvanbhṛkuṭīm kvacit*
prasannavadano nityam sarvabhūtahite rataḥ
jaṅgamājaṅgamam sarvamavihiṃsaṃścaturvidham
svāsu prajāsviva sadā samaḥ prāṇabhṛtām prati (I.110.10–11)

8. These are discussed in more detail in Sutton (2000, 98–105).

9. Though not all *yogins* are ascetics, and not all ascetics are *yogins*. These points are made, for example, by Frauwallner (1973) and Bronkhorst (1998).

10. The many works of J. C. Heesterman argue this point. See especially 1964.

11. Heesterman (1964, 1978, 1982) argues for a Vedic origin, and Heesterman's arguments are favoured by H. P. Schmidt (1968). Others, however, have argued for a completely non-Aryan origin to the ascetic traditions of India, and hence of the heterodox traditions of Buddhism and Jainism. Chief among these is Johannes Bronkhorst (1998). For more on the discussion and the evidence offered on both sides, see Jacobi (1884), Buhler (1879), Muller (1879), P. Deussen (1906), Sprockhoff (1979, 1987), and the many works of Patrick Olivelle (particularly 1995, 162–64).

12. 1973.

13. Jamison (1996, 16).

14. Romila Thapar makes this point in "Householders and Renouncers" (1982, 273–98).

15. Thapar's definition would therefore be too narrow to describe the phenomenon of *Mahābhārata* asceticism: "The term ascetic refers to a person who has opted out of society, renounced social mores and cast himself away. Ostensibly he has also taken upon himself the goal of discovering the ecstasy (*ānanda*) in the comprehension of the ultimate reality and of characterizing this search by resorting to austerity (*tapas*) and meditation (*dhyāna*) with the final aim of union with the ultimate reality (*yoga*)" (57). Similarly, Denton's definition would be too limited for the classical period of the epic: "An ascetic is a person who has been initiated into a tradition of asceticism by a recognized preceptor or teacher (*guru*). Typically the ritual of initiation into asceticism marks three things: the rejection of, or separation from, householdership; a commitment to a particular path towards salvation; and the entry into a community of fellow aspirants" (214).

16. In this latter vocational sense, it is called *naiṣṭhikabrahmacārya*, to distinguish it from the student stage, which is temporary (Olivelle, 1978b, 29).

17. Although in Narada's case, the *Mahābhārata* alludes in two instances to a marriage with Sukumārī.

18. 1991.

19. *Kuṭumbam putradāram ca śarīram dravyasaṃcayaḥ*
pārakyamadhruvā sarvam kim svam sukṛtaduṣkṛtam

yadā sarvam parityajya gantavyamavaśena te
anarthe kim prasaktastvam svamartham nānutiṣṭhasi (XII.316.32–33).

20. *Nibandhanī rajjureṣā yā grāme vasato ratiḥ* (XII.316.37).

21. *Tyaja dharmamadharmam ca ubhe satyānṛte tyaja*
ubhe satyānṛte tyaktvā yena tyajasi tam tyaja (XII.316.40).

22. Later Hindu tradition concurs that Vyāsa, despite his numerous extraordinary achievements, does not reach the level of realization of his son. As Brown says of Vyāsa's efforts, the epic and the Purāṇas "attribute [a] . . . higher sanctity to his son," who becomes "universally recognized as a model of human perfectability, an ideal renunciate with complete knowledge of the Absolute" (1992, 158).

23. One exceptional instance is the episode in which they disagree with the gods on the use of animals in sacrifice. See Chapter One.

24. In Bronkhorst's analysis, the *parivraja* is a renunciant but not an ascetic: "In this enumeration, no painful mortifications are included. The life of the *parivraja* is no doubt simple, extremely simple, but the only remaining thing that interests him is not the capacity to endure hardship but rather to find his self" (1998, 14).

25. See Olivelle (1981).

26. Olivelle (1995, 9).

27. C. McKenzie Brown compares the different trajectories of Śuka's journey to *mokṣa* to be found in the *Mahābhārata* and the Purāṇas (1992).

28. It is unclear what are the rules for such practice, but in several cases, there is reference to a *dīkṣā,* or ritual initiation. Through the *dīkṣā,* individuals resolve to undertake ascetic vows for the fulfillment of particular purposes. They are then formally initiated into the ascetic mode for a limited period. For the duration of that period, they must abide by the rules of ascetic life. When they have acquired what they seek, the *dīkṣā* is concluded, and they may return to ordinary householder life. Kṛṣṇa follows this course when he practices asceticism for the birth of his son, Sāmba. His ascetic practices are directed at the great god Śiva. Kṛṣṇa is initiated into the practice, and guided by the *vānaprasthin* ascetic Upamanyu (XIII.15.4). When he has acquired the boons that he seeks, through the blessings of Umā and Maheśvara, he returns to his ordinary life.

29. While most texts on *vānaprasthya* suggest that in this stage a man abandons his wife, as in the *Upaniṣadic* paradigm of Yājñavalkya and Maitreyī, where the former gives his wives the choice of whether or not to accompany him, the MBh. says of *vānaprasthya* that "It is the mode in which wives afflict themselves by means of austerities. It is the mode practised by those that live as forest recluses" (XII.236.2).

30. This is not, obviously, to say that they do not participate in the same lifecycle as their male counterparts, as Olivelle notes (1993, 182). It simply means that their activities are not religiously or theologically recognized.

31. See Wade H. Dazey (1990). Catherine Ojha, however, points out that "While according to the strict rules of this monastic institution, women were not allowed membership, it is a fact that individual *saṃnyāsins* have taken the liberty over

the past centuries to give initiation into *saṃnyāsa* to women" (1981, 260). She further points out that six of the ten orders of the *Daśanāmis* now allow women (261).

32. Mudgala follows the vow of gleaning (*silonchvṛtti*), which, according to Bronkhorst, characterizes certain "Vedic" *vānaprasthins* (1998, 34) and whose reward is usually heaven. Mudgala however, gains liberation through his practice of *dhyānayoga*. According to Hiltebeitel, *unchavṛtti* represents the highest type of practice valorized by the epic, resulting in liberation.

33. This, incidentally, is another point of parallel between Brahmā and Vyāsa, a point made by Bruce Sullivan (1990).

34. *avidvāṃsamalam loke vidvāṃsamapi vā punaḥ*
nayante hyatpatham nāryaḥ kāmakrodhavaśānugam
svabhāvaścaiva nāriṇām narāṇāmiha dūṣaṇam
ityartham na prasajjante pramadāsu vipaścitaḥ (XIII.48.36–37).

35. *rakṣaṃsi caitāni caranti putra rūpeṇa tenādbhutadarśanena*
atulyarupāṇyatighoravanti vighnam sadā tapasaścintayanti (III.113.1)

36. *yoṣitām na kathāḥ śrāvya na nirīkṣyā nirambaraḥ*
kadāciddarśanādasām durbalānāviśedrajaḥ (XII.207.12).

37. *kṛtya hyetā ghorarūpā mohayantyavicakṣaṇān* (XII.206.9).

38. *punarājanmalokaugham putrabāndhavapattanam* (XII.290.67).

39. *dṛḍhaiśca pāśairbahubhirvimuktaḥ prajānimittairapi daivataiśca*
yadā hyasau sukhaduḥkhe jahāti muktastadāgyām gatimetyaliṅga
(XII.212.45)

40. D. P. Vora points to the essentially ethical content of the concept of *tapas* (1959, 187–89).

41. *svapne 'pyevam yathābhyeti manaḥsaṃkalpajam rajaḥ*
śukramasparśajam dehātsṛjantyasya manovahā (XII.207.22).

42. *naivākāśe na paśuṣu nayonau na ca parvasu*
indriyasya visargam te 'rocayanta kadācana (XII.221.44).

43. *ātmabhāvam tathā strīṣu muktameva punaḥ punaḥ*
yaḥ paśyati sadā yukto yathāvanmukta eva saḥ (XII.277.28).

44. *nirindriyā amantrāśca striyo 'nṛtamiti śrutiḥ* (XIII.40.11).

45. *rajasyantarhitā mūrtirindriyāṇām sanātanī* (XII.206.9).

46. An interesting counterpoint to this is found in the Pali canon, in which male members of the *saṃgha* are also challenged by their desire for women, and are taught various techniques for loosening their hold on this desire. As Bernard Faure's book *The Red Thread* points out (1998, 207–40), however, male desire in the *saṃgha* frequently found expression in sexual acts with other men, but the male image is never deconstructed in these texts as is the female. Whereas the Buddhist tradition develops techniques of meditation aimed at loosening a man's desire for a woman by representing her in her least desirable states, there is no parallel meditation developed for disengaging a man's desire for another man, or even for disengaging a woman's desire for a man. Similar arguments are made by Liz Wilson (1996).

47. *sahavāsam na yāsyāmi kālametaddhi vañcanāt*
vañcito 'smyanayā yaddhi nirvikāro vikārayā (XII.295.32).

48. Olivelle (1993, 188; 189).

49. Ojha (1981, 254). For another portrait of contemporary female asceticism, see Lynn Teskey Denton (1992), and Meera Khandelwal (2004).

50. There is some debate about this for the earlier period; scholars interpret *Aṣvalāyana Gṛhasūtra* 3.8.11–15 differently. See Schmidt (1987, 26); Olivelle (1993, 184); Mary McGee's discussion of the "Gender Implications of *Adhikara,*" in Mīmāṃsā raises similar questions (2002, 32–50).

51. Stephanie Jamison makes a similar point about the ancient Vedic tradition, that theoretically women were barred from studying the Veda, but "their presence at and participation in Vedic solemn ritual attests to the fact that they were not prevented from hearing it or indeed from speaking Vedic *mantras*" (1996, 14).

52. *bṛhaspatestu bhaginī varastrī brahmacāriṇī*
yogasiddhā jagatsarvamasaktam vicaratyuta (I.60.26).

53. *tapasvinīm mahābhāgām vṛddham dīkṣāmanuṣṭhitām*
dṛṣṭvā sā tvayā tatra sampūjya caiva yatnataḥ (XIII.19.24).

54. *atraiva brāhmaṇī siddhā kaumārabrahmacāriṇī*
yogayuktā divam yatā tapaḥsiddhā tapasvinī (IX.53.6).

55. *babhuva śrīmatī rājanśāṇḍilyasya mahātmanaḥ*
sutā ghṛtavratā sādhvī niyatā brahmacāriṇī
sā tu prāpya param yogam gatā svargamanuttamam
bhuktvāśrame 'śvamedhasya phalam phalavatam śubhā
gatā svargam mahābhāgā pūjita niyatātmabhiḥ (IX.53.8).

56. *subhrūḥ sā hyath kalyāṇī puṇḍarīkani bhekṣaṇā*
mahatā tapasogreṇa kṛtvāśramamaninditā (IX.51.5).
sā pitrā dīyamānāpi bhartre naicchadaninditā
ātmanaḥ sadṛsam sā tu bhartāram nānvapaśyata
tataḥ sā tapasogreṇa pīdayitvātmanastanum
pitṛdevārcanaratā babhuva vijane vane (IX.51.7–8).

57. *Tāḥ sughoram tapaḥ kṛtvā devyo bharatasattama*
deham tyaktvā mahārāja gatimiṣṭām yuyustadā (I.119.12)

58. *gaccha tvam tyāgamāsthāya yuktā vasa tapovane* (I.119.8)

59. *Evam siddhiḥ parā prāpta arundhatyā viśuddhyā*
yathā tvayā mahābhāge madartham saṃśitavrate
viśeṣo hi tvayā bhadre vrate hyasminsamarpitaḥ (IX.47.47–49).

60. Olivelle documents other references to female ascetics in the *sūtra* and *śāstra* literature: *Manu* (8.363), *Yāj.* (II.293), *Arthaśāstra* (4.13.36), *Viṣṇu* (36.7), *Nārada* (12.73–74) (1993, 189). More recently, Stephanie Jamison discusses the presence of female ascetics in the period "Between the Empires" (2003).

61. 1991, 213–14.

62. *akāmāḥ kāmarūpeṇa dhūrtā narakarūpiṇaḥ*
napunarvañcayiṣyanti pratibuddhāsmi jāgrmi . . .
saṃbuddhāham nirākārā nāhamadyājitendriyā
sukham nirāśaḥ svapiti nairāśyam paramam sukham
āśāmanāśām kṛtvā hi sukham svapiti piṅgalā (XII.168.50–52).

63. *kā hi kāntamihāyāntamayam kānteti maṃsyate* (XII.168.49)

64. *unmattāhamanunmattam kāntamanvavasam ciram*
antike ramaṇam santam nainamadhyagamam purā (XII.168.48).

65. *moktukāmām tu tām dṛṣṭvā śarīram nārado 'bravīt*
asaṃskṛtāyāḥ kanyāyāḥ kuto lokāstavānadhe (IX.51.11).

This, incidentally, is not a consistently held position in the *Mahābhārata*, for many unmarried men and women do go to heaven. Bhīṣma certainly does, as do many of the *bālabrahmacārinī*s discussed in this chapter.

66. *hīnayālakṣaṇaiḥ sarvaistathāninditayā mayā*
ācāram pratigṛhṇantyā siddhiḥ prāpteyamuttamā (V.111.14).

67. *na ca te garhaṇṇīyāpi garhitavyāḥ striyāḥ kvacit* (V.111.16).

68. *atha dharmayuge tasminyogadharmamanuṣṭhitā*
mahımanucacāraikā sulabhā nāma bhikṣukī (XII.308.7).

69. *sulabhā tvasya dharmeṣu mukto neti sasaṃśayā*
sattvam sattvena yogajñā praviveśa mahīpate (XII.308.16).

70. *na ca kāmasamāyukte mukte 'pyasti tridaṇḍakam*
na rakṣyate tvayā cedam na muktasyāsti gopanā (XII.308.56).

71. *varṇapravaramukhyāsi brāhmaṇī kṣatriyo hyaham*
nāvayorekayogo 'sti mā kṛthā varṇasaṃkaram (XII.308.59).

72. *ātmanyevātmanātmānam yathā tvamanupaśyasi*
evamevātmanātmānamanyasminkim na paśyasi
yadyātmani paraṃsmiśca samatāmadhyavasyasi (XII.308.126).

73. *priye caivāpriye caiva durbale balavatyapi*
yasya nāsti samam cakṣuḥ kim tasminmuktalaksaṇam (XII.308.130).

74. 1993, 190.

75. Meena Khandelwal (2004, 3).

76. *Naiva strī na pumānetannaiva cedam napuṃsakam* (XII.242.22).

77. *naitajjñātvā pumānstrā vā punarbhavamavāpnuyāt*
abhavapratipattyarthametadvartma vidhīyate (XII.242.23).

78. *pārāvaryam tu bhūtānām jñānenaivoplabhyate*
vidyayā tāta sṛṣṭānām vidyaiva paramā gatiḥ (XII.229.10).

79. *api varṇāvakṛṣṭastu nārī vā dharmakāṅkṣiṇī*
tāvapyetena mārgeṇa gacchetā paramam gatim (XII.232.32).

80. *Mām hi pārtha vyapāśritya ye 'pi syuḥ pāpayonayaḥ*
striyo vaiśyās tathā śūdrās te 'pi yānti parām gatim (BG IX:32).

Chapter Three. Wedding and Bedding in *Pravṛtti Dharma*

1. This is symbolized in *śrauta* ritual. See Smith (1991) and Jamison (1996).

2. *ye tu mūḍhā durācārā viyonau maithune ratāḥ*
puruṣeṣu suduṣprajñāḥ klībatvamupayānti te (XIII.133.51).

3. The *Āpastamba Dharmasūtra*, for example, states: "So long as his wife participates in religious rites and bears children, a man may not take another wife." If she is wanting in either of these, he may take another prior to establishing his sacred fires, for a wife who participates in the ritual establishment of his sacred fires becomes associated with the rites to which the establishment of the sacred fires is only supplementary" (II.11.12–14).

4. "There is no division of property between a husband and a wife, because from the time of their marriage they are linked together in the performance of religious rites as also in receiving the rewards of their meritorious deeds and in acquiring wealth; for while the husband is away people do not consider it a theft for the wife to make a gift when the occasion demands" (ĀpDh.II.14.16–20).

5. Some of the *Dharmasūtras* state that she may do this after the passage of merely three menstrual periods (GDh. 18.20–23)

6. *bhāryā hi paramo nāthaḥ puruṣasyeha paṭhyate*
asahāyasya loke 'sminllokayātrāsahāyinī
tathā rogābhibhūtasya nityam kṛcchragatasya ca
nāsti bhāryāsamam kiṃcinnarasyārtasya bheṣajam
nāsti bhāryāsamo bandhurnāsti bhāryāsamā gatiḥ
nāsti bhāryāsamo loke sahāyo dharmasādhanaḥ (XII.142.8–10).

7. *ardham bhāryā manuṣyasya bhāryā śreṣṭhatamaḥ sakhā*
bhāryā mūlam trivargasya bhāryā mitram mariṣyataḥ
bhāryāvantaḥ kriyāvantaḥ sabhāryā gṛhamedhinaḥ
bhāryāvantaḥ pramodante bhāryāvantaḥ śriyānvitāḥ
sakhāyaḥ praviviktesu bhavantyetāḥ priyaṃvadāḥ
pitaro dharmakāryeṣu bhavantyārtasya mātaraḥ (I:68.40–42).

8. *bhāryāpatyorhi saṃbandhaḥ strīpuṃsostulya eva saḥ*
ratiḥ sādhārano dharma iti cāha sa pārthivaḥ (XIII.45.10).

9. *ṛte na puruṣeṇeha strī garbham dhārayatyuta*
ṛte striyam na puruṣo rūpam nirvartayettathā
anyonyasyābhisaṃbandhādanyonyaguṇasaṃśrayāt

10. *daṃpatyoḥ samaśīlatvam dharmaśca gṛhamedhinām* (XIII.128.43).

11. *brāhmaṇī tu bhavejjyeṣṭhā kṣatriyā kṣatriyasya tu* (XIII.44.11).
"A *brāhmaṇa* wife is senior to a *kṣatriya*, a *kṣatriya* to a *vaiśya*, and so on".

12. *vaiṣamyādatha vā lobhātkāmādvāpi paraṃtapa*
brāhmaṇasya bhavecchūdrā na tu dṛṣṭantataḥ smṛtā

śūdrām śayanamāropya brāhmaṇaḥ pīḍito bhavet
prāyaścittīyate cāpi vidhhidṛṣṭena hetunā
tatra jāteṣvapatyeṣu dviguṇam syādyudhiṣṭhira (XIII.47.8–10)

13. *param śavādbrāhmaṇasyaiṣa putrā śūdrāputram pāraśavam tamāhuḥ* (XIII.48.5). The same sort of characterizations are found in more detail in the *Dharmasūtras* and *śāstras*.

14. This is the principle followed in most *Dharma* texts, although there is some discussion that the paternity of the child reverts to the biological father on his death. See ĀpDh. II.13.6: When we are in the abode of Death, they say, a son belongs to the man who fathered him. After he dies, the man who deposited the seed takes the son to himself in the abode of Death.

15. *nekṣetādityamudyantam na ca nagnām parastriyam* (XII.186.16).

16. *sutastriyā ca śayanam sahabhojyam ca varjayet* (XII.186.23).

17. *devastrīṇāmadhīvāse nṛtyagītaninādite*
prājāpatye vasenpadma varṣāṇāmagnisaṃnibhe (XIII.110.8).

18. Doniger (1995, 160).

19. These are summarized, for example, in Jayal (70)

20. *Śīlavṛtte samājñāya vidyām yonim ca karma ca*
adbhireva pradātavyā kanyā guṇavate vare (XIII. 44.3–4).

"Only after having informed himself about the conduct and learning of the man, his birth and his accomplishments, should [the father] bestow the girl upon a worthy husband."

21. "No practical example of this method is . . . found in the epics," Jayal (81).

22. In Olivelle's translation (1999, 162).

23. Summarized in *The Laws of Manu* (III.21–31); Meyer (55–58); Jayal (69–84), Altekar (35–48).

24. R. S. Sharma draws attention to this phenomenon (1958).

25. Interestingly, aristocratic women are also wont to make use of the sexual labor of female slaves. As evident in the stories of Ambikā and Sudeṣṇā, for example, both escape unpleasant sexual situations by employing their female slaves to substitute for themselves.

26. *tathaiva paradārānye kāmavṛttānrahogatān*
manasāpi na hiṃsanti te narāḥ svargagāminaḥ (XIII.132.32).

27. *paradāreṣu ye mūḍhāścakṣurduṣṭaṃ prayunjate*
tena duṣṭasvabhāvena jātyandhāste bhavanti ha
manasā tu praduṣṭena nagnām paśyanti ye striyam
rogārtāste bhavantīha narā duṣkṛtakarmiṇaḥ (XIII.133.50).

28. The *Dharmasūtras* seem to concur that women are purified of such sins through their menstrual periods: Women have an unparalleled means of purification and they never become sullied, for month after month their menstrual flow washes away their sins" (BDh.2.4.4).

29. *yāvanto romakūpāḥ syuḥ strīṇām gātreṣu nirmitāḥ*
tāvadvarṣasahasrāṇi narakam paryupāsate (XIII.107.480*).

30. "And if his wife wants it, he may have sex with her between the seasons as well, in accordance with the Brahmaṇa passage" (ĀpDh.2.1.16–19).

31. *Bhāryām gacchanbrahmacārī ṛtau bhavati brāhmaṇaḥ* (XII.214.10).

32. *anṛtau jaṭī vratinyām vai bhāryāyām saṃprajāyatu* (XIII.96.27).

33. Patton analyzes this myth in relation to its Vedic antecedents and finds it to represent a diminution of the stature of the woman. "In the stereotype of the manipulative wife," she makes her demands. Here, Lopamudra is a "cardboard cut-out" of the Vedic poet, who articulates her desire for sex and progeny and persuades her husband to fulfill it (1996, 34).

34. Biardeau reads Nala as *Nara*, "Man." Nala is representative of Man, of Humanity, in his susceptibility to the forces of *daiva*, fate, and in his alienation from himself (1984, 1985).

35. *śāśvato ayam dharmapathaḥ sadbhirācaritaḥ sadā*
yadbhāryām parirakṣanti bhartāro alpabalā api (III.13.60).

36. *bhartavyā rakṣaṇīyā ca patnī hi patinā sadā* (III.67.13).

37. *api kīṭapantagānām mṛgāṇām caiva śobhane*
striyo raksayāśca poṣyāśca naivam tvam vaktumarhasi
anukampito naro naryo puṣṭo rakṣita eva ca
prapatedyaśaso dīptānna ca lokānavāpnuyāt (XIV.93.21–22).

38. *mayi jīvati yattātaḥ keśagrahamavāptavān*
kathamanye kariṣyanti putrebhyaḥ putriṇaḥ spṛhām (VII.166.1360*)

39. *yadyevamahamajñāsyamaśaktānrakṣaṇe mama*
putrasya pāṇḍupāncālānmayā gupto bhavettataḥ (VII.150.74).
aho vaḥ pauruṣam nāsti na ca vo asti parākramaḥ
yatrābhimanyuḥ samare paśyatām vo nipātitaḥ (VII.50.76).

40. *ṛtukāle svakām patnīṃ gacchatām yā manasvinām*
na cānyadārasevīnām tām gatim vraja putraka (VII.155.28).

41. "When his wife is in season, he must have sexual intercourse with her as required by his vow" (ĀpDh.2.1.17).

42. This point is also made by Julia Leslie in her discussion of female sexuality in Tryambakayajvan's *Strīdharmapaddhati*: "A man who fails in his duty to his wife should put on the skin of a donkey with the hair turned outwards and go to seven houses calling (out to each in turn): '(Give) alms to to a man who has failed in his duty to his wife!' And this should be his livelihood for six months." As Leslie notes, this penalty is the same as the one prescribed for a man who commits adultery (1994, 75–76).

43. *sahadharmacarīm dāntam nityam matṛsamām mama*
sakhāyam vihitām devairnityam paramikām gatim
mātrā pitrā ca vihitām sadā gārhasthyabhāginīm
varayitvā yathānyāyam mantravatpariṇīya ca (I.145.31–32).

44. *Na ca bhāryāsamam kiṃcidvidyate bhiṣajam matam*
auṣadham sarvaduḥkhesu satyametadbravīmi te (III.58.27).

45. *atmānaṃ ca viśeṣeṇa praśaṃsāmyanapāyini*
yasya me tvam viśālakṣi bhāryā sarvaguṇānvitā (XII.348.19).

46. *gāndhārī hataputreyam dhairyeṇodīkṣate ca mām* (XV.5.15).

47. This is certainly the case in the *Dharmasūtras*; see GDh.23.12.

48. See ĀpDh.2.12–22; GDh.15.18, 18.18; BDh.2.1.39–40; VaDh.1.18.

49. Such passages are also to be found in the *Dharma* literature; see, for example, VaDh.20.7–8.

50. Theoretically, Bhīma has been through one marriage, with the *rākṣasī* Hiḍimbā. That marriage, however, is clearly unorthodox, with the understanding that it will conclude with the birth of a son. Accordingly, when Ghaṭotkaca is born, the marriage dissolves of its own accord. Hiḍimbā leaves with Ghaṭotkaca, and only Ghaṭotkaca is seen periodically after that.

51. Indeed, as Fitzgerald remarks, "there can be only one reason the MBh emphasizes *varṇadharma* and *svadharma* as strongly as it does—these principles were not as widely followed nor as widely recognized as the authors and editors of the text would wish" (2003c, 6–7).

52. *pitṛbhirbhrātṛbhiścaiva śvaśurairatha devaraiḥ*
pūjyā lālayitavyāśca bahukalyāṇamīpsubhiḥ (XIII.46.3).

53. *na hyakāmena saṃvādam manurevam praśaṃsati*
ayaśasyamadharmyam ca yanmṛṣā dharmakopanam (XIII.44.22).

54. *nāniṣṭāya pradātavya kanyā ityṛṣicoditam* (XIII.44.35).

55. *striyo mānanamarhanti tā mānayata mānavāḥ*
strīpratyayo hi vo dharmo ratibhogāśca kevalāḥ
paricaryānnasaṃskārāstadāyattā bhavantu vaḥ
utpādanamapatyasya jātasya paripālanam
prītyartham lokayātrā ca paśyata strīnibandhanam (XIII.46.8–10).

56. *Na caitebhyaḥ pradātavyā na voḍhavyā tathāvidhā*
na hyeva bhāryā kretavyā na vikreyā kathaṃcana
ye ca krīṇanti dāsīvadye vikrīṇatejanāḥ
bhaveteṣām tathā niṣṭhā lubdhānām pāpacetasām (XIII.44.46).

57. *saṃśayam param prāpya vedanāmatulāmapi*
prajāyante sutānnāryo duḥkhena mahatā vibho
puṣṇanti cāpi mahatā snehena dvijasattama (III.196.10)

58. These observations are supported by parallel injunctions in Manu: "If a virgin makes love with a man of a superior class (the king) should not make her pay any fine at all; but if she makes love with a man of the rear classes, he should have her live at home in confinement. If a man of the rear classes makes love with a virgin of the highest class, he should be given corporal or capital punishment; if he makes love with a virgin of the same class as his own, he should pay the bride-price, if her father should wishes it (8.365–66).

59. This is at least the case in rhetoric. There are just a few cases of *brāhmaṇa* women marrying *kṣatriya*s that pass without comment: Devayānī with Yayāti, Śakuntalā with Duḥṣanta, Pramadvarā with Ruru. In all of these cases, the women are brought up in forest hermitages by their fathers, who are gurus and sages. They

involve *gandharva* unions with prominent royal figures, and possibly escape reproof because of the political stature of the men involved. *Brāhmaṇa* and *kṣatriya* unions are in general treated as being less offensive than unions between high and low classes.

60. *śreyāṃsam śayane hitvā yā pāpīyāṃsamṛcchati*
śvabhiratām khādayedrājā saṃsthāne bahusaṃvṛte (XII.159.59).

61. *pumāṃsam bandhayetprājñaḥ śayane tapta āyase*
apyādadhīta dārūṇi tatra dahyeta pāpakṛta (XII.159.60).

62. *kulakṣaye praṇaśyanti kuladharmāḥ sanātanāḥ*
dharme naṣṭe kulam kṛtsnam adharmo 'bhibhavaty uta
adharmābhibhavāt kṛṣṇa praduṣyanti kulastriyaḥ
strīṣu duṣṭāsu vārṣṇeya jāyate varṇasaṃkaraḥ (BG I.40–41).

63. *ye vai śukragatiṃ vidyurbūtasaṃkarakārikam*
virāgā dagdhadoṣaste nāpnuyurdehasaṃbhavam (XII.207.24).

64. "One of the fundamental concerns of the entire MBh and of its chartering of proper kingship is the primacy of *varṇadharma*, the social hierarchy which grounds and preserves what is, ideally, a theocratic monopoly" (Fitzgerald 2003c, 5–6).

65. See 12.91.30–38 for the evils of *varṇasaṃkara*.

66. *mā śucaḥ putra caṇḍālastvādhitiṣṭhati*
brāhmaṇe dāruṇam nāsti maitro brāhmaṇa ucyate (XIII.28.10–11).

67. Uma Chakravarti draws attention to the category of *dāsīs* in her provocative article, "Whatever Happened to the Vedic *Dāsī*?" (1989).

Chapter Four. The Unruly Desire of Women

1. Laurie Patton, 1996, 24.

2. Bal 2001, 153.

3. White, 14.

4. Julia Leslie for example concludes that: "At its simplest, this view maintains that women are inherently wicked, that they are possessed of an incontrollable and threatening inborn sexuality, and that they are innately impure" (1994, 63).

5. This of course is unlikely history. As Brockington says, "The occasional references to an original situation of sexual promiscuity are clearly intended as means of persuasion rather than as fact" (1998, 223).

6. *Anāvṛtāḥ kila purā striya āsanvarānane*
kāmacāravihāriṇyaḥ svatantrāścārulocane
tāsām vyajcaramāṇānām kaumārātsubhage patīn
nādharmo 'bhūdvarārohe sa hi dharmaḥ purābhavat (I.113.4–5).

7. *Strīṇāmanugrahakaraḥ sa hi dharmaḥ sanātanaḥ* (I.113.7).

8. The character Śvetaketu is familiar from the Chāndogya Upaniṣad, where he is represented as a comically brash young man, "swollen headed, arrogant, thinking

himself learned." He requires the temperance and instruction of his father who imparts to him some of the loftiest teachings of the Upanisads, each ending in *Tat tvam asi* Śvetaketu. "That's how you are." The fact that the MBh. uses Śvetaketu of all characters as the source for such a ruling, and moreover, Śvetaketu at a young age still needing the restraining hand of his father, suggests that the rule originated by him is intended to appear hasty and impetuous, even irrational. The fact that Pāṇḍu cites it to support his argument suggests that we are to understand Pāṇḍu's arguments as sophistical.

9. *mā tāta kopan kārṣīstvameṣa dharmaḥ sanātanaḥ*
anāvṛtam hi sarveṣām varṇānāmaṅganā bhuvi
yathā gāvaḥ sthitāstāta sve sve varṇe tathā prajāḥ (I.113.13–14).

10. *Vyujcarantyāḥ patim nāryā adya prabhṛti pātakam*
bhrūṇahatyākṛtam pāpam bhaviṣyatyasukhāvaham (I.113.17).

11. *bhāryām tathā vyujcarataḥ kaumārīm brahmacāriṇīm*
pativratāmetadeva bhavitā pātakam bhuvi (I.113.18).

Then Pāṇḍu slips in the subject closest to his heart, "A wife who is bidden by her husband to do something for his sake and refuses shall incur the same fate"
patyā niyuktā yā caiva patnyapatyārthameva ca
na kariṣyati tasyāśa bhaviṣyatyetadeva hi (I.113.19).

12. To borrow a phrase from Bal, 155.

13. *īpsitaśca gunaḥ strīṇāmekasyā bahubhartṛtā*
tam ca prāptavatī kṛṣṇā na sa bhedayitum sukham (I.194.8).

14. This is the perspective offered, for example, by N. K. Basu and S. N. Sinha, 1994.

15. See, for example, Doniger, 1973.

16. *rajasvalāsu nārīṣu yo vai maithunamācaret*
tameṣā yāsyati kṣipram vyatu vo mānaso jvaraḥ (XII.283.44).

17. *bhavatyā gūḍhamantratvātpīḍito asmītyuvāca tāṃ*
śaśāpa ca mahātejaḥ sarvalokeṣu ca striyāḥ
na guhyam dhārayiṣyantītyatiduḥkhasamanvitaḥ (XII.6.10).

18. *Teṣāmantargatam jñātvā devānām sa pitāmahaḥ*
mānavānām pramohartham kṛtyā nāryo 'sṛjatprabhuḥ (XIII.40.7).

19. *tābhyaḥ kāmānyathākāmām pradāddhi sa pitāmahaḥ*
tāḥ kāmalubdhaḥ pramadāḥ prāmathnanta narāmstadā (XIII.40.9).

20. *śayyāsanamalaṃkāramannapānamanāryatām*
durvāgbhāvaṃ ratiṃ caiva dadau stribhyaḥ prajāpatiḥ (XIII.40.12).

21. *pūrvasarge tu kaunteya sādhvyo nārya ihābhavan*
asādhvyastu samutpannā kṛtyā sargātprajāpateḥ (XIII.40.8).

22. In the words of Wendy Doniger (1976, 16).

23. Kaikeyī and Śūrpanakhā have been proposed as models of aggressive female sexuality, who are brutally disciplined by the patriarchal culture in which they live. See Kathleen Erndl, 1991; and Sutherland, 1992.

24. *Na hi strībhya param putra pāpīyaḥ kiṃcidasti vai*
agnirhi pramadā dīpto māyāśca mayajā vibho
kṣuradhārā viṣam sarpo mṛtyurityekataḥ striyaḥ (XIII.40.4).

25. *nirindriyā amantrāśca striyo 'nṛtamiti śrutiḥ* (XIII.40.11).

26. *rajasyantarhitā mūrtirindriyāṇām sanātanī* (XII.206.9).

27. *strīṇām buddhayupaniṣkarṣādarthaśāstrāṇi śatruhan*
bṛhaspatiprabhṛtibhirmanye sadbhiḥ kṛtāni vai

"The sciences of cunning policy devised by Bṛhaspati and others of his ilk were devised through observation of the intelligence of women" (XIII.39.9).

28. *na brahmacāryadhīyāta kalyāṇī gaurna duhyate*
na kanyādvahanam gaccedyadi daṇḍo na pālayet (XII.15.37).

29. *anarthitvānmanuṣyāṇām bhayātparijanasya ca*
maryādāyāmaryādāḥ striyastiṣṭhanti bhartṛṣu
nāsām kaścidagamyo sti nāsām vayasi saṃsthitiḥ
virūpam rūpavantam va pumānityeva bhuñjate (XIII.38.15–17).

30. *Na śakṣyāmi strī satā ninditum striyaḥ* (XIII.38.7); *satye doṣo na vidyate* (XIII.38.9).

31. *strīṇāmagamyo loke sminnāsti kaścinmahāmune* (XIII.30.21).

32. *kulīnā rūpavatyaśca nāthavatyaśca yoṣitaḥ*
maryādāsu na tiṣṭhanti sa doṣaḥ strīṣu nārada (XIII.38.11).

33. *nāgnistṛpyati kāṣṭhānām nāpagānām mahodadhiḥ*
nāntakaḥ sarvabhūtānām na puṃsām vāmalocanāḥ (XIII.38.25).

34. *striyam hi yaḥ prārthayate saṃnikarṣam ca gacchanti*
īṣajca kurute sevām tamevecchanti yoṣitaḥ (XIII.38.15).

35. *striyaḥ puṃsām paridade manurjigamiṣurdivam*
abalāḥ svalpakaupīnāḥ suhṛdaḥ satyajiṣṇavaḥ (XIII.46.7).

36. *samājñātānṛddhimataḥ pratirūpānvaśe sthitān*
patīnantaramāsādhya nālam nāryaḥ pratīkṣitum (XIII.38.13).

37. Apparently she still retained some male privileges!

38. Niles Newton, quoted with approbation by Adrienne Rich, 1976, 274.

39. The dangers of this dynamic are discussed by Uma Narayan 1989.

40. *śīśoḥ śuśrūṣaṇācchuśrūmātā dehamanantaram*
cetanāvānnaro hanyādyasya nāsuśiram śiraḥ (XII.258.31).

41. *sā vai tasyābhavanmātā pitā ceti hi naḥ śrutam*

42. *mātaraṃ caiva śocāmi kṛpaṇāṃ putragṛddhinīṃ*
yasmākam nityamāśāaste mahattvamadhikam paraiḥ
katham nu tasyānāthāyā madvināśādbhujangam
aphalāste bhaviṣyanti mayi sarve manorathāḥ (III.176.35–36)

43. *guruṇām caiva sarveṣām janitrī paramo guruḥ* (I.188.14).

44. Sally Sutherland argues the need to "rehabilitate" Kaikeyī in Hinduism, and to update her reputation to "something of a cryptic feminist heroine" (1992, 250).

45. *yathā kuntī tathā mādrī viśeṣo nāsti me tayoḥ*
matṛbhyām samamicchāmi (III.297.73).

46. *pitṛdaśa tu mataikā sarvam vā pṛthivīmapi*
gurutvenābhibhavati nāsti matṛsamo guruḥ (XII.109.16).

47. *mātā gurutara bhūmeḥ pitā ujcataraśca khāt* (III.297.41).

48. *na tu mātrābhiśaptānām mokṣo vidyeta pannagāḥ* (I.33.5).

49. The Matṛkās have been studied at length in the works of David Kinsley, 1988, 1997.

50. *lohitasyodadheḥ kanyā krūrā lohitabhojanā* (III.215.22).

51. "It is evident . . . that the male guardianship of females [indicated in Manu's famous '*rakṣati* verse] is directed in a special way at their sexual life. A husband should guard his wife carefully, says an ancient *Brāhmaṇa*, "lest in my womb, in my world somebody else come into existence" (*Jaiminīya Brāhmaṇa* 1.17, cited in Olivelle, 1993, 185). Also, *Āpastamba Dharmasūtra* 2.12.6 cites a Vedic text: "After his death the man who planted the seed carries off his son into Yama's world; fearful of another man's seed, therefore, they guard their wives. Take vigilant care over (the procreation of your children, lest the seed of others be sown on your soil" [Olivelle 1993, 185, n. 8]).

52. Gupta cites the *Manusmṛti* as a case in point (1992, 90).

53. This pattern seems to be identified by Mieke Bal in her discussion of "the emergence of the female character," when she speaks of the "formation of characters and their features by opposition and analogy" (152).

Chapter Five. Disciplining Desire

1. These scenes bear an unmistakable resemblance to the scene encountered by Hanumān on his visit to Laṅka in the *Vālmīki Rāmāyaṇa*. There also women are represented in an unflattering way, but the context is different; the negative characterization is intended to show that the *rākṣasas* are fundamentally barbaric in nature.

2. See Wilson, particularly Chapter Three.

3. As translated by Murcott, 26.

4. *Yogavasiṣṭha* 1.21.11, 12, 18, 12; cited in Olivelle (1995), 198.

5. "*Nāradaparivrājaka Upaniṣad,*" *Saṃnyāsa Upaniṣads,* 160 (cited in Olivelle 1995, 198).

6. Wilson makes a similar observation about the scarcity of male objects of contemplation in Buddhism: "There is, to my knowledge, only one post-Aśokan tale of a male body causing an aha experience in a woman, and it involves the disciple Ānanda" (18).

7. (Quote from Liberation in the Palm of Your Hand by Phabongka Rinpoche, trans. Michael Richards, Boston, Wisdom Publications, 1993.)

8. "*Nāradaparivrājaka Upaniṣad,*" *Saṃnyāsa Upaniṣads* 144 (cited in Olivelle 1995, 191).

9. *Vaitaraṇyām ca yadduḥkham patitānām yamakṣaye*
yonīṣu ca vicitrāsu saṃsāranaśubhāṃstathā
jaṭhare caśubhe vāsam śoṇitodakabhājane
śleṣmamūtrapūrīṣe ca tīvragandhasamanvite
śukraśoṇitasaṃghāte majjāsnāyuparigrahe
sirāśatasamākīrṇe navadvāre pure a śucau (XII.290.31–33)
10. *Mātāpitṛsahasrāṇi putridāraśatāni ca*
anāgatānyatītāni kasya te kasya vā vayam
na teṣām bhavata kāryam na kāryam tava tairapi
svakṛtaistāni yātāni bhavāṃscaiva gamiṣyati (XII.309.84–85)
11. *mithilāyām pradīptāyām na me dahyati kiñcana* (XII.17.18)
12. *na caivārtirvidyate asmadvidhānām dharmāramaḥ satataṃ sajjano hi*
nityāyasto bālajano na cāsti dharmo hyeṣa prabhavāmyasya nāham
na brāhmaṇām kopo asti kutaḥ kopājca yātanā
mārdavātkṣamyatām sādho mucyatāmeṣa pannagaḥ (XIII.1.19–20)
13. *devo manuṣyo gandharvo yuvā cāpi svalaṃkṛtaḥ*
dravyavānabhirūpo vā na me anyaḥ puruṣo mataḥ
nābhuktavati nāsnāte nāsaṃviṣṭe ca bhartari
na saṃviśāmi nāśnāmi sadā karmakāreṣvapi
kṣetrādvanādvā grāmadvā bhartāram gṛhamāgatam
pratyutthāyābhinandāmi āsanenodakena ca (III.222.22–24).
Niratāham sadā satye bhartṇāmupasevane
Sarvathā bhartṛrahitam na mameṣṭam kathaṃcana
Yadā pravasate bhartā kuṭumbarthena kenacit
Sumanovarṇakapetā bhavāmi vratacāriṇī
yajca bhartā na pibati yajca bhartā na khādati
yajca nāśnati me bhartā sarvam tadvarjayāmyaham (III.222.28–30).
14. *Pradyumnasāmbāvapi te kumārau nopāsitavyau rahite kadācit* (XII.223.10)
15. *patyāśrayo hi me dharmo mataḥ strīṇām sanātanaḥ*
sa devā sa gatirnānyā tasya kā vipriyam caret (XII.222.35)
16. *naitadṛśam daivatamasti satye sarveṣu lokeṣu sadaivateṣu* (III.223.2).
17. *yadyakāryamadharmam vā yadi vā prāṇanāśanam*
patirbruyāddaridro vā vyādhito vā kathaṃcana
āpanno ripusaṃstho vā brahmaśāpārditopi vā
āpaddharmānanupreksya tatkāryamaviśaṅkayā (XIII.134.53–54).
18. *daridram vyādhitam dīnamaghvanā parikarśitam*
patim putramivopāste sā nārī dharmabhāginī (XIII.134.40).
19. *śrutvā svaram dvāragatasya bhartuḥ pratyutthitā tiṣṭha gṛhasya madhye*
dṛṣṭvā praviṣṭam tvaritāsanena pādyena caiva pratipūjya tvam
saṃpreṣitāyāmatha caiva dāsyāmutthāya sarvam svayameva kuryaḥ
jānātu kṛṣṇastava bhāvametam sarvātmanā mām bhajatīti satye
(III:223:6–7).

20. *Notthāpyāmi bhartāram sukhasuptamaham sadā*
ātureṣvāpi kāryeṣu tena tuṣyati me manaḥ (XIII.124.18).

21. *kalyotthānaratā nityam guruśuśrūṣaṇe ratā*
susaṃmṛṣṭkṣayā caiva gośakṛtkṛtalepanā
agnikāryaparā nityam sadā puṣpabalipradā
devatātithibhṛtyānām nirupya patinā saha
śeṣānnamupabhuñjānā yathānyāyam yathāvidhi
tuṣṭapuṣṭajanā nityam nārī dharmeṇa yujyate
śvaśrūśvaśurayoḥ pādau toṣayanti guṇānvitā
mātāpitṛparā nityam yā nārī sā tapodhanā (XIII.134.44–47)

22. *nityamāryamaham kuntīm vīrasūm satyavādinīm*
svayam paricarābhyekā snānācchādanabhojanaiḥ
naitāmatiśaye jātu vastrabhūṣaṇabhojanaiḥ
nāpi parivade cāham tām pṛthām pṛthivīsamām (III.222.38–39).

23. *Kutumbārthe samānītam yatkiṃcitkāryameva tu*
prātarutthāya tatsarvam kāryāmi karomi ca (XIII.124.15).

24. *priyāṃśca raktāṃśca hitāṃśca bhartustānbhojayethā vividhairupayaiḥ*
dveṣyairapakṣairahitaiśca tasya bhidyasva nityam kuhakoddhataiśca
(III.223.9).

25. *naitadṛśam daivatamasti satye sarveṣu lokeṣu sadaivateṣu*
yathā patistasya hi sarvakāmā labhyāḥ prasāde kupitaśca hanyāt
tasmādapatyam vividhaśca bhogāḥ śayyāsanānyadbhutadarśanāni
vastrāṇi mālyāni tathaiva gandhāḥ svargaśca loko viṣamā ca kīrtiḥ
(III:223:2–3).

26. *mitam dadāti hi pitā mitam mātā mitam sutaḥ*
amitasya tu dātāram bhartāram kā na pūjayet (XII.144.6).

27. *nāsti bhṛtṛsamo nātho na ca bhartṛsamam sukham*
visṛjya dhanasarvasvam bhartā vai śaraṇam striyāḥ (XII.144.7).

28. See, for example, Altekar 1959, and Jayal 1966.

29. See Jamison, 1996. Frederick M. Smith, however, argues to the contrary, that the woman's role in Vedic sacrifice was being diminished (1992).

30. The various works of Werner F. Menski dwell on the subject of Hindu marriage, from its ancient times to its contemporary manifestations. See, for example, 1992, 1987, 1985.

31. This phenomenon is also noted by Patton in her discussion of Ṛgvedic hymns and their commentators: "One can . . . see a progression from negotiated gender identity to regulated gender identity in the treatment of the hymn by later commentators. Through a deft use of exegetical techniques, the later Vedic scholars, writing at a time when the maintenance of Brahminical norms were paramount, 'clean up' the offensively free sexual dialogues in an effort to make them acceptable" (1996a). Olivelle remarks for the *Dharmaśāstras*: "The history of Brahmanical theology is a

constant movement in the direction of an ever increasing restrictive ideology regarding the status and role of women" (1993, 184).

32. *Nāsti yajñaḥ striyaḥ kaścinna śrāddham nopavāsakam* (XIII.46.12).

33. *mām cābhigamya kṣīṇo yam kāmādbharatasattamaḥ*
tamucchindyāmasya kāmam katham nu yamasādane (I.116.26)

34. *na kāryamiha me nātha jīvitena tvayā vinā* (XII.144.8).

35. *patihīnāpi kā nārī satī jīvitumutsahet?* (XII.144.8).

36. "But this is . . . not the standard *sati* pattern, since this even occurs years after their husbands' deaths" (Brockington 1996, 218). Four of Vasudeva's wives Devakī, Bhadrā, Rohiṇī, and Madirā prepare to mount his pyre and die with him (16.8.18–24), but Akrūra's wives go forth as wanderers (*pravavrajuh*; 16.8.70). Rukmiṇī and other names wives enter fire, but Satyabhāmā and others enter the forest (16.8.71–72).

37. *yā yāḥ patikṛtaṃllokānicchanti paramastriyaḥ*
tā jāhnavījalaṃkṣipramvagāhantyatandritāḥ (XVI.41.18).

38. *yāpi caivaṃvidhā nārī bhartāramanuvartate*
virājate hi sā kṣipram kapotīva divi sthitā (XII.145.15).

39. Jayal, 180.

40. Hiltebeitel suggests that as a pattern, it is only junior wives who become *satis*, but this is not so apparent in the above.

41. *mayā caitatpratijñātam raṇamūrdhani keśava*
abhimanyau hate vīra tvāmeṣyāmyacirāditi
tajca nākaravaṃ kṛṣṇa nṛśaṃsā jīvitapriyā
idānīmāgatām tatra kim nu vakṣyati phālguniḥ (XIV.67.23–24).

42. This may simply be a narrative device used by the author to further the story, but the prevalence of widow remarriage in ancient India has been argued by other scholars as well. See Altekar, Chakladar, and Jayal.

43. The reasons for a man's prerogative to remarry are, however, complex. As noted, the male householder is the primary agent of the Vedic sacrificial system. It was critical to the efficacy of the sacrifice that he be married. As one scholar points out, for example, quite apart from reasons of personal grief, "No greater calamity could befall a Vedic householder than the untimely death of his wife. The household fire now burns her mortal remains, and becomes no better than the funeral fire (*śavāgni*). The widower must set up a new fire and seek a new partner at the daily offerings. Two courses are open to him—either he must forsake the world and become a forest-recluse (*vānaprastha*), or he must marry immediately on the expiry of the period of impurity, if he prefers to continue in the householder's state, because the paramount duty of the householder, the daily offering of the *agnihotra* cannot be carried on without the wife" Chakladar, 574.

44. *Na cāpyadharmaḥ kalyāṇa bahupatnīkatā nṛṇām*
strīṇāmadharmaḥ sumahānbhartuḥ pūrvasya laṅghane (I.146.34–35).

45. *sarva vai vidhavā nārī bahuputrāpi khecara*
śocyā bhavati bandhūnām patihīnā manasvinī (XII.144.2).

46. *śūpaśca sumahāṃstasya dattaḥ suragaṇaistadā*
kukṣau punarbhvāṃ bhāryāyām janayitvā cirātsutān
nirayam prāpsyati mahatkṛtaghno 'yamiti prabho (XII.167.17).

47. *nāham kāṣāyavasanā nāpi valkaladhāriṇī*
na ca muṇḍa na jaṭilā bhūtvā devatvamāgatā
ahitāni ca vākyāni sarvāṇi paruṣāṇi ca
apramattā ca bhartāram kadācinnāhamabruvam (XIII.124.8–9)

48. find (III.183.14–15).

49. Damayantī's Self-assured and active identity is contrasted with the Self-forgetful tendencies of Nala by David Shulman, 1994. Shulman also remarks the many parallels between Damayantī and Draupadī.

50. *patirhi devo nārīṇām patirbandhuḥ patirgatiḥ*
patyā samā gatirnāsti daivatam vā yathā patiḥ (XIII.134.51).

51. *sa tu deveśaḥ pratipūjya gireḥ sutām* (XIII.134.56).

52. *punyametattapaścaiva svargaścaiṣa sanātanaḥ*
yā nārī bhartṛparamā bhavedbhartṛvratā śivā (XIII·134.50).

53. *yathāham naiṣadhādanyam manasāpi na cintaye*
tathāyam patatām kṣudraḥ parāsurmṛgajīvanaḥ (III.60.37).

54. Vidyut Aklujkar (2000).

55. *Cilappatikaram*

56. *pitā mātā guravaścaiva ye 'anye dehasyāsya prabhavanti pradāne*
nāham dharmam lopayiśyāmi loke strīṇām vṛttam pūjyate deharakṣā
mayā mantrabalā jñātumāhūtastvam vibhāvāso
bālyādbāleti kṛtvā tatkṣantumarhasi me vibho (III.290.22–23).

57. *na cāhamīṣā dehasya tasmānnṛpatisattam*
samīpaṃ nopagacchāmi na svatantrā hi yoṣitaḥ (I.161.16).

58. *viddhi mām bhagvankanyām sadā pitṛvaśānugām*
tvatsaṃyogājca duṣyeta kanyābhāvo mamānagha
kanyātve dūṣite cāpi kathaṃ śakṣye dvijottama
gantum gṛham gṛhe cāham dhīmānna sthātumutsahe
etatsaṃcintya bhagavanvidhatsva yadanantaram (I.57.61–62).

"Sir, know me for a virgin who has always been in her father's care. Consorting with you, blameless lord, would destroy my virginity. And when my virginity is lost, how could I go home?"

59. *nārīṇām ciravāso hi bāndhaveṣu na rocate*
kīrticāritradharmaghnastasmānnayata māciram (I.68.12).

56. 0*na candrasūryau na tarum punnāmno yā narīkṣate*
bhartṛvarjam varārohā sā bhaveddharmacāriṇī (XIII.134.39).

61. *pitā rakṣati kaumare bhartā rakāati yauvane*
putrāśca sthavirībhāve na strī svātantryamarhati (XIII.21.19).

This is, of course, also the infamous dictum of Manu invariably cited in all texts of Hindu women.

62. Liz Wilson, in her work *Charming Cadavers*, argues something similar for Buddhist women. She says, "Buddhist women living in South Asia in the first millennium of the Common Era were subordinated to men not so much by rules that enshrine male privilege and circumscribe women's rights but by representational practices that would have made it difficult for a woman to imagine herself following in the footsteps of highly revered Buddhist saints" (4).

63. *dharme sthito dharmasutaśca rājā dharmaśca sūkṣamo nipuṇopalabhyaḥ*
vācāpi bhartuḥ paramāṇumātram necchāmi doṣam svaguṇānvisṛjya
(II.60.31).

64. *dīrghāyuratha vālpayuḥ saguṇo nirguṇopi vā*
sakṛtvrato mayā bhartā na dvitīyam vṛṇomyaham
manasā niścayam kṛtvā tato vācābhidhīyate
kriyate karmaṇā paścātpramāṇam me manastataḥ (III.278.26–27).

65. Some more than others! Draupadī, for example, an ideal *pativratā* in various respects, is voluble in her complaints about the injustices she has suffered, but women such as Kuntī, Gāndhārī, and Sāvitrī are of outstanding scruple and forbearance.

Chapter Six. *Āpaddharma*

1. *hīne paramake dharme sarvalokātilaṅgini*
adharme dharmatām nīte dharme cādharmatām gate
maryādāsu prabhinnāsu kṣubhite dharmaniścaye
rājabhiḥ pīḍite loke corairvāpi viśām pate
sarvāśrameṣu mūḍhesu karmasūpahateṣu ca
kāmānmohājca lobhājca bhayam paśyatsu bhārata
aviśvasteṣu sarveṣu nityabhīteṣu pārthiva
nikṛtyā hanyamāneṣu vañcayatsu parasparam
saṃpradīpteṣu deśeṣu brāhmaṇye cābhipīḍite
avarṣati ca parjanye mitho bhede samutthite
sarvasmindasyusādbhūte pṛthivyāmupajīvane
kena svidbrāhmaṇo jīvejjaghanye kāla āgate (XII.139.1–6)
kathamāpatsu varteta tanme brūhi pitāmaha (XII.139.7)

2. *śreyastatra anṛtam vaktum satyāditi* (XII.110.15).

3. *advaidhyajñaḥ pathi dvaidhe saṃśayam prāptumarhati*
buddhidvaidham veditavyam purastādeva bhārata (XII.140.8)

4. *yugakṣayātparikṣīṇe dharme loke ca bhārata*
dasyubhiḥ pīdyamā ca katham stheyam pitāmaha (XII.138.1)

5. That dogs were held is low esteem is apparent, for example, in the numerous statements that equate sacrificial food licked by dogs with the state of the highest

impurity. In a story from the *Ādiparva*, Saramā, the prototypical mother dog, finding that her son has beaten, immediately assumes that the beating was a result of his having licked sacrificial food (I.3.5).

6. *nirāhārasya sumahān mama kālo abhidhāvataḥ*
na vidyate abhyupāyaṣca kiścin me prāṇadhāraṇe
yena tena viśeṣeṇa karmaṇā yena kenacit
abhyujjīvetsīdamānaḥ samartho dharmamācaret (XII.139.58–59)

7. *yathā yathā vai jīveddhi tatkartavyampīḍayā*
jīvitam maraṇācchreyo jīvandharmamavāpruyat (XII. 139.61)

8. As the story unfolds, after all their preparations, they do not in fact eat the corpse; they are interrupted before it has finished cooking, and the story moves in another direction.

9. *vyajcarantyapi duḥśīlā dāsaiḥ paśubhireva ca* (III.186.55).

10. *bhartṇām vacane caiva na sthāsyanti* (III.188.77).

11. *sūdayiṣyanti ca patīnstriyaḥ putrānapāśritāḥ* (III.188.78).

12. *keśaśūlāḥ striyaścapi bhaviṣyanti yugākṣaye* (III.188.51).

13. *āpaddharmamavekṣasva vaha paitāmahīm dhuram* (I.97.21)

14. The text is hesitant to allege actual infertility in a man, though it would seem to be the obvious problem in some cases, such as Kalmāṣapāda Saudāsa and Balin; indeed, while the subject of female infertility is discussed in various texts and represents a legitimate reason for a man to abandon his wife or to take another, a discussion of male fertility is hardly to be encountered in the *dharma* literature.

15. There is some discussion about whether *niyoga* was limited to the younger brother—Meyer and Jayal assume this to be the case (Meyer, 162 ff.; Jayal, 161 ff.). Emeneau and van Nooten have demonstrated, however, that in the earliest times, from the *Ṛgveda* through classical Hinduism, the brother was not specified; the use of the word *devara* to connote "husband's younger brother" can be dated back "to the fifth or sixth century at the earliest" (490).

16. Children born of such unions are *kṣetraja*, "born of the field" of the husband (Jayal, 156 ff.). As Pāṇḍu anxiously seeks advice from the forest sages, "How can I have children? Should I have offspring in my field, just as I myself was begotten by the great-spirited seer in my father's field?" (I.111.17).

17. Manu, for example, is highly ambivalent, condemning it in IX.64–70, and permitting it in IX.57–63, where he enters the following caveat: (1) the husband, whether living or dead, must have no son; (2) the gurus in a family council should decide to appoint the widow to raise issue for the husband; (3) the person appointed must be either the husband's brother, or a member of the same caste and lineage; (4) the person appointed and the widow must be motivated not by desire, but only by a sense of duty; (5) the person must not speak with or kiss or engage in amorous merriment with the woman; and (6) the relationship must end after the birth of one son, or according to others, two. Ultimately, "when the purpose of the appointment with the widow has been completed in accordance with the rules, the two of them should behave toward each other like a guru and a daughter-in-law (IX. 57–62).

18. I have argued elsewhere that this is an important consideration for interpreting why the Bharata widows are punished for their reactions with congenitally flawed children (2003).

19. As in some cases she is alleged to do: Pāṇḍu's cites the example of Śaradaṇḍāyiṇī. She is said to be a widow who stood at an intersection and chose a wise *brāhmaṇa* to father children with her. Through his co-operation, she obtained three children, all of whom went on to be the progenitors of illustrious lineages (I.111.32–36). In this telling, Śaradaṇḍāyiṇī would appear to be acting upon her own initiative, making her own decisions and finding her own mate. It is questionable, however, whether this rosy picture isn't painted by Pandu to achieve his own ends—persuading Kunti to agree to niyoga.

20. *ṛtum vai yācamānāyā na dadāti pumānvṛtā*
bhūṇahetyucyate brahmansa iha brahmavādibhiḥ (I.78.32).

21. *ṛtavṛtau rājaputri striyā bhartā yatavrate*
nātivartavya ityevam dharmam dharmavido viduḥ (I.113.25).

22. *atrerbhāryāpi bhartāram saṃtyajya brahmavādinī*
nāham tasya munerbhūyo vaśagā syām kathaṃcana
ityuktva sā mahādevamagacchaccharaṇam kila (XIII.14.65)

23. *tāmabravīddhasandevo bhavitā vai sutastava*
vaṃśe tavaiva nāmnā tu khyātim yāsyati cepsitām (XIII.14.67)

24. *devaram praviśetkanyā tapyedvāpi mahattapaḥ*
tamevānuvratā bhūtvā pāṇigrahasya nāma sā (XIII.44.50)

25. *aham saptarṣipatnīnām kṛtvā rūpāṇi pāvakam*
kāmayiṣyāami kāmartam tāsāam rūpeṇa mohitam
evam kṛteprītirasya kāmāvāptiśca me bhavet (III.213.52)

26. The *Anuśāsanaparva* recounts a tale where we learn that Jamadagni used to practise archery in the forest, and his wife used to run and gather his arrows for him after he shot them. One time, the sun was so hot that she scorched her head and feet, and was compelled to sit under the shade of a tree to rest. "The black-eyed and graceful Renukā, having rested for only a moment, feared the curse of her husband and therefore returned to her task of retrieving the arrows. Taking them with her, the celebrated and graceful woman returned, distressed in mind and her feet in pain. Trembling with fear, she approached her husband, but the seer, consumed with anger, repeatedly badgered his wife, demanding, 'What took you so long to return?'" The terrified Renukā explains her reasons, and pleads with her husband not to be angry with her (XIII.97.6–16).

27. The Indo-European roots of this myth are analyzed by Dumézil, 1968, and Hiltebeitel, 1976.

28. This is also apparent in the *Dharma* literature, which advocates harsh penalties for rapists. See (primary texts) and Basu and Sinha, 111.

29. *ṛtavṛtau rājaputri striyā bhartā yatavrate*
nātivartavya ityevam dharmam dharmavido viduḥ (I.113.25).

30. *niveśam tu bhavettena sadā tārayitā pitn*
na tu striyā bhavetdoṣo na tu sā tena lipyate
striyastvāśaṅkitāḥ pāpairnopagamyā hi jānatā
rajasā tā viśudhyante bhasmanā bhājanaṃ yathā (XII.36.25, 27).
31. *Evam strī nāparādhnoti nara evāparādhyati*
vyujcaraṃśca mahādoṣam nara evāparādhyati (XII.258.36).
32. *Yaścanokto hi nirdeśaḥ striyā maithunatṛptaye*
tasya smārayato vyaktamadharmo nātra saṃśayaḥ (XII.258.38).
33. *Naitacchuddhāgamadeva tava dharmānuśāsanam*
prajñāsamavatāro ayam kavibhiḥ saṃbhṛtam madhu
bahvayaḥ pratividhātavyāḥ prajñā rajñā tatastaḥ
naikaśākhena dharmeṇa yatraiṣā saṃpravartate (XII.140.3–5).

Conclusion

1. Gitomer, 1992, 222.
2. Fitzgerald, 1983, 613.
3. Fitzgerald, 1985.
4. *Naiva strī na pumānetannaiva cedam napuṃsakam* (XII.242.22).

Selected Bibliography

Primary Texts

The Bhagavadgītā in the Mahābhārata. J. A. B. van Buitenen, trans. and ed. Chicago: The University of Chicago Press. 1981.

The Buddhacarita. Trans. E. H. Johnston. Delhi: Motilal Banarsidass. 1968.

Dharmasūtras. The Law Codes of Ancient India. Trans. and ed. Patrick Olivelle. Oxford University Press. 1999.

The Mahābhārata (Crit. Ed.). 19 vols. V. S. Sukthankar et al., eds. Poona: Bhandarkar Oriental Research Institute, 1927–59.

The Mahābhārata (Bombay Ed.). 12 vols. K. M. Ganguli, trans. and ed. (first published 1883–1896 by P. C. Roy). New Delhi: Munshiram Manoharlal Publishers Pvt. Ltd., 1970–1981.

The Mahābhārata (Crit. Ed.). 5 vols. J. A. B. van Buitenen, trans. and ed. Chicago: The University of Chicago Press. 1973–1978.

The Law Code of Manu. Trans. Patrick Olivelle. Oxford University Press. 2004.

The Laws of Manu. Wendy Doniger with Brian K. Smith, trans. and ed. Penguin Books, 1991.

The Rāmāyaṇa of Vālmīki. Critical Edition. 7 vols. Baroda: Oriental Institute. General Editors: G. H. Bhatt and U. P. Shah. 1960–1975.

Saṃnyāsa Upaniṣads: Hindu Scriptures of Asceticism and Renunciation. Patrick J. Olivelle, trans. and ed. New York: Oxford University Press, 1992.

The Upaniṣads. Patrick Olivelle, trans. and ed. New York: Oxford University Press, 1996.

Apte, V. S. *The Practical Sanskrit-English Dictionary*. Delhi: Motilal Banarsidass. 1965.

Secondary Sources

Aklujkar, Vidyut. "Anasūyā: a *Pativratā* with Panache." *Faces of the Feminine in Ancient, Medieval and Modern India.* OUP 2000. 56–68.

———. "Sāvitrī: Old and New." *Essays on the Mahābhārata.* Arvind Sharma, ed. Leiden: E. J. Brill (1991): 324–33.

Altekar, A. S. *The Position of Women in Hindu Civilization.* Delhi: Motilal Banarsidass, 1959.

Angier, Natalie. *Woman: An Intimate Geography.* Boston: Houghton Mifflin Co., 1999.

Babb, Lawrence A. "Marriage and Malevolence: The Uses of Sexual Opposition in a Hindu Pantheon." *Ethnology* IX:2 (1970).

Bailey, Gregory. "Suffering in the *Mahābhārata*: Draupadī and Yudhiṣṭhira." *Inde et Littératures: Études Reunies Par Marie-Claude Porcher*, Paris: Écoles des Hautes Études en Science Sociale (1983): 109–29.

———. *The Mythology of Brahma.* Delhi: Motilal Banarsidass. 1983.

———. *Materials for the Study of Ancient Indian Ideologies: Pravṛtti and Nivṛtti.* Torino: Publicazioni di Indological Taurinensia. 1985.

Basu, N. K.& Sinha, S. N. *History of Prostitution in India.* New Delhi: Cosmo Publications, 1994.

Bhargava, Deepali. *Manu Smriti: A Sociological Analysis.* Jaipur: Rawat Publications, 1989.

Bhattacharya, Birendra Kumar. "The *Mahābhārata*—An Epic of *Śāntarasa.*" *The Mahābhārata Revisited.* R. N. Dandekar, ed. New Delhi: Sahitya Akademi (1990): 95–100.

Biardeau, Madeleine. "Nala et Damayantī, Heros Épiques." *Indo-Iranian Journal* 27, (1984): 247–74 and 28 (1985): 1–34.

———. "The Salvation of the King in the *Mahābhārata*." *Way of Life: King, Householder, Renouncer*: Essays in Honour of Louis Dumont. T. N. Madan, ed. Delhi: Vikas Publishing House (1982): 75–98.

Biardeau, Madeleine. *Hinduism: The Anthropology of a Civilization.* Trans Nice, Richard. Delhi: Oxford University Press, 1995 (first published 1981).

———. *Études de mythologie hindoue I: cosmogonies purāṇiques; Études de mythologie hindoue II: bhakti et avatāra.* Pondichéry: Publication de l'ecole francaise d'extreme-orient, 1994.

———. *Le Mahābhārata.* Tome I et II. Paris: Editions du Seuil. 2002.

———. "La Dcapitation de Renukā dans le Mythe de Paraśurāma." Pratidanam: Indian, Iranian, and Indo-European Studies Presented to Franciscus Bernardus Jacobus Kuiper on his Sixtieth Birthday. Eds. Heesterman, J. C., Schokker, G. H., Subramoniam, V. I. The Hague: Mouton, 1968. 563–72.

——— and Malamoud, Charles. *Le Sacrifice dans l'Inde Ancienne*. Paris, 1976.

Bleier, Ruth. "Sex Differences Research: Science or Belief?" In *Feminist Approaches to Science*. Ruth Bleier, ed. New York: Pergamon Press. 1988. 147–66.

Brockington, J. L. *The Sanskrit Epics*. Leiden: E. J. Brill, 1999.

Bronkhorst, Johannes. *The Two Sources of Indian Asceticism*. Delhi: Motilal Banarsidass, 1998 (first published 1993).

Brown, C. Mackenzie. "Modes of Perfected Living in the *Mahābhārata* and the *Purāṇa*: The Different Faces of Śuka the Renouncer." *Living Liberation in Hindu Thought*. Andrew O. Fort and Patricia Y. Mumme, eds. Albany: SUNY (1996): 157–83.

———. *The Triumph of the Goddess*. Albany: SUNY Press, 1990.

Bryant, Edwin F. *In Quest of the Origins of Vedic Culture: The Indo-Aryan Invasion Debate* New York: Oxford University Press, 2001.

Caldwell, Sarah. *Oh Terrifying Mother*. New York: Oxford University Press. 1995.

Chakladar, H. C. "Some Aspects of Social Life in Ancient India," in *The Cultural Heritage of India*, vol. II, *Itihāsas, Purāṇas, Dharma, and Other Śāstras*. Calcutta: The Ramakrishna Mission Institute of Culture (1962, first published 1937): 557–81.

———. *Social Life in Ancient India: A Study of Vatsyāyana's Kāmasutra*. Calcutta: Susil Gupta (India) Limited, 1954 (first published 1929).

Chakravarti, Uma. "Whatever Happened to the Vedic *Dāsī*?" *Recasting Women: Essays in Colonial History*. Kumkum Sangari and Sudesh Vaid, eds. New Delhi: Kali for Women (1989), 27–87.

———. "Saffroning the Past: Of Myths, Histories, and Right-Wing Agendas." *Economic and Political Weekly*, vol. 33, no. 5 (January 31 1998): 225–32.

———. "The World of the South Indian *Bhaktin*." *Manushi Special Issue: Women Bhakta Poets*. New Delhi: Manushi Trust (Jan.–June, 1989): 18–29.

Chapple, Christopher Key. *Nonviolence to Animals, Earth, and Self in Asian Traditions*. Albany: SUNY Press, 1993.

Chatterjee, A. K. Political History of Pre-Buddhist India. Calcutta: Indian Publicity Society, 1980.

Chaudhuri, Jatindrabimal. *The Position of Women in the Vedic Ritual*. London and Calcutta: Pracyavani Research Series, 1956.

Coburn, Thomas. *Devī Māhātmya* (Delhi: Motilal Banarsidass, 1985), *Encountering the Goddess* (Albany: SUNY Press, 1991).

Coward, Rosalind. *Female Desire. Women's Sexuality Today*. London. Paladin. 1984

Dabbe, Vijaya and Zydenbos, Robert. "Akka Mahadevi." *Manushi Special Issue: Women Bhakta Poets*. New Delhi: Manushi Trust (Jan.–June, 1989): 39–44.

Dandekar, R. N. "Inaugural Address" to *The Mahābhārata Revisited*. New Delhi: Sahitya Akademi (1990): 7–18.

Das, Veena. "On Female Body and Sexuality." *Contributions to Indian Sociology*, vol. 21, no. 1 (1987): 57–66.

Dazey, Wade H. "Tradition and Modernization in the Organization of the *Daśanāmi Saṃnyāsin*s." *Monastic Life in the Christian and Hindu Traditions: A Comparative Study*. Austin B. Creel and Vasudha Narayanan, eds. Lewiston: The Edwin Mellen Press (1990): 281–321.

Denton, Lynn Teskey. "Varieties of Hindu Female Asceticism." *Roles and Rituals for Hindu Women*. Julia Leslie, ed. Delhi: Motilal Banarsidass (1992): 211–31.

Dhand, Arti. "Women, Smelly Ascetics, and Reproductive Method: Reflections on a Theme in the *Mahābhārata*." Paper Presented at the AAR San Francisco. March (1999): 1–40.

Doniger, Wendy (as O'Flaherty). *Śiva, the Erotic Ascetic*. London: Oxford University Press, 1973.

———. *The Origins of Evil in Hindu Mythology*. Berkeley: University of California Press, 1976.

———. *Women, Androgynes, and Other Mythical Beasts*. Chicago: University of Chicago Press, 1980.

Doniger, Wendy. "Begetting on the Margin: Adultery and Surrogate Pseudo-marriage in Hinduism." *From the Margins of Hindu Marriage*. Ed. by Lindsey Harlan and Paul B. Courtright. New York: Oxford University Press. 1995: 160–83.

———. *Tales of Sex and Violence: Folklore, Sacrifice, and Danger in the Jaiminiya Brāhmaṇa*. Chicago: University of Chicago Press, 1985.

Doniger, Wendy. "Medical and Mythical Constructions of the Body in Hindu Texts." *Religion and the Body*. Sarah Coakley, ed. Cambridge: Cambridge University Press (1997): 167–84.

Doniger, Wendy. *Splitting the Difference: Gender and Myth in Ancient Greece and India*. Chicago: University of Chicago Press, 1999.

Donovan, Josephine. *Feminist Theory: The Intellectual Traditions of American Feminism*. New York: Frederick Ungar Publishing Co., 1985.

Dumézil, Georges. *Mythe et Épopée: l'idéologies des trois fonctions dans les épopees des peuples indo-européens*: 3 vols. Paris: Editions Gallimard, 1968.

———. *The Destiny of the Warrior*. Alf Hiltebeitel, trans. Chicago: University of Chicago Press, 1970.

———. *The Destiny of a King*. Alf Hiltebeitel, trans. Chicago: University of Chicago Press, 1973.

Elder, Joseph W. "Some Roots and Branches of Hindu Monasticism." *Monastic Life in the Christian and Hindu Traditions: A Comparative Study*. Austin B. Creel and Vasudha Narayanan, eds. Lewiston: The Edwin Mellen Press (1990): 1–36.

Emeneau, M. B. and van Nooten, B. A. "The Young Wife and Her Husband's Brother: *Ṛgveda* 10.40.2 and 10.85.44." *Journal of the American Oriental Society*, vol. 111, no. 3 (July-September 1991): 481–94.

Erndl, Kathleen. *Victory to the Mother*. New York: Oxford University Press. 1993.

———. "The Mutilation of Surpanakha." *Many Ramayanas*. Berkeley: University of California Press (1991): 67–88.

Falk, Nancy. "Draupadī and the *Dharma*." *Beyond Androcentrism: New Essays on Women and Religion*. Rita Gross, ed. Scholars Press (1977): 89–114.

Fauré, Bernard. *The Red Thread: Buddhist Approaches to Sexuality*. Princeton: Princeton University Press, 1998.

Feldhaus, Anne. *Water and Womanhood: Religious Meaning of Rivers in Maharashtra* (New York: Oxford University Press, 1995).

Fitzgerald, James L. "The Great Epic of India as Religious Rhetoric: A Fresh Look at the *Mahābhārata*." *Journal of the American Academy of Religion* 51:4 (1983): 611–30.

———. "The Position of Brahmins in the *Mahābhārata*: New Perspectives on the Development and Growth of the Epic Between the Empires." Paper presented at *Between the Empires* Conference at the University of Texas, April 2003c.

———. "Making Yudhisthira the King: the Dialectics and Politics of Violence in the *Mahābhārata*." *Rocznik Orientalistyczny* LIV (2001): 63–92.

———. "Sanskrit Pita and Saikya/Saikya: Two Terms of Iron and Steel Technology in the *Mahābhārata*." *JAOS*, vol. 120, no. 1, Jan.–March 2000: 44–62.

———. "The *Mahābhārata*: A Play Based upon the Indian Classic Epic." *Soundings*, vol. LXX, no.1–2, Spring/Summer 1987, 539–51.

———. "Nun Befuddles King, Shows Karmayoga Does Not Work." Sulabha's Refutation of King Janaka at MBh 12.308, annotated translation of MBh 12.308, to appear in the *Journal of Indian Philosophy*. 2003a

———. "The Many Voices of the *Mahābhārata: A Review Article of Rethinking The Mahābhārata: A Reader's Guide to the Education of the Dharma King* by Alf Hiltebeitel (Chicago: University of Chicago Press, 2001), *Journal of the American Oriental Society*, 132.4.2003b: 803–18.

———. "What the *Mahābhārata* Tells Us About *Dharma*." Special issue on dharma edited by Patrick Olivelle. *Journal of Indian Philosophy* 2004.

———. "The Rāma Jāmadagnya Thread of the *Mahābhārata*: A New Survey of Rāma Jāmadagnya in the Pune Text." Mary Brockington, ed., *Stages and Transitions: Temporal and Historical Frameworks in Epic and Puranic Literature*, Proceedings of the Second Dubrovnik International Conference on the Sanskrit Epics and *Purāṇas*, August, 1999 (Zagreb, Croatian Academy of Sciences and Arts, 2002). 89–132.

———. "Some Storks and Eagles Eat Carrion; Herons and Ospreys Do Not: Kankas and Kuraras (and Badas) in the *Mahābhārata*." *Journal of the American Oriental Society.* 1998 Apr.–June. 118(2): 257–61.

———. "India's Fifth Veda: the *Mahābhārata*'s Presentation of Itself." *Journal of South Asian Literature* 20, 1 (1985): 125–40.

Flax, Jane. 1987. "Postmodernism and Gender Relations in Feminist Theory." *Signs* 12/4: 621–43.

Foucault, Michel. *History of Sexuality*. 3 vols. Roberty Hurley, trans. New York: Pantheon Books, 1978–1986.

Gandhi, Ramchandra. "*Brahmacārya*." *Way of Life: King, Householder, Renouncer: Essays in Honour of Louis Dumont*. T. N. Madan, ed. Delhi: Vikas Publishing House (1982): 205–22.

Gitomer, David L. "*Rākṣasa* Bhīma: The Wolf-Belly Among Ogres and Brahmans in the Sanskrit *Mahābhārata* and the *Veṇīsaṃhāra*." *Essays on the Mahābhārata*. Arvind Sharma, ed. Leiden: E. J. Brill (1991): 296–323.

Gitomer, David L. "King Duryodhana: The *Mahābhārata* Discourse of Sinning and Virtue in Epic and *Dharma*." *Journal of the American Oriental Society*. 112:2 (1992): 222–32.

Gold, Ann Grodzins and Raheja, Gloria. *Listen to the Heron's Words*. Berkeley: University of California Press, 1994.

Goldman, Robert. *Gods, Warriors, and Priests: The Bhṛgus of the Mahābhārata*, New York: Columbia University Press, 1971.

Goldman, Robert P. "Esa Dharmah Sanatanah: Shifting Moral Values and the Indian Epics." *Relativism, Suffering, and Beyond: Essays in Memory of Bimal K. Matilal*. Eds. Bilimoria, P., Mohanty, J. N. Delhi: Oxford University Press. 1997. 187–223.

———. "Transsexualims, Gender, and Anxiety in Traditional India." *JAOS* 113/3. 1993. 374–401.

———. "Karma, Guilt, and Buried Memories: Public Fantasy and Private Reality in Traditional India." *JAOS* 105/3. 1985. 413–25.

———. "Fathers, Sons and Gurus: Oedipal Conflict in the Sanskrit Epics." *Journal of Indian Philosophy*. 6. 1978. 325–92.

———. "Gods in Hiding: The *Mahābhārata*'s Virata Parvan and the Divinity of the Indian Epic Hero." *Modern Evaluation of the Mahābhārata*. Delhi: Nag Publishers. 73–100.

Gupta, Sanjukta Gombrich. "The Goddess, Women, and Their Rituals in Hinduism." Leslie, *Roles and Rituals for Hindu Women*. Delhi: Motilal Banarsidass, 1991. 87–106.

Halbfass, Wilhelm. *India and Europe*. Albany: SUNY Press. 1988.

Hales, Dianne. Just Like a Woman: How Gender Science Is Redefining What Makes us Female. New York: Bantam Books, 1999.

Haynes, Edward S. "From Sagara to Sanjay: The Ksatriya Alternative and Feudal Authoritarianism in Indian History." *Boeings and Bullock-Carts: Studies in Change and Continuity in Indian Civilization*. Delhi: Chankya Publications (1985): 63–89.

Heesterman, J. C. "*Veda* and *Dharma*." *The Concept of Duty in South Asia*. New Delhi: Vikas Publishing House Pvt. Ltd. 1978. 80–95.

———. "Householder and Renouncer." *Way of Life: King, Householder, Renouncer: Essays in Honour of Louis Dumont*. T. N. Madan, ed. Delhi: Vikas Publishing House (1982): 251–72.

Hiltebeitel, Alf. "The *Mahābhārata* and Hindu Eschatology." *History of Religions*. 12:2 (1972): 95–135.

———. "Comparing Indo-European Epics." *History of Religions*. 15:1 (August 1975): 90–99.

———. *The Ritual of Battle: Kṛṣṇa in the Mahābhārata*. Ithaca: Cornell University Press, 1976.

———. "The Burning of the Forest Myth." *Hinduism: New Essays in the History of Religions*. Bardwell L. Smith, ed. Leiden: E. J. Brill (1976): 208–24.

———. "Draupadī's Garments." *Indo-Iranian Journal*. 22 (1980): 97–112.

———. "Śiva, the Goddess, and the Disguises of the Pāṇḍavas and Draupadī." *History of Religions*. 20:1 and 2 (1980): 147–74.

———. "Draupadī's Hair." *Autour De La Déesse Hindoue: Puruṣārtha 5, 1980: Etudes Reunies Par Madeleine Biardeau*. Paris: Editions de l'Ecole des Haute Etudes en Sciences Sociales (1980): 179–213.

———. "Sexuality and Sacrifice: Convergent Subcurrents in the Fire-Walking Cult of Draupadī." *Images of Man: Religion and Historical Processes in South Asia*. Fred Clothey, ed. Madras: New Era (1982): 72–111.

———. "Brothers, Friends, and Charioteers: Parallel Episodes in the Irish and Indian Epics." *Journal of Indo-European Studies*. Homage to Georges Dumézil. Edgar C. Palome, ed. Monograph no. 3 (1982): 85–111.

———. "Toward a Coherent Study of Hinduism." *Religious Studies Review*. 9:3 (July 1983): 206–12.

———. "The Two Kṛṣṇas on One Chariot: *Upaniṣad*ic Imagery and Epic Mythology." *History of Religions* 24:1 (1984): 1–26.

———. "Purity and Auspiciousness in the Sanskrit Epics." *Purity and Auspiciousness in Indian Society*. John B. Carman and Frederique Apffel Marglin, eds. Leiden: E. J. Brill (1985): 41–54.

———. "Two Kṛṣṇas, Three Kṛṣṇas, Four Kṛṣṇas, More Kṛṣṇas: Dark Interactions in the *Mahābhārata*." *Essays on the Mahābhārata*. Arvind Sharma, ed. Leiden: E. J. Brill (1991): 101–09.

———. Interview with Steven J. Rosen. *Vaiṣṇavism: Contemporary Scholars Discuss the Gaudiya Tradition*. New York: Folk Books (1992): 49–59.

———. "Religious Studies and Indian Epic Texts." *Religious Studies Review*. 21:1 (January 1995): 26–31.

———. "Rethinking Bhrguization." Brockington and Schreiner, eds. *Composing a Tradition: Concepts, Techniques and* Relationships. Proceedings of the First Dubrovnik Internation Conference on the Sanskrit Epics and Puranas. August 1997. Zagreb: Croatian Academy of Sciences and the Arts. 155–68.

———. *Rethinking the Mahabharata: A Guide to the Education of the Dharma King*. Chicago: University of Chicago Press, 2000.

Holdrege, Barbara. "Body Connections: Hindu Discourses of the Body and the Study of Religion." Paper Presented to the Annual Conference of the American Academy of Religion (Orlando, 1998): 1–56.

Hopkins, E. W. *The Great Epic of India*. Calcutta: Punthi Pustak, 1969.

Hubbard, Ruth. "Science, Facts, and Science." In *Feminism and Science*. Indiana: Indiana University Press, 1989 (1199–131).

Humm, Maggie, ed. *Modern Feminisms: Political, Literary, Cultural*. New York: Columbia University Press, 1992.

Jacobsen, Knut A. Theory and Practice of Yoga: Essays in Honour of Gerald James Larson. Leiden: E. J. Brill. 2005.

Jamison, Stephanie W. *Sacrificed Wife Sacrificer's Wife: Women, Ritual, and Hospitality in Ancient India*. New York: Oxford University Press, 1996.

Jamison, Stephanie W. "Penelope and the Pigs: Indic Perspectives on the Odyssey." *Classical Antiquity* 18/2 1999.

———. "Women 'Between the Empires' and 'Between the Lines.'" Paper read at the "Between the Empires" Conference. April. 2003.

Jash, Pranabananda. *History of the Parivrājaka.* Delhi: Ramanand Vidya Bhawan, 1991.

Jayal, Shakambari. *The Status of Women in the Epics.* Delhi: Motilal Banarsidass, 1966.

Johnsen, Gosta. "Varuṇa and Dhṛtarāṣṭra." *Indo-Iranian Journal* 9 (1965–66): 245–65.

Jung, Patrica Beattie, Hunt, Mary E., Balakrishnana, Radhika, eds. *Good Sex: Feminist Perspectives from the World's Religions.* Rutgers University Press, 2001.

Kakar, Sudhir. *Intimate Relations: Exploring Indian Sexuality.* Chicago: University of Chicago Press, 1990.

Kalyanov, V. I. "The Image of the Indian Woman in the *Mahābhārata.*" *Annals of the Bhandarkar Oriental Research Institute.* Diamond Jubilee Volume (1977–78): 161–72.

Kane, P. V. *History of Dharmaśāstra.* 5 vols. Poona: Bhandarkar Oriental Research Institute, 1968–77.

Katz, Ruth Cecily. *Arjuna in the Mahābhārata: Where Krishna Is, There Is Victory.* Delhi: Motilal Banarsidass, 1990.

———. "The *Sauptika* Episode in the Structure of the *Mahābhārata.*" *Essays on the Mahābhārata.* Arvind Sharma, ed. Leiden: E. J. Brill (1991): 130–49.

Klaes, Norbert. *Conscience and Consciousness: Ethical Problems of the Mahābhārata.* Bangalore: Dharmaram College, 1975.

Kinsley, David. *Hindu Goddesses: Visions of the Divine Feminine in the Hindu Religious Tradition.* Berkeley: University of California Press, 1988.

———. *Tantric Visions of the Divine Feminine: The Ten Mahāvidyās.* Berkeley: University of California Press, 1997.

Kishwar, Madhu. "From Manusmrti to Madhusmrti: Flagellating a Mythical Enemy." *Manushi.* March–April, 2000.

Knipe, David. *In the Image of Fire: Vedic Experiences of Heat.* Delhi: Motilal Banarsidass. 1975.

Kuiper, F. B. J. "The Basic Concept of Vedic Religion." *History of Religions.* 15:2. (1975): 107–20.

Kumari, Ranjana. *Female sexuality in Hinduism.* Delhi: Published for the Joint Women's Programme ISPCK. 1988.

Lacan, Jacques. *Female Sexuality: Jacques Lacan and the école freudienne.* Josephine Rose, trans. Juliet Mitchell and Josephine Rose, eds. London: W. W. Norton and Company, 1982.

Laine, James, W. "Out of Character: Marginal Voices and Role-Transcendence in the *Mahābhārata*'s Book of the Forest." *Journal of Indian Philosophy* 19 (1991): 273–96

———. "Hinduism and the *Mahābhārata*." *Wiener eitschrift fur die Kunde Sudasiens: Und Archiv fur Indische Philosophie*. 30 (1986): 73–83.

Lath, Mukund. "The Concept of Anrsamsya in the *Mahābhārata*." *The Mahābhārata Revisited*. R. N. Dandekar, ed. New Delhi: Sahitya Akademi (1990): 113–19.

Law, Jane Marie, ed. *Religious Reflections on the Human Body*. Bloomington: Indiana University Press, 1997.

Leslie, Julia. "Some Traditional Indian Views on Menstruation and Female Sexuality." *Sexual Knowledge, Sexual Science: The History of Attitudes to Sexuality*. Roy Porter and Mikula Teich, eds. Cambridge: Cambridge University Press (1994): 63–81.

Leslie, Julia I. *Roles and Rituals for Hindu Women*. Delhi: Motilal Banarsidass, 1991.

Lincoln, Bruce. "Theses on Method." *Method and Theory in the Study of Religion* 8, 3 (1996): 225–27.

Madan, T. N. "Domesticity and Detachment." *Monastic Life in the Christian and Hindu Traditions: A Comparative Study*. Austin B. Creel and Vasudha Narayanan, eds. Lewiston: The Edwin Mellen Press (1990): 497–540.

Marglin, Frédérique Apffel. "Power, Purity, and Pollution: Aspects of the Caste System Reconsidered." *Contributions to Indian Sociology* n.s., vol. 11, no. 2, (1977): 245–70.

———. "Female Sexuality in the Hindu World." *Immaculate and Powerful*. Clarissa W. Atkinson, Constance H. Buchanan and Margaret R. Miles, eds. Boston: Beacon Press (1985): 39–59.

———. "Kings and Wives: the Separation of Status and Royal Power." *Way of Life: King, Householder, Renouncer*: Essays in Honour of Louis Dumont. T. N. Madan, ed. Delhi: Vikas Publishing House (1982): 155–82.

———. *Wives of the God-King*.Oxford: Oxford University Press. 1985.

Matilal, B. K. "Elusiveness and Ambiguity in Dharma-Ethics." In *Ethics and Epics: The Collected Works of Bimal Krishna Matilal*, Ed. Jonardon Ganeri, New Delhi: OUP 2002.36–48.

———. "Kṛṣṇa: In Defence of a Devious Divinity." *Essays on the Mahābhārata*. Arvind Sharma, ed. Leiden: E. J. Brill (1991): 401–18.

———, ed. *Moral Dilemmas in the Mahābhārata*. Simla: Indian Institute of Advanced Study, 1989.

Menski, Werner F. "Marital Expectations as Dramatized in Hindu Marriage Rituals." *Rules and Rituals for Hindu Women*. Delhi: Motilal Banarsidass (1992): 47–67.

———. "Legal Pluralism in the Hindu Marriage." *Hinduism in Great Britain*. Richard Burghart, ed. London: Tavistock (1987): 180–200.

———. "Solemnization of Hindu Marriages: The Law and Reality." *Kerala Law Times,* Journal Section (1985): 1–10.

Meyer, J. J., *Sexual Life in Ancient India: A Study in the Comparative History of Indian Culture*. London: Routledge and Kegan Paul, 1930.

Minkowski, C. Z. "Janamejaya's *Sattra* and Ritual Structure." *Journal of the American Oriental Society*. 109:3 (1989): 401–20.

Misra, Vidya Niwas. "Keynote Address." *The Mahābhārata Revisited*. New Delhi: Sahitya Akademi (1990): 19–36.

Mishra, Saraswati. *Status of Indian Women*. New Delhi. Gyan Publishing House. 2002.

Moorthy, K. Krishna. "Socio-Cultural Milieu of the *Mahābhārata*." *The Mahābhārata Revisited*. New Delhi: Sahitya Akademi (1990): 139–50.

Mukherjee, Prabhati. "Widowhood and *Niyoga* in the *Arthaśāstra* and *Manusmṛti*." *Our Heritage* 11.1 (1963): 1–11.

Murcott, Susan. *The First Buddhist Women: Translations and Commentary on the Therīgāthā*. Berkeley: Parallax Press, 1991.

Nanda, Serena. *Neither Man Nor Woman: The Hijras of India*. Belmont, Calif.: Wadsworth Pub. Co., 1990.

Narayanan, Janudha. "Hinduism," *Women, Religion, and Sexuality: Studies on the Impact of Religous Teachings on Women* (Geneva: WCC Publications, 1990).

Nelson, James B. and Longfellow, Sandra P., eds. *Sexuality and the Sacred: Sources for Theological Reflection*. Louisville: Westminster/John Knox Press, 1993.

Ojha, Catherine. "Feminine Asceticism in Hinduism: Its Tradition and Present Condition." *Man in India*. 61:3 (September 1981): 254–88.

Olivelle, Patrick. "The Integration of Renunciation by Orthodox Hinduism." Journal of the Oriential Institute, Baroda. 28/1, 1978a. 27–36.

———. "Young Svetaketu: A Literary Study of an Upanisadic Story." *Journal of the American Oriental Society* 119, 1999: 46–70.

———. "Amrta: Women and Indian Technologies of Immortality," *Journal of Indian Philosophy* 25, 1997: 427–49.

———. "Ritual Suicide and the Rite of Renunciation," Wiener Zeitschrift für die Kunde Südasiens 22, 1978b: 19–44.

Olivelle, J. Patrick. "A Definition of World Renunciation." In *Wiener Zeitschrift fur die Kunde Sudasiens*. vol. 19 (1975): 75–83.

———. "Contributions to the Semantic History of *Saṃnyāsa*." *Journal of the American Oriental Society*. 101:3 (1981): 265–74.

———. "Renouncer and Renunciation in the *Dharmaśāstras*." *Studies in Dharmaśāstra*, Richard W. Lariviere, ed. Calcutta: Firma KLM (1984).

———. "Village vs. Wilderness: Ascetic Ideals and the Hindu World." *Monastic Life in the Christian and Hindu Traditions: A Comparative Study*. Austin B. Creel and Vasudha Narayanan, eds. Lewiston: The Edwin Mellen Press (1990): 125–60.

———. *The Āśrama System: The History and Hermeneutics of a Religious Institution*. New York: Oxford University Press, 1993.

———. 1995. "Deconstruction of the Body in Indian Asceticism." *Asceticism*. Vincent L. Wimbush and Richard Valantasis, eds. New York: Oxford University Press (1995): 188–210.

Orr, Leslie. "Women's Wealth and Worship: Female Patronage of Hinduism, Jainism and Buddhism in Medieval Tamilnadu." *Faces of the Feminine in Ancient, Medieval and Modern India*. OUP 2000. 124–47.

Orr, Leslie C. *Donors, Devotees, and Daughters of God: Temple Women in Medieval Tamilnadu*. New York: Oxford University Press. 2000.

Pande, G. C. "The Socio-Cultural Milieu of the *Mahābhārata*: An Age of Change." *The Mahābhārata Revisited*. R. N. Dandekar, ed. New Delhi: Sahitya Akademi (1990): 121–37.

Parrinder, Geoffrey. *Sex in the World's Religions*. New York: Oxford University Press, 1980.

Patton, Laurie L. Dis-solving a Sebate: Toward a Practical Theory of Myth, with a Case Study in Vedic Mythology. *Religion and Practical Reason*. Albany: State University of New York Press, 1994. 213–62.

———. "The fate of the female Rsi." In *Myths and Mythmaking in India*, Ed. Julia Leslie. London: Curzon Press, 1996a.

———, ed. *Myth and Method*. University of Virginia. 1996b. Patton, Laurie L. ed. *Authority, Anxiety, and Canon: Essays in Vedic Interpretation*. Albany: SUNY Press, 1994.

———. ed. *Jewels of Authority: Women and Textual Tradition in Hindu India*. Oxford, 2002.

Pinkham, Mildred Worth. *Woman in the Sacred Scriptures of Hinduism*. New York: AMS Press, 1967, c1941.

Rajagopalachari, C. "Avvaiyar, the Fearless Wanderer." *Manushi Special Issue: Women Bhakta Poets*. New Delhi: Manushi Trust (Jan.–June, 1989): 30–31.

Ramanujan, A. K. "Repetition in the *Mahābhārata*." *Essays on the Mahābhārata*. Arvind Sharma, ed. Leiden: E. J. Brill (1991).

Raychaudhuri, Hemchandra. "The *Mahābhārata*: Some Aspects of Its Culture." *The Cultural Heritage of India*. vol. II, Calcutta: The Ramakrishna Mission Institute of Culture (1962, first ed. 1937): 71–79.

Ricoeur, Paul. *Interpretation Theory: Discourse and the Surplus of Meaning*. 1976.

Scheuer, Jacques. "Śiva dans le *Mahābhārata*: L'Histoire d'Ambā/Śikhaṇḍin." *Puruṣārtha* vol. 2 (1975): 67–86.

Schmidt, Hanns-Peter. "Ahimsa and Rebirth." *Inside the Texts Beyond the Texts: New Approaches to the Study of the Vedas*. Ed. Witzel, Michael. Cambridge 1997. 207–34.

Sen, Nabaneeta Dev. "Lady Sings the Blues." *Manushi* 108.

Shah, Shalini. *The Making of Womanhood: Gender Relations in the Mahābhārata* New Delhi: Manohar Publishers, 1995.

Sharma, Arvind. *The Hindu Gita: Ancient and Classical Interpretations of the Bhagavadgītā*. La Salle. Open Court, 1986.

———, ed. *Essays on the Mahābhārata*, Leiden: E. J. Brill, 1991.

———. "Homosexuality and Hinduism," in *Homosexuality in the World Religions*. Arlene Swidler, ed. Philadelphia: Trinity Press International (1993): 47–80.

Sharma, R. S. *Śūdra*s in Ancient India. Delhi: Motilal Banarsidass, 1958.

Shulman, David. "Devana and Daiva." *Ritual, State and Hinstory in South Asia: Essays in Honour of J. C. Heesterman*. Eds. Van den Hoek, A. W., Kolff, D. H. A., Oort, M. S. Leiden: E. J. Brill, 1992. 350–65.

———. "The Yakṣa's Questions." *Untying the Knot: On Riddles and Other Enigmatic Modes*. Eds. Hasan-Rokem, Galit, and Shulman, David. New York: Oxford Univesity Press. 1996.151–67.

———. "Towards a Historical Poetics of the Sanskrit Epics." *International Folklore Review* 8. London, 1991. 9–17.

———. "On Being Human in the Sanskrit Epic: the Riddle of Nala." *Journal of Indian Philosophy*. 22 (1994): 1–29.

———. "Asvatthaman and Brhannada: Brahmin and Kingly Paradigms in the Sanskrit Epic. *The Origins and Diversity of Axial Age Civilizations*. Albany: SUNY Press. 1986. 407–26.

Sinha, Braj M. "Arthaśāstra Categories in the *Mahābhārata*: from *Daṇḍanītī* to *Rājadharma*." In *Essays on the Mahābhārata*. Arvind Sharma, ed. Leiden: E. J. Brill (1991): 369–83.

Skurzak, Ludwik. "Indian Asceticism in its Historical Development." *The Adyar Library Bulletin*. Vols. XXXI–XXXII, 1967–68, Dr. V. Raghavan Felicitation Volume. 203–10.

Smith, Frederick M. "Indra's Curse, Varuṇa's Noose, and the Suppression of the Woman in the Vedic Śrauta Ritual." *Roles and Rituals for Hindu Women*. Julia Leslie, ed. Delhi: Motilal Banarsidass (1992): 17–46.

Smith, Mary Carroll. "Epic Parthogenesis." *Journal of South Asian* Literature. 20, 1 (1985): 79–92.

Sorensen, Soren. *Index to the Names in the Mahābhārata*. Delhi: Motilal Banarsidass, 1978 (first printed 1904).

Staal, Frits. "Indian Bodies." *Self as Body in Asian Theory and Practice*. Thomas P. Kasulis, with Roger T. Ames and Wimal Dissanayake, eds. Albany: SUNY Press (1996): 59–102.

Strauss, Otto. Éthische Probleme aus dem *Mahābhārata Giornale della Societa Asiatica Italiana*. 24: 193–335.

Sullivan, Bruce M. "The Epic's Two Grandfathers, Bhīṣma and Vyāsa." *Essays on the Mahābhārata*. Arvind Sharma, ed. Leiden: E. J. Brill (1991): 204–11.

———. *Kṛṣṇa Dvaipāyana Vyāsa and the Mahābhārata: A New Interpretation*. Leiden: E. J. Brill, 1990.

Sukthankar, V. S. "The Bhṛgus and the Bhārata: A Text-Historical Study." ABORI, XVIII (1950): 1–76.

Sukthankar, V. S. "*Critical Studies in the Mahābhārata*." *Sukthankar Memorial Edition*. P. K. Gode, ed. Bombay: Karnatak Publishing House (1944) 263–67.

———. *On the Meaning of the Mahābhārata*. Bombay: The Asiatic Society of Bombay, 1957.

Sutherland, Sally. "Sītā and Draupadī: Aggressive Behaviour and Female Role-Models in the Sanskrit Epics." *Journal of the American Oriental Society*. 109 (1) (1989): 63–79.

———. "Seduction, Counter-Seduction, and Sexual Role-Models: Bedroom Politics and the Indian Epics." *Journal of Indian Philosophy*. 20 (1992): 243–51.

Sutton, Nicholas. *Religious Doctrines in the Mahabharata*. Delhi: Motilal Banarsidass. 2000.

———. "Ashoka and Yudhisthira: A Historical Setting for the Ideological Tensions in the *Mahābhārata*." *Religion* vol. 27, no. 4. October 1997.

Thapar, Romila. "Householders and Renouncers in the Brahmanical and Buddhist Tradition." *Way of Life: King, Householder, Renouncer: Essays in Honour of Louis Dumont*. T. N. Madan, ed. Delhi: Vikas Publishing House (1982): 273–98.

———. "Dissent and Protest in the Early Indian Tradition." *Studies in History*. vol. I, no. 2. (1979): 177–95.

———. *Ancient Indian Social History: Some Interpretations*. Hyderabad: Orient Longman, 1978.

Thomas, Lynn. "The Identity of the Destroyer in the *Mahābhārata*." *Numen* 41/3. 1994. 255–72.

Tubb, Gary. "*Śāntarasa* in the *Mahābhārata*." *Essays on the Mahābhārata*. Arvind Sharma, ed. Leiden: E. J. Brill (1991): 171–203.

Upadhyay, Govind Prasad. *Brāhmaṇas in Ancient India: A Study of the Role of the Brāhmaṇa from c. 200 B.C. to c. 500 A.D.* New Delhi: Munshiram Manoharlal, 1979.

Urban, Hugh. *The Economics of Ecstasy*. OUP 2001.

Vaidya, P. L. and Pusalker, A. D. "The *Mahābhārata*: Its History and Character." *The Cultural Heritage of India*, vol. II, Calcutta: The Ramakrishna Mission Institute of Culture (1962, 1st ed. 1937): 51–70.

Valverde, Mariana. *Sex, Power and Pleasure*. Toronto: Women's Press, 1985.

van Buitenen, J. A. B. "On the Structure of the *Sabhāparvan* of the *Mahābhārata*." India Major: Congratulatory Volume Presented to J. Gonda. J. Ensink and P. Gaeffke, eds. Leiden: E. J. Brill (1972): 68–84.

van Nooten, Barend A. *The Mahābhārata attributed to Kṛṣṇa Dvaipāyana Vyāsa*, New York: Twayne Publishers, 1971.

Vassilkov, Yaroslav. "Kālavāda (the doctrine of Cyclical Time) in the Mahābhārata and the concept of Heroic Didactics." *Composing a Tradition: Concepts, Techniques, and Relationships*. Eds. Brockington, Mary, and Schreiner, Peter. Zagreb: Academia Scientiarum et Artium Croatia. 1999. 17–33.

Vassilkov, Yaroslav V. "Parable of a Man Hanging in a Tree and Its Archaic Background." *Jadavpur Journal of Comparative Literature*. 1995. 32. 38–51.

Vora, Dhairyabala P. *The Evolution of Morals in the Epics (Mahābhārata and Rāmāyaṇa)*. Bombay: Popular Book Depot, 1959.

Wadley, Susan and Jacobson, Doranne. *Women in India: Two Perspectives* Delhi: Manohar, 1970.

Weeks, Jeffrey. *Sexuality*. London: Tavistock, 1986.

White, David G. *The Alchemical Body*. Chicago: University of Chicago Press. 1996.

White, David Gordon. "Transformations in the Art of Love: Kāmakalā Practices in Hindu Tantric and Kaula Traditions." *History of Religions*. 38:2 (November 1998): 172–98.

White, Hayden. 1987. *The Content of the Form: Narrative Discourse and Historical Representation*. Baltimore: Johns Hopkins.

Wilson, Liz. *Charming Cadavers: Horrific Configurations of the Feminine in Indian Buddhist Hagiographic Literature*. University of Chicago Press. 1996.

Woods, Julian. *Destiny and Human Initiative in the Mahābhārata*. Doctoral dissertation. McGill University, Montreal, 1993.

———. "Hinduism and the Structural Approach of Madeleine Biardeau." *Hermeutical Paths to the Sacred Worlds of India*. Katherine K. Young, ed. Georgia: Scholars Press (1994): 160–85.

Wulff and Hawley, eds., *The Divine Consort*: *Rādhā and the Goddesses of India*. Berkeley: Berkeley Religious Studies Series. 1993.

———, eds., *Devī*. Berkeley: University of California Press. 1996.

Index